# Basic FORTRAN

## Hayden Computer Programming Series

PROBLEM-SOLVING PRINCIPLES FOR PROGRAMMERS: Applied Logic, Psychology, and Grit
*William E. Lewis*

BASIC COMPUTER PROGRAMS FOR BUSINESS
*Charles D. Sternberg*

BASIC FORTRAN
*James S. Coan*

BASIC BASIC: An Introduction to Computer Programming in BASIC Language (Second Ed.)
*James S. Coan*

ADVANCED BASIC: Applications and Problems
*James S. Coan*

DISCOVERING BASIC: A Problem Solving Approach
*Robert E. Smith*

PROGRAMMING PROVERBS
*Henry F. Ledgard*

PROGRAMMING PROVERBS FOR FORTRAN PROGRAMMERS
*Henry F. Ledgard*

FORTRAN WITH STYLE: Programming Proverbs
*Henry F. Ledgard and Louis J. Chmura*

COBOL WITH STYLE: Programming Proverbs
*Louis J. Chmura and Henry F. Ledgard*

BASIC WITH STYLE: Programming Proverbs
*Paul A. Nagin and Henry F. Ledgard*

PASCAL WITH STYLE: Programming Proverbs
*Henry F. Ledgard, Paul A. Nagin, and John F. Hueras*

THE BASIC WORKBOOK: Creative Techniques for Beginning Programmers
*Kenneth E. Schoman, Jr.*

BASIC FROM THE GROUND UP
*David E. Simon*

APL: An Introduction
*Howard A. Peelle*

Z-80 AND 8080 ASSEMBLY LANGUAGE PROGRAMMING
*Kathe Spracklen*

SOFTWARE ENGINEERING FOR MICROS: The Electrifying Streamlined Blueprint Speedcode Method
*T. G. Lewis*

# Basic FORTRAN

JAMES S. COAN

HAYDEN BOOK COMPANY, INC.
Rochelle Park, New Jersey

**Library of Congress Cataloging in Publication Data**

Coan, James S
Basic FORTRAN.

(Hayden computer programming series)
Includes index.
1. FORTRAN (Computer program language)
2. Mathematics—Data processing. I. Title.
QA76.73.F25C62 001.64'24 80-23839
ISBN 0-8104-5168-9



*Printed in the United States of America*

| 2 | 3 | 4 | 5 | 6 | 7 | 8 | 9 | PRINTING |
|---|---|---|---|---|---|---|---|---|
| 81 | 82 | 83 | 84 | 85 | 86 | 87 | 88 | YEAR |

# Preface

Wouldn't it be nice to learn a programming language and not later have to unlearn all of the bad programming habits that the book taught us or at least allowed us to learn? That is exactly what this book tries to accomplish. A program doesn't have to be long to be worth designing well. An effort has been made to foster readable programs.

Wouldn't it be nice to be able to write a FORTRAN program the first day? The reader will find that enough is presented so that meaningful programs may be written immediately. People generally do not attempt to learn to drive a car on an eight-lane superhighway. Many people start out learning to drive in an empty parking lot. But they do drive the first day! Then, after the new driver develops confidence, streets and roads with a few other cars may be attempted. And finally, the transition is made to the insanity of superhighway driving. So it may be with computer programming.

With the introduction of the microcomputer, the world of computing suddenly became available to a tremendous number of people. Now a vast number of companies, schools, and colleges that previously couldn't budget for computer facilities have from one to a dozen or more computers at their disposal—many of them capable of supporting FORTRAN programming. In addition, large numbers of people are acquiring microcomputers for their own use at home. An astonishing amount of significant and uncompromised data processing can be accomplished on some of these "small" machines.

This book is an attempt to bring computer programming in FORTRAN to all who want to learn. The general approach is to begin with short, complete programs and then build them into longer, more comprehensive ones. Over 80 complete program examples are included. At first, we will avoid worrying about the myriad of fussy little language details that might scare off the beginner (and indeed some experienced programmers). Later, when we have some successful programming experience under our belts, we may begin to use some of those "fussy little details" to our advantage.

While you can learn a great deal about FORTRAN and programming by merely reading this book, you really ought to have access to a real live computer. Try learning to drive a car without a car.

Many of the problems in the book are intended to lead the reader to pursue interesting mathematical concepts and computing situations based on results of program execution. The supreme joy of learning to program a computer comes when the learner begins to formulate new problems to solve. The computer will serve as an impartial and unyielding judge as to the correctness of the program form for the solution. It is the programmer who must verify the correctness of the actual solution that the program produces. The programmer is in control at all times. So be alert for problems that might be appropriate for a computer program.

The first five chapters introduce FORTRAN language features. Chapters 6 through 11 emphasize applications. The first five chapters may be studied in conjunction with, or at any time following, first-year algebra. The applications chapters cover many of the popular precalculus topics, with all of the required algorithms developed in the text. Thus, this book is suitable for use as a supplementary text to be incorporated into existing mathematics courses, or as a text for a course or unit to cover programming in FORTRAN, or for anyone who wishes to learn FORTRAN on his or her own.

Appendix A is a table of FORTRAN-supplied functions. Appendix B is an index of the over 80 program examples in the text. Each program is listed by program name and program number, i.e., 3-4 is the fourth program in Chap. 3. Appendix C presents a Z80 random number generating function. And possible solution programs are given in Appendix D for the even-numbered problems to give the student an indication of the correctness of his or her program without being required to compile and execute every program. However, particularly in the beginning, a far greater benefit will be derived from seeing programs compile and execute (or not compile and not execute) than from any other programming activity.

I wish to thank Scott Banks for program suggestions; my wife Clara for doing without a husband; Louisa, Margaret, and Anya for doing without a father; Dianne Littwin for suggesting the project in the first place; and the people at Cromemco for patiently answering my many questions and providing other assistance.

Philadelphia JAMES S. COAN

# To the Student

You are about to embark on an exciting adventure. You will be well advised to look upon the computer as something to be mastered and not as some impersonal monster that is out to do you in. Everything the computer does is explainable and predictable. You should take care to evaluate the results the computer produces. Do not blindly accept computer results as faultless, which is not to say that the computer is going to make many mistakes. In fact, under normal conditions, the computer will execute your instructions exactly. Mistakes in the results of a program execution are usually caused by errors in the instructions written by the programmer. Occasionally, (almost never) the program that processes your program statements is at fault. Don't count on it. This is the absolute last resort.

Learning to program a computer is not that complicated. You will probably find that an iterative process works best: read some, try some on the computer, and go back to read some more. There are certain things that you cannot possibly know without being told and some things just make sense based on what is known so far. You will find that reading the text will help with writing the next program and writing and executing a program will help with reading the text.

I hope that you are soon stimulated by your work in programming to bring to the computer your new and exciting problems to be solved. Above all, to be successful, you will have to be an active participant. Actually write programs. Compile and execute them. Then try to see how what you have learned fits into the picture of the FORTRAN language and programming in general. Good luck to you!

# Contents

# 1

# Introduction to FORTRAN

To work with a computer, you, the programmer, must communicate with the computer. In order to do that, you have to use a language that the computer will "understand." It is through the proper use of a computer language that programmers cause computers to perform useful tasks. A number of languages have been written for this purpose. The computer language of this text is FORTRAN, which comes from FORmula TRANslation. FORTRAN IV is a "mature" language that has been in extensive use for many years. Over the years, attempts have been made to create a "standard" language. You will find that many computers "understand" FORTRAN IV, with a specified list of exceptions and extensions, which vary from one computer to the next.

In 1966 a standard FORTRAN IV was specified. In 1977 a standard FORTRAN 77 was specified. Unfortunately, there probably is no computer that exactly implements either language. For the most part, this book utilizes features defined by FORTRAN IV along with some of the features defined by FORTRAN 77. It is our intent to get you writing programs as soon as possible. In order to do that, we will introduce as little detail as seems reasonable to produce the desired result. This is the deserted parking lot concept. When the time seems right, we will introduce additional detail.

Now that we have selected what language to use, we need some physical apparatus with which to actually carry out the communication. Traditionally, the medium of communication was the punch card and a high-speed card reader. This is generally referred to as *batch mode*. More recently, time-sharing computers have enabled us to communicate through the keyboard of a remote terminal such as a teletypewriter or a video terminal—often over telephone lines. Most recently, the microcomputer has made it possible for many of us to communicate with our own dedicated computer through a teletypewriter, a video terminal, or even a simple keyboard and a modified TV receiver. These last two computing environments may be referred to as *interactive*. All of the programs that appear in this book have been developed and executed on a Cromemco microcomputer.

Regardless of which of these methods is used, the principles of developing sound programs remain the same.

## 1-1 Getting Started

Regardless of how complicated a particular set of instructions is going to be, eventually you will have to tell the computer to produce some kind of printed output. Therefore, let us make our first program one to write a message. If you want the computer to type the following statement:

THIS IS MY FIRST FORTRAN PROGRAM

you could type or keypunch what is shown in Program 1-1.

```
      WRITE ( 5, 440 )
440      FORMAT ( 33H THIS IS MY FIRST FORTRAN PROGRAM )
      END
```

**Program 1-1.** My first FORTRAN program.

The three lines in Program 1-1 constitute a complete FORTRAN program. Each line is a statement of the program. Upon execution of your program, the computer will do exactly what you have set out to do. Even though we have not discussed the steps required for program execution, we show the results of execution right from the start.

```
[Begin execution]

THIS IS MY FIRST FORTRAN PROGRAM
```

**Fig. 1-1.** Execution of Program 1-1.

### *FORMAT*

The second statement in our first FORTRAN program is a FORMAT statement. Every FORMAT statement must have a statement label, which consists of from one to five digits, at least one of which must be nonzero. In our example the statement label is 440. The statement label is required so that WRITE and READ statements (to be discussed later) can reference the appropriate FORMAT statement. The contents of the parentheses following the word FORMAT specify the exact arrangement of the output generated by the referencing WRITE statement. Note that a FORMAT statement may be referenced by more than one WRITE statement.

### *H-format*

In the FORMAT statement of our program, the 33H causes the 33 characters following the H to be output exactly as they were originally typed, including spaces, with the exception of the first character on a line. This is called *H-format* (after Herman Hollerith, who invented the punch card) and is the first of many FORMAT types that we will be using to specify output. The general form for H-format is nH, where n designates the number of characters to be output.

### *Carriage Control*

The first character on every line of output is used to control vertical spacing and is not itself printed. In this example we have used a blank space to indicate single spacing. A '0' (zero) in this position specifies double spacing. A'1' (one) in this position causes the line printer to start at the top of a new page. And a '+' (plus) causes no vertical spacing, to allow overprinting on the same line (see Table 1-1).

**Table 1-1.** Printer control symbols in FORTRAN

| *Symbol* | *Result* |
|---|---|
| ' ' (blank) | Single spacing |
| '0' (zero) | Double spacing |
| '1' (one) | New page |
| '+' (plus) | No vertical spacing |

Note: The printer control as outlined in Table 1-1 is not limited to H-format but applies to all output format types in FORTRAN.

### *WRITE*

The first statement in our first FORTRAN program is the WRITE statement. The minimum WRITE statement is

```
WRITE ( i, j )
```

where the i designates the device to which the output is to be sent by the computer. Possible devices include the console, terminal, high-speed printer, card punch, disk, mag tape, or even a plotter. Each of these devices will have its own device number, which is assigned by the people who set up and maintain the particular computer in question. Before writing your programs, you must decide where you want your output to go and determine the appropriate device number to use. On the computer used for this book, device "5" is one of those assigned to the console. The j in WRITE ( i, j ) refers to the statement label of the FORMAT statement that specifies exactly how the output will be arranged.

### *END*

The third statement in our three-statement program is the FORTRAN END statement. It must be physically the last statement of every FORTRAN program. This is particularly significant if you are using card input and there are stacks of cards for more than one program in the card reader. Some computer installations may require an additional statement to actually terminate the program execution. Typically either CALL EXIT or STOP may be required. The difference between END and CALL EXIT or STOP is that END notifies the computer that this is the last statement of the program, while CALL EXIT or STOP signifies that the program execution may terminate with this statement.

Many computers limit alphabetic characters in FORTRAN programs to uppercase letters. Note that in the printed listing of our program, the digit ''Ø'' has a slash while the letter ''O'' does not, so that they are distinguishable. Some output devices use the reverse convention. On some output devices, the letter ''O'' is a rectangle, while the digit ''Ø'' is elliptical. Some output devices use a diamond shape for one and not the other. It should be a simple matter to type some sample characters to determine how your output device makes this distinction. It is not uncommon for programs to fail just because of mistyping one for the other. So be cautious.

## 1-2 Arithmetic Replacement

One of the major uses of computers is to perform numeric calculations. In order to instruct the computer to perform these, we also must provide somewhere for the computer to put the ''answer.'' One of the necessary components of any computer is its *memory,* which consists of storage locations or cells. A portion of this memory is occupied by our program itself. Some of what remains

```
          NUMBER = 51 * 63
          WRITE ( 5, 19Ø ) NUMBER
    19Ø      FORMAT ( 1ØH 51 * 63 =, I5 )
          END
```

**Program 1-2.** Writing a numeric value.

is available for us to use by simply selecting a name for each data storage location desired. These names are referred to as *variables*. Variables in computer programs can be used to temporarily save the numeric result of a numeric calculation. Most computers supporting FORTRAN will permit up to six-character variable names, which must begin with a letter of the alphabet and contain only letters and digits. So NUMBER = 51 * 63 in a FORTRAN program will direct the computer to multiply 51 by 63 and save the product (3213) in a storage location called NUMBER. Note the use of the symbol ''*'' to indicate multiplication. We may now see the product by referring to NUMBER in an appropriate WRITE-FORMAT statement, as shown in Program 1-2. The value of the variable NUMBER is established in the first line of our four-line program. We can get the computer to output the value of NUMBER by naming NUMBER in a WRITE statement. In fact, we will see later that we may name several variables in a WRITE statement by separating them with commas.

### *I-format*

Now we must provide a new FORMAT capability, as shown in statement 190 in Program 1-2. The I5 there directs the computer to output an integer in the next five columns on the paper, screen, or card. Iw calls for w columns. This is referred to as *I-format* (for Integer-format). FORTRAN will place results in the rightmost columns of the field width specified. This is called *right justification*. Since we have specified two FORMATs (H-format and I-format) in the same statement, they are separated by a comma.

```
[Begin execution]

51 * 63 = 3213
```

**Fig. 1-2.** Execution of Program 1-2.

## 1-3 Getting Numbers into a Program

### *READ*

Often we write a computer program to solve a general problem for which the data is known only as the program is being run. The READ statement exists for the purpose of entering data during the execution of a program. READ behaves like WRITE in that the READ statement must reference a FORMAT statement and specify a device from which the data will be read. Among other possibilities, this device may be a card reader in batch mode, or the keyboard of a terminal in interactive mode. We will use the keyboard of our terminal for many of our programs. Of course, on an expensive batch processor we would use punch cards and a card reader for entering data during program execution. For demonstration purposes, let us simply read two integers and output them and their product. Examine Program 1-3.

```
      WRITE ( 5, 100 )
100      FORMAT ( 21H INPUT TWO INTEGERS ? )
      READ ( 5, 200 ) NUMB1, NUMB2
200      FORMAT ( I5, I5 )
      WRITE ( 5, 300 )
300      FORMAT ( 21H  NUMB1  NUMB2   MULT )
      MULT = NUMB1 * NUMB2
      WRITE ( 5,400 ) NUMB1, NUMB2, MULT
400      FORMAT ( 2X, I5, 2X, I5, 2X, I5 )
      END
```

**Program 1-3.** Introduce the READ statement.

The first line in Program 1-3 directs the computer to print a request for data on device 5 according to the H-format of the statement labeled 100. The third line in our program

READ ( 5, 200 ) NUMB1, NUMB2

causes the computer to read from device 5, two numbers named NUMB1 and NUMB2 according to the FORMAT statement labeled 200. The FORMAT statement labeled 200 requires two integers with up to five digits each. If we were providing data on punched cards, then those two integers would have to be right-justified in columns 1–5 and 6–10 respectively. However, on our terminal, we may simply type the two integers separated by a comma. The fifth line of our program

WRITE ( 5, 300 )

causes the characters after the 21H in the FORMAT statement labeled 300 to be printed on our terminal. The seventh statement

MULT = NUMB1 * NUMB2

causes the product of NUMB1 and NUMB2 to be stored in a storage location in memory identified by our name MULT.

### *X-format*

Next,

WRITE ( 5, 400 ) NUMB1, NUMB2, MULT

directs the computer to type out the values stored in our three variables according to the specification of the FORMAT statement labeled 400. That FORMAT statement

400 FORMAT ( 2X, I5, 2X, I5, 2X, I5 )

contains the new format type referred to as *X-format*.

The general form for X-format is nX: nX provides n spaces except for the first space on a new line, which will be interpreted as calling for single spacing in the same way that the first space in H-format calls for single spacing.

```
[Begin execution]

INPUT TWO INTEGERS ?25,39

  NUMB1  NUMB2   MULT
     25     39    975
```

**Fig. 1-3.** Execution of Program 1-3.

There are a number of things we can do to simplify (or at least shorten) our Program 1-3. First of all, in the FORMAT statement labeled 200 we have repeated I-format. We can accomplish the same result by replacing I5, I5 with 2I5. The general form is rIw, where r designates the number of times to repeat the Iw field.

### *Slash (/) in a FORMAT Statement*

Next, note that we have specified the two lines of output with two WRITE-FORMAT statement pairs. These can be easily combined by using a slash (/) to instruct the computer to start a new line (often referred to as *record* in FORTRAN reference manuals). Lastly, note that 2X, I5 is written three times in statement 400. This also can be accomplished by simply placing 2X, I5 in parentheses preceded by a 3. The combined result would be

```
400     FORMAT ( 21H NUMB1   NUMB2   MULT / 3( 2X, I5 ) )
```

When a slash is used in this way, it serves the function of a comma separater. Thus it may be used to replace a comma.

Consider the following simplified program to produce the same results as Program 1-3.

```
      WRITE ( 5, 100 )
100       FORMAT ( 21H INPUT TWO INTEGERS ? )
      READ ( 5, 200 ) NUMB1, NUMB2
200       FORMAT ( 2I5 )
      MULT = NUMB1 * NUMB2
      WRITE ( 5, 400 ) NUMB1, NUMB2, MULT
400       FORMAT ( 21H  NUMB1  NUMB2   MULT / 3( 2X, I5) )
      END
```

**Program 1-4.** Demonstrate repeat and slash in FORMAT.

```
[Begin execution]

INPUT TWO INTEGERS ?61,58

 NUMB1  NUMB2   MULT
    61     58   3538
```

**Fig. 1-4.** Execution of Program 1-4.

There are two schools of thought about the placement of FORMAT statements in a program. One school places all FORMAT statements together at the end of the program. The other places each FORMAT statement immediately following the READ or WRITE line that references it, unless there are several such references. If a FORMAT is referenced more than once, then it goes at the end of the program. The latter convention is used for this book.

## 1-4 Running Your Programs

### *Preparation*

We will have to prepare programs for entry into the computer either by keypunching cards so that each line of our program is on a single card or by typing our program into a computer file using a source code or text editor. We might be creating such a file in a microcomputer or on a large computer in a time-sharing mode. Regardless of the particular apparatus used, similar concepts are involved. Every system has its advantages and disadvantages. If we are using cards, then any necessary corrections or changes are made by replacing the erroneous cards. Lines are inserted by inserting a new card into its proper location in the deck of cards. With cards, lines are deleted by simply removing the unwanted cards. If we are using a source code or text editor, there may be commands available that allow us to insert lines, remove lines, insert characters, remove characters, and make corrections by simply replacing incorrect characters with correct ones.

There are certain rigid rules that must be followed for the layout of a FORTRAN program statement. It is better to master the rigid rules than to let them master you. Knowledge is your most powerful weapon. It may be helpful, at least for your first few programs, to use a FORTRAN coding form similar to the one shown in Fig. 1-5.

### *A FORTRAN Line*

A FORTRAN program line consists of 72 character positions or columns, divided into three fields. There are 80 columns on punch cards and on coding forms. However, columns 73–80 are ignored by the computer.

### *Statement Label*

The first field consists of columns 1–5 and is reserved for a statement label, if needed.

### *Continuation Line*

The second field consists of column 6. If column 6 contains any character other than blank or zero and columns 1–5 are blank, then the current line is taken to be a continuation of the previous line. We may wish to carry a FORTRAN statement over more than one line because it simply won't fit or because the meaning of the statement is clearer if we group (ungroup?) parts of the statement on different lines. We may use 1, 2, etc., to indicate first continuation line, second continuation line, and so on. Some programmers like to use a "+" in column 6 to indicate all continuation lines. We will use this convention throughout, which will clearly distinguish continuation lines from FORTRAN statements that have labels. Just don't use a zero.

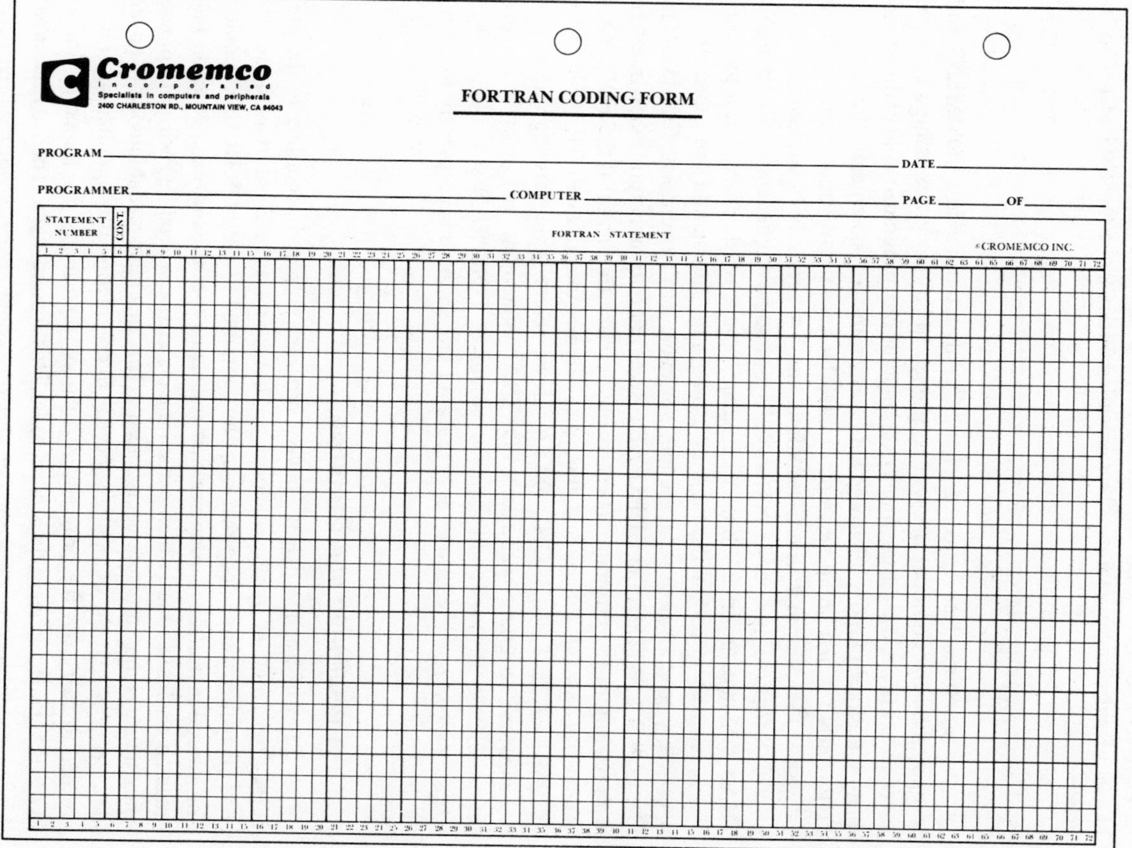
Cromemco
incorporated
Specialists in computers and peripherals
2400 CHARLESTON RD., MOUNTAIN VIEW, CA 94043

FORTRAN CODING FORM

PROGRAM ________ DATE ________

PROGRAMMER ________ COMPUTER ________ PAGE ____ OF ____

STATEMENT NUMBER | CONT. | FORTRAN STATEMENT

©CROMEMCO INC.

Fig. 1-5. FORTRAN coding form. (Courtesy of Cromemco, Inc.)

### *Statement Field*

The third field consists of columns 7–72 and is used to contain the FORTRAN statement itself. Since in this field blanks are ignored, we may insert blanks to enhance readability. This is called PRETTYPRINTING and is to be encouraged.

### *COMMENT*

If column 1 contains the letter "C," then the line is a COMMENT and is ignored by the compiler but will be printed in any program listing. Thus we have the ability to insert comments throughout our programs to explain to humans the exact purpose of statements and groups of statements. In addition, FORTRAN 77 and some versions of FORTRAN IV will treat a line with an asterisk (*) in column 1 as a COMMENT line. An entirely blank line also may be a COMMENT line in FORTRAN 77 and some implementations of FORTRAN IV. Inserting blank lines to separate groups of statements in a program makes it easier to follow the logic of a program. You should use COMMENT lines freely to document source code; however, don't overdo it. COMMENTs like LOAD Y WITH 45 or SUBTRACT 8 are not only unhelpful, they interfere with reading of the program. They should describe the intent of the FORTRAN statements, not the action, and should say things like COMPUTE INTEREST or TABULATE LEVEL ONE DATA. If we select good variable names and organize our programs well, each FORTRAN statement will describe its own action. COMMENTs should apply to groups of FORTRAN statements. They require no computer resources at execution time; so there is no penalty for using them.

### *Compilation and Execution*

Let us assume that we have a program prepared according to the previous discussion. In its present form, we have what is referred to as the *source code*. It is this source code that must be submitted to the FORTRAN compiler. The compiler is itself a program that translates the human readable code into machine readable code (which some humans also can read). (Well, all humans can read it, some humans understand it.) This machine-readable code is called the *object code*. If the computer succeeds in completing the compilation, it may proceed to carry out the program instructions represented by the collection of FORTRAN statements in the source code. This second stage is called *execution*.

Occasionally, the compiler will find some errors in your source code. These are syntactic in nature. Spelling and typing errors may cause much grief. Statements may be in the wrong order. You might mistakenly begin a statement before column 7. The more skilled we become at writing FORTRAN programs, the more infrequently the compiler will find such errors. The compiler will list any errors it finds. It may print a list of error numbers, which you must look up in a chart for the computer you are using, or you may be fortunate enough to have a compiler that provides written messages that will indicate the nature of the error. You may instantly see the problem or require the patient assistance of someone with more experience. Soon you will be that someone. Having found the error(s) and either typed new cards for your batch system or used the text editor for your interactive system to make corrections, you may once again submit your source code to the computer.

At the time you submit your source code to the computer, there may be options available to you. You may want the computer to print the source code on a high-speed printer or at your terminal. You may even want to have the object code printed. You may want to save the object code on a storage medium such as disk, floppy, mag tape, or cassette. These options are exercised by using JOB CONTROL CARDS preceding the source code cards or by typing appropriate command lines on the console or terminal. These options and the commands required depend on the computer you are using and the rules established by the people responsible for its operation. This may even be between you and your microcomputer. You should obtain the necessary literature describing the operation of the computer you are using before you intend to submit your first program.

## 1-5 F-format, REAL

Suppose you worked 7 3/4 hours at $4.32 per hour and must pay 19 percent in Federal Income Taxes and 6.05 percent in Social Security Taxes. What should the amount of the check be? Program 1-5 will provide the answer.

We have used COMMENTs and spacing here to inform the reader about the program. Note the use of F-format in statement 200. F stands for *external Fixed-point* and is used to specify formatting for real number data. The 5.2 specifies five columns for the contents of whatever variable is output, two of which must be to the right of the decimal point. The column occupied by the decimal point counts as one of the five. The general form for F-format is rFw.d, where r is called the repeat factor, w is the field width, and d is the number of digits to the right of the decimal point.

We also have introduced the use of the plus sign (+) to direct the computer to perform addition and the minus sign (−) to direct the computer to perform subtraction.

We could have written the tax deduction statement in the form

```
WTHOLD = PAY * ( TAXRAT + FICA )
```

using parentheses to force the addition to be performed first. We could even combine the three computations in Program 1-5 into the single arithmetic replacement statement

```
AMOUNT = HOURS * RATE * ( 1.0 - TAXRAT - FICA )
```

using parentheses as in algebra to force subtraction to be performed before multiplication. However, that single statement is not quite as readable as the three statements we did use. For our sample program, there is no significant benefit in doing this, but if this statement were to be executed thousands (or even millions) of times, it is worth noting that we would save the computer one multiplication every time the statement executed. Whether or not this is important will depend on the execution speed of the computer you are using and the size of the program you are running. Note that in order for the constant 1.0 to be treated properly by the compiler, we explicitly typed the decimal point to designate it as a real number. In addition we typed the zero there to make it easier for humans to read.

```
C  **  THIS SHORT PROGRAM COMPUTES NET PAY

C  **  ESTABLISH BASIC FACTORS
      HOURS  = 7.75
      RATE   = 4.32
      TAXRAT = Ø.19
      FICA   = Ø.Ø6Ø5

C  **  COMPUTE NET PAY
      PAY    = HOURS * RATE
      WTHOLD = PAY * TAXRAT + PAY * FICA
      CHECK  = PAY - WTHOLD

C  **  OUTPUT THE AMOUNT OF THE CHECK
      WRITE ( 5, 1ØØ ) CHECK
  1ØØ    FORMAT ( 12H AMOUNT = $ , F5.2 )

      END
```

**Program 1-5.** Calculate a paycheck.

```
[Begin execution]

AMOUNT = $ 25.Ø9
```

**Fig. 1-6.** Execution of Program 1-5.

We may use a slash in an arithmetic assignment statement to indicate division. For example,

AVERAG = ( 93.2 + 81.0 + 76.9 ) / 3.0

would store the average of those three numbers in the variable AVERAG. Thus we have *, +, −, and / to indicate multiply, add, subtract, and divide respectively.

## 1-6 Variable Convention

We have used real and integer variables. There are some important differences between the way in which the computer works with these two kinds of variables. For example, for a real number, the computer must keep track of the position of the decimal point and the significant digits of the number. Since the decimal point is said to float, real numbers are sometimes designated as *floating-point numbers,* and calculations carried out on real numbers are designated as *floating-point arithmetic*. In contrast, for integer arithmetic, the decimal point is always just to the right of the rightmost digit in the number. It should be clear that integer arithmetic is much simpler than floating-point arithmetic. Just consider division—integer arithmetic may simply ignore any results to the right of the decimal point, while floating-point arithmetic must continue to carry out additional calculations.

There are two factors involved in the distinction between integers and reals. One is that the two kinds of numbers "look" different as they are stored in the computer memory and on an external storage device, such as a disk, since one requires that the location of the decimal point be stored and the other does not. Thus integers and reals have different storage representations. And the other factor is that different calculation procedures are required to process those different storage representations.

It is because of these differences that the computer must at all times "know" exactly which type of variable or constant is in use. The first letter of the variable name determines this for variables. It is the presence or absence of a decimal point that determines this for constants. All variables that begin with one of the letters I, J, K, L, M, or N designate integer storage and integer arithmetic. All other first letters designate real storage and real arithmetic. FORTRAN is said to "default" all variable names beginning with one of these letters to integer storage and all other variable names to real storage. This convention is sometimes referred to as the IN convention. Since this often results in peculiar variable names, we will soon use the FORTRAN REAL and INTEGER type declaration statements to override the default assignment and select variable names without regard to first letter. The exact storage size and numeric value ranges will depend on the computer you are using.

## Summary

We have used the WRITE-FORMAT statement pair to output data and the READ-FORMAT statement pair to input data. The FORTRAN statement label enables us to refer to a given statement from another statement in the same program. Four format types have been introduced. They are nH, nX, rIw, and rFw.d. We have seen how to repeat single format types and groups of format types. We have seen that a slash (/) may be used to generate more than one line of output with a single FORMAT statement. The required END statement has been used to designate the physical end of all programs. The statements STOP or CALL EXIT may be used to designate the end of execution of a program. The arithmetic replacement statement enables us to assign the value of an arithmetic expression to a variable. The arithmetic operators *, +, −, and / have been used for multiplication, addition, subtraction, and division respectively. We have described the compilation of source code to produce object code that can be executed. The COMMENT statement has been demonstrated. The proper use of COMMENT statements and proper selection of meaningful variable names contribute significantly to the readability of FORTRAN programs. We have seen that variable names beginning with I, J, K, L, M, or N are automatically considered to be integer variables, while all other first letters are automatically considered to be real variables.

## Problems for Chap. 1

You should not feel that you must limit yourself to the problems offered here. As you get some programming under your belt, you should find lots of interesting problems to try on the computer. Learning to program is unique in that the computer will provide you with a measure of your success. You do not need an answerbook for that.

1. Write a program to print the sum of 1234, 2081, 6820, 11610, and 72.
2. Write a program to print the sum of the first ten counting numbers.
3. Write a program to print the sum of 2081, 682, 1161, and 72.08.
4. Write a program to print the product of the first ten counting numbers. (Should you use integer or real?)
5. Have the computer print all possible arrangements of three digits using one FORMAT statement and six WRITE statements.
6. You drove 129 kilometers on 20 liters of gasoline (gasohol?), selling for 31.9 cents per liter. Write a program to print the kilometers per liter and the cost per kilometer.
7. Write a program to convert the metric measures of problem 6 to miles and gallons and compute the miles per gallon and cents per mile. One mile equals 1.6093 kilometers and 1 gallon equals 3.7853 liters.
8. Write a program to print a real approximation of 2/3. Also print 2/3 using integer arithmetic.
9. Have the computer request the numerator and denominator for two fractions to be multiplied. Print the numerator and the denominator of the product.
10. Do problem 9 for adding fractions.
11. Write a program to print a decimal value for

    $$[(1/2) + (1/3)]/[(1/3) - (1/4)]$$

12. Write a program that will multiply two binomials. In other words, for (AX + B) (CX + D), you will enter the four numbers A, B, C, and D and you want

the computer to print the three numbers that are the coefficients in the trinomial product, $aX^2 + bx + c$, where $a = AC$, $b = (BC + AD)$, and $c = BD$.

13. Write a program to add 20000 and 0.000001 using only information in this chapter. Comment on the result.

# 2

# Writing a FORTRAN Program

In Chap. 1 we looked at some programs and tried to analyze them, but our primary purpose was to familiarize you with just enough FORTRAN program statements and rules so that you could get your feet wet by running a few programs. We do not want to be inundated with a myriad of technical programming language details. But we do want to write correct programs. By writing even a few short programs it should have become clear that by taking a careful stepwise approach to things you can save many unsuccessful trips to the compiler.

This might be a good time to point out that it is much easier to make changes in programs while the program statements are still committed only to pencil and paper. Once the code has been typed on cards or into a computer file, we will be tempted to fix up the program with patches rather than incorporate changes as though they were part of the original design.

If we approach programming with care and attention to detail, we will probably find that writing a program in FORTRAN is not only easy, but very rewarding. If we simply write down FORTRAN statements with little thought or care, we will doubtless have many program failures and will soon rate the language as difficult to learn. The true culprit in that case would be our own faulty approach. Admittedly, some features of FORTRAN are awkward to work with, but remember how hard it was learning to tie your shoes. If you could do that as a child, you also can master this computer programming language.

In writing program solutions for the problems of Chap. 1, the primary decisions to be made were whether to use INTEGER or REAL type variable names and, correspondingly, whether to type constants as INTEGER or REAL values. Beyond that, we needed only to decide how many digits to specify in output formatting. In this chapter we will introduce some principles of programming, aids to planning our programs, and some additional FORTRAN statements that will greatly increase the flexibility and power available for problem solving with FORTRAN programs.

## 2-1 Flowcharting

Flowcharting is one of the computer-related subjects about which many reasonable people disagree. People with very important credentials may be found who have very strong and opposite opinions. Experiments have shown flowcharting to be detrimental to good programming. Some publications will not accept programs for publication unless accompanied by a flowchart. If you find flowcharting to be a useful tool, then by all means do it, but do not feel obligated to produce flowcharts unless you have an instructor who insists.

If you are faced with the choice between good flowcharts and good program code, then clearly, until computers are able to read flowcharts, your effort should go into good program code. It seems reasonable to say that the need for flowcharts has been overemphasized in the past; even so, the detailed discussion required for them also is useful for writing programs.

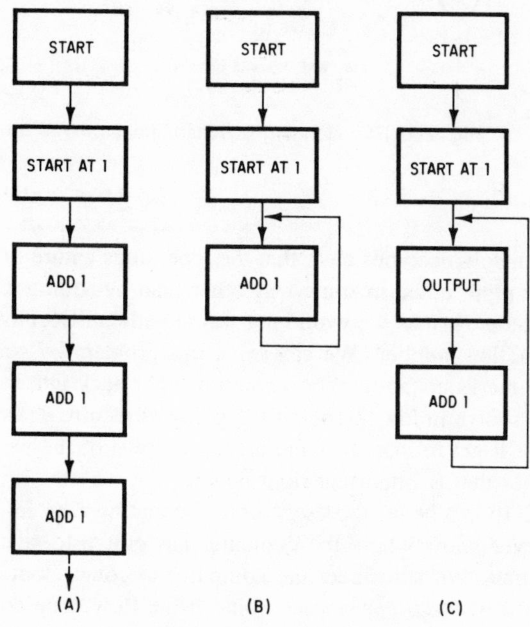


**Fig. 2-1.** Diagram for counting.

Suppose we want to write a program that will direct the computer to "count." Counting should be simple enough to explain, since surely we know very well how to do it. A thorough understanding of the problem at hand is always very important for writing computer programs. It is highly unlikely that we can write a program to solve a problem we do not understand. We usually count by starting with the number 1 and repeatedly add 1 to get the next counting number in sequence. Thus, our first flowchart might look like Fig. 2-1a.

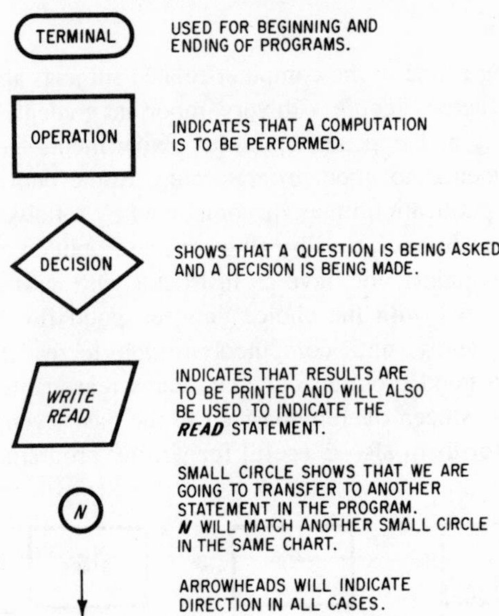


**Fig. 2-2.** Five standard flowchart shapes.

It immediately becomes clear that the repetitious nature of the counting process has to be represented in some way other than by adding a box for each new counting number, just as we would not want to add a FORTRAN statement for each new counting number. We can solve this problem by simply drawing an arrow leaving the first ''add 1'' box pointing right back into the entrance to the same box, as shown in Fig. 2-1b. This is going to require a new FORTRAN statement, but we'll get to that. It is the breaking down of the problem into its fundamental pieces that is important right now.

Figure 2-1b is a better representation of counting than Fig. 2-1a. However, we will never know where the computer has gotten to since there is no provision for output. We can direct the computer to count ''out loud'' by inserting an output box at the appropriate point in the flow. The correct point at which to place the output box is between the ''start at 1'' box and the ''add 1'' box (see Fig. 2-1c). Note that placing the output box after the ''add 1'' box would produce 2 as the first output rather than 1.

If all of the boxes are identical rectangles, it is difficult to tell much about a flowchart from an overall view. It is helpful to have the shapes of the boxes convey specific meaning. Therefore, a system of standardized shapes has been developed to convey certain functions. Some of them are presented in Fig. 2-2. Plastic templates are available that make the drawing of flowcharts easy. Using the standard shapes, the diagram of Fig. 2-1c. is presented in Fig. 2-3.

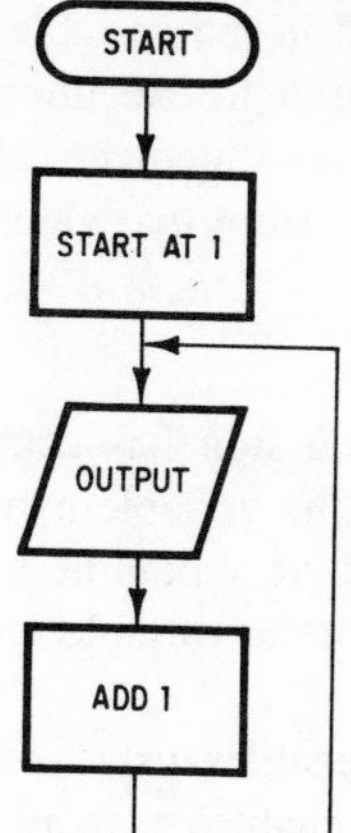


**Fig. 2-3.** Flowchart for counting, using standard shapes.

## 2-2 Program Control

### *GO TO*

In order to write a program to implement the counting of the last section, we need the ability to alter the sequence of execution of FORTRAN statements from that of simply executing statements in the order in which they appear in the program. The first such statement we will consider that has this ability is the statement

GO TO label

This statement will direct the computer to execute next the statement bearing the designated statement label, which may either precede or follow the GO TO statement in the program. The GO TO statement is referred to as an *unconditional transfer* statement and allows us to draw an arrow from one box to the entrance of another not directly in line.

One other step listed for directing the computer to count that requires further discussion is "add 1." One possible procedure for doing this would be the following pair of FORTRAN statements:

```
COUNT1 = COUNT + 1
COUNT  = COUNT1
```

However, it is not necessary in FORTRAN to use the temporary second variable COUNT1 to accomplish this. The following single statement does the same thing more compactly:

```
COUNT = COUNT + 1
```

We now see that the equals sign in FORTRAN does not declare that two quantities have the same value, but that the result of a calculation carried out on the right is to be stored in the variable named on the left. The variable COUNT contains one value prior to execution of this statement and a second value following execution of this statement. The prior value is replaced by the new value. A variable may not store two values simultaneously.

### *Type Declaration*

Since this whole discussion has centered around counting, we have naturally selected COUNT as the variable name to use, but that variable name will default to REAL-type and we should be using an INTEGER-type variable. The time has come to introduce the variable type declaration statement in FORTRAN.

The type statement enables us to override the variable type default convention of FORTRAN and enables us to avoid the awkwardness of a variable name like ICOUNT. We may now use a type statement to declare COUNT to be an integer variable. The statement to accomplish this is simply

INTEGER COUNT

This is called a *declaration* or *specification statement*. It is not executable and must appear before any statements that are executable. REAL variables may be specified with a statement such as

REAL NUMBER, JOKER

It is recommended that all variable names be mentioned in a type statement.

Having thoroughly discussed all facets of counting and writing a program to count in FORTRAN, we should be able to create the simple program in Program 2-1.

```
C  **  THIS PROGRAM DIRECTS THE COMPUTER TO COUNT
C  **  USING COUNT AS AN INTEGER VARIABLE

       INTEGER  COUNT
       COUNT = 1

10     WRITE ( 5, 12 ) COUNT
12        FORMAT ( 1H , I3 )
       COUNT = COUNT + 1
       GO TO 10

       END
```

**Program 2-1.** Directing the computer to count.

Several comments and one *WARNING* are in order here. Since Program 2-1 has no natural termination and even the flowchart has the appearance of hanging in midair, don't try to execute this program unless you know where the panic button is! This program will run forever on many computers and that could be very expensive if you are paying for computer time. In order to make this a useful counting program, we need to replace the unconditional statement GO TO 10 with one that can make a decision. This brings us to the logical IF statement.

### *Logical IF*

Our counting program would be more useful if we just had some way for it to terminate when a predetermined number has been reached. FORTRAN has the ability to alter the order in which statements are executed depending on the outcome of a decision. This is called a *conditional transfer*. There are six options, called *relational operators,* provided. They are as follows:

| | | |
|---|---|---|
| .LT. | less than | < |
| .LE. | less than or equal to | <= |
| .EQ. | equal to | = |
| .NE. | not equal to | <> |
| .GT. | greater than | > |
| .GE. | greater than or equal to | >= |

In our counting program, if we would like the computer to count to 7, we may replace the statement GO TO 10 with

```
IF ( COUNT .LE. 7 ) GO TO 10
```

Any FORTRAN expression may appear on either side of the relational operator. The statement to be evaluated as "true" or "false" must be placed in parentheses. The periods before and after the two letter mnemonics are necessary so that those letters cannot be mistaken for parts of variable names. If the contents of the parentheses evaluate as true, then the next statement executed will be the statement with the label 10. If the evaluation result is false, then the next statement physically in line will be executed.

Now let us modify the flowchart in Fig. 2-3 to show the decision. At the same time, we list the FORTRAN statements that implement the verbal instructions in the boxes (see Fig. 2-4).

At last we have a program that has a natural termination! The flowchart has a more satisfactory structure, in that it has clear beginning and ending points. We simply insert the specification statement INTEGER COUNT and an appropriate FORMAT statement labeled 12 in our program of Fig. 2-4b and now we may submit our source code to the compiler in the form of Program 2-2.

## 2-3 A Potpourri of FORTRAN Information

This section expands upon some of the ideas expressed in the last section and introduces several additional FORTRAN capabilities.

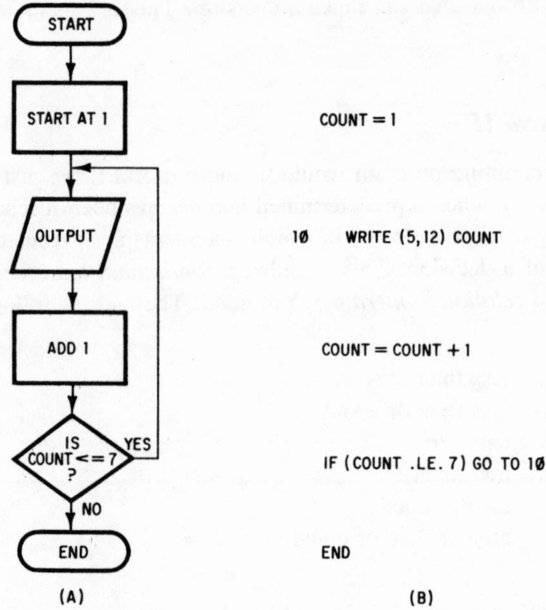


**Fig. 2-4.** Flowchart for counting from 1 to 7.

```
C   **  PROGRAM TO COUNT FROM 1 TO 7

        INTEGER COUNT

        COUNT = 1

  1Ø    WRITE ( 5, 12 ) COUNT
  12        FORMAT ( 9H NUMBER =, I3 )
        COUNT = COUNT + 1
        IF ( COUNT .LE. 7 ) GO TO 1Ø

        END
```

**Program 2-2.** Counting from 1 to 7.

## *PROGRAM*

The PROGRAM statement enables us to give programs names internally without the use of a COMMENT statement. The PROGRAM statement is optional and is followed by a program name (usually up to six characters) selected by the programmer. In FORTRAN 77, if a PROGRAM statement is present, it must be the first statement of the program. We will employ the PROGRAM statement for the rest of this book.

```
[Begin execution]

NUMBER =  1
NUMBER =  2
NUMBER =  3
NUMBER =  4
NUMBER =  5
NUMBER =  6
NUMBER =  7
```

**Fig. 2-5.** Execution of Program 2-2.

## *Apostrophe*

Apostrophe editing may be used in place of H-format. Characters enclosed within two apostrophes will be handled by FORTRAN in the same manner that the characters following nH are handled. To cause the printing of an apostrophe using apostrophe editing, simply enter two adjacent apostrophes. One advantage to using apostrophe editing is that we do not have to count the number of characters, as we do with H-format. Apostrophe editing is not part of the FORTRAN IV standard, but it is found on many FORTRAN IV implementations and it is part of the FORTRAN 77 standard.

Let us incorporate all of these features into Program 2-2, naming it COUNT1 (see Program 2-3).

```
      PROGRAM COUNT1
C  **  PROGRAM TO COUNT FROM 1 TO 7
C  **  WITH:  PROGRAM STATEMENT,
C  **         INTEGER DECLARATION, AND
C  **         APOSTROPHE EDITING.

      INTEGER  COUNT

      COUNT = 1

10    WRITE ( 5, 12 ) COUNT
12       FORMAT ( ' NUMBER =', I3 )
      COUNT = COUNT + 1
      IF ( COUNT .LE. 7 ) GO TO 10

      END
```

**Program 2-3.** Counting with new features.

Suppose we expand our counting problem a bit. Let us write a program to compute the sum of the counting numbers from 1 to 10, from 1 to 100, and from 1 to 200 all in the same execution of the same program. It looks as though we need three logical IF statements to route the computer along a path that writes out the intermediate sums, followed by another logical IF to see if we need to send the computer back into the path that continues counting. We might draw a flowchart such as that shown in Fig. 2-7. And our first attempt at a program might look like Program 2-4 named SUM1.

```
[Begin execution]

NUMBER =  1
NUMBER =  2
NUMBER =  3
NUMBER =  4
NUMBER =  5
NUMBER =  6
NUMBER =  7
```

**Fig. 2-6.** Execution of Program 2-3.

Examine the FORMAT statement labeled 42 in Program SUM1. The first item within parentheses is a pair of apostrophes surrounding a blank space.

```
      PROGRAM SUM1
C  **  PROGRAM TO SUM THE COUNTING NUMBERS FROM 1 TO
C  **  10, 100, AND 200.  THIS IS OUR FIRST PROGRAM DESIGN
C  **  FOR THIS PROBLEM.

      INTEGER COUNT, SUM

      SUM   = 0
      COUNT = 1

20    SUM = SUM + COUNT
       IF ( COUNT .EQ. 10 )  GO TO 40
       IF ( COUNT .EQ. 100 ) GO TO 40
       IF ( COUNT .EQ. 200 ) GO TO 40
30    COUNT = COUNT + 1
      GO TO 20

40    WRITE ( 5, 42 ) COUNT, SUM
42       FORMAT ( ' ', 'AT COUNT =', I4, ' THE SUM IS', I6 )
      IF ( COUNT .LT. 200 ) GO TO 30

      END
```

**Program 2-4.** To sum counting numbers.

That space is the printer control character for standard single spacing. Some programmers tend to ''bury'' that character within other format specifications. That burial is poor practice. Don't do it that way. We will always explicitly separate that control character to make it visible.

Program SUM1 does produce the correct results, but it could be better structured. Any of the three IF statements may transfer control to the line labeled 40. Following this, control usually passes to line 30 and then to line 20; or, if none of the three logical IF statements diverts control to line 40, then control passes to line 30, since it is physically next in line. That flow of control is circuitous and difficult to follow merely by reading the program. It is difficult to describe. Even the flowchart has lots of arrows and diversions. We will see that by using several additional FORTRAN capabilities, a clearer program may be written.

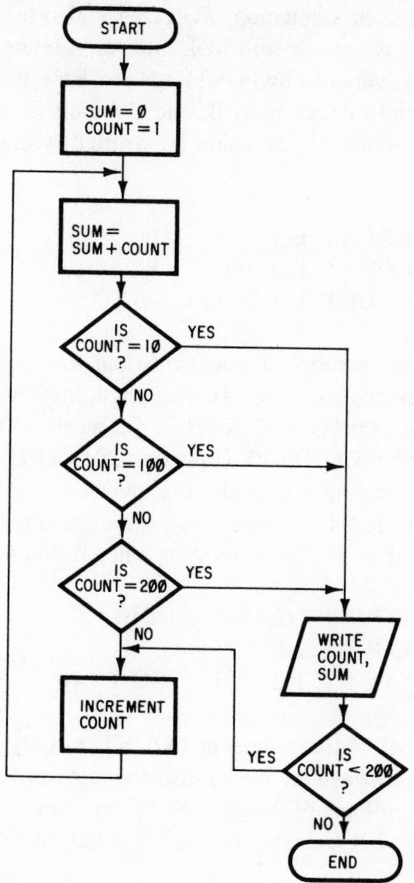


**Fig. 2-7.** Flowchart for writing sums from 1 to 10, from 1 to 100, and from 1 to 200.

```
AT COUNT =  1Ø THE SUM IS    55
AT COUNT = 1ØØ THE SUM IS  5Ø5Ø
AT COUNT = 2ØØ THE SUM IS 2Ø1ØØ
```

**Fig. 2-8.** Execution of Program 2-4.

## *Logical Operators*

A slight improvement could be gained in Program SUM1 by combining the three logical IF statements into one by joining the three relational expressions, using FORTRAN logical operators. FORTRAN provides the logical operator .OR. for just such a situation. FORTRAN also provides .NOT., .AND. and .XOR., each of which we will look into for solutions to future problems. A .OR. B .OR. C is evaluated by FORTRAN as TRUE if any of the expressions A, B, or C is true and FALSE if A, B, and C are all false. So the three logical IF statements of Program SUM1 could be written (with continuation lines) as follows:

```
      IF  ( ( COUNT .EQ. 10 )    .OR.
     +      ( COUNT .EQ. 100 )   .OR.
     +      ( COUNT .EQ. 200 ) ) GO TO 40
```

That only reduces the number of statements that reference line 40. It does not improve the fundamental structure. Another slight improvement could be gained by inserting the line COUNT = COUNT + 1 after the FORMAT statement and changing GO TO 20 to GO TO 30. However, that GO TO 20 can be eliminated entirely by simply creating a structure that bypasses the WRITE statement for all those values of COUNT for which we do not desire output. For that we must convert the logical IF to the form not A and not B and not C. One form is

```
      IF  ( ( COUNT .NE. 10 )    .AND.
     +      ( COUNT .NE. 100 )   .AND.
     +      ( COUNT .NE. 200 ) ) GO TO 40
```

where 40 is the label of the statement COUNT = COUNT + 1. We can see clearly the contrast between the messy decision logic of Program SUM1 and the crisp explicit decision logic of Program SUM2 by comparing the two flowcharts of Fig. 2-7 and Fig. 2-9 (see also Program 2-5 named SUM2).

```
      PROGRAM SUM2
C  **  WE FIND THE SUMS OF THE COUNTING NUMBERS FROM 1 TO
C  **  10, 100, AND 200 USING AN IMPROVED CONTROL STRUCTURE.

      INTEGER COUNT, SUM

      SUM   = 0
      COUNT = 1

20    SUM = SUM + COUNT
      IF (( COUNT .NE. 10 )   .AND.
     +     ( COUNT .NE. 100 ) .AND.
     +     ( COUNT .NE. 200 )) GO TO 40
       WRITE ( 5, 32 ) COUNT, SUM
32        FORMAT ( ' ', 'AT COUNT =', I4, ' THE SUM IS', I6 )

40    COUNT = COUNT + 1
      IF ( COUNT .LE. 200 ) GO TO 20

      END
```

**Program 2-5.** Program SUM1 with improved control.

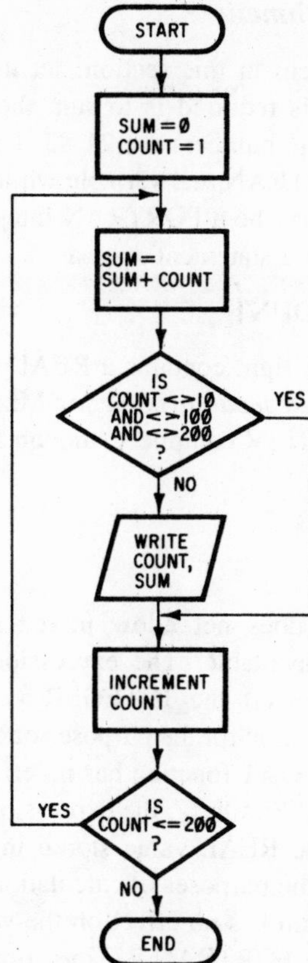


**Fig. 2-9.** Flowchart for improved control in SUM1.

Now we have only two statements that alter the flow of control through the program. One statement directs the computer to bypass the output statement except for the three desired values of COUNT and the other directing the computer to continue counting until 200 is reached.

```
[Begin execution]

AT COUNT =  1Ø THE SUM IS    55
AT COUNT = 1ØØ THE SUM IS  5Ø5Ø
AT COUNT = 2ØØ THE SUM IS 2Ø1ØØ
```

**Fig. 2-10.** Execution of Program 2-5.

Program SUM2 provides a smoother flow of control than does Program SUM1. Note that we eliminated a GO TO statement in the process of redesigning our program. GO TOs are necessary in FORTRAN but, we will find that any effort to minimize their number results in improved program logic.

### *Mixed Mode Arithmetic*

As our final problem in this section, let us compute the average for some test results. All that is required is to sum the results and divide by the number of tests. Suppose the numbers are 21.83, 62.41, 59.2, 50, and 31.92. The sum will require a FORTRAN real variable while the variable used to count the number of test results may be a FORTRAN integer variable. So we will be computing the average with a statement such as

```
AVG = SUM / COUNT
```

Since the expression on the right contains a REAL variable and an INTEGER variable, this is called *mixed mode arithmetic*. Mixed mode arithmetic is not allowed on some FORTRAN IV compilers, though FORTRAN 77 does permit it.

### *FLOAT, IFIX*

If your compiler does not allow mixed mode arithmetic, then the FLOAT function will be available. The expression FLOAT( COUNT ) will direct the computer to convert the INTEGER value stored in the variable COUNT to REAL representation for the purposes of calculation in the expression in which it appears. The FLOAT function has no effect on the variable COUNT or its storage representation. Similarly, the expression IFIX( ZETA ), will direct the computer to convert the REAL value stored in the variable ZETA to INTEGER representation for the purposes of calculation in the expression in which it appears. The IFIX function has no effect on the variable ZETA or its storage representation. When using FORTRAN 77, the corresponding functions REAL and INT are recommended. We may now use the statement

```
AVG = SUM / FLOAT( COUNT )
```

Statements such as this, which utilize the FLOAT or IFIX conversions, also clearly document what is going on.

### *DATA Initialization*

So far we have discussed entering data into our programs either through the arithmetic assignment statement, by typing numbers at a keyboard in response to a READ statement or through cards in response to a READ statement. Another useful method for entering data into programs is through the DATA initialization statement. The DATA initialization statement in FORTRAN directs the compiler to enter the desired values into memory so that they will be available at program execution time. The intended purpose of this is really to enable us to enter constant data, such as look up tables or charts, rather than as a source of data that will change from one execution of our program to the next. However, we introduce this statement as a means of making the data visible in a listing of our demonstration programs. We will soon see other methods of displaying the data used for calculation during a particular run of a program.

The statement

DATA SUM/ 0.0/ COUNT/ 1/

or the statement

DATA SUM, COUNT/ 0.0, 1/

each has the same result as the two statements

SUM = 0.0
COUNT = 1

We will demonstrate a use of the DATA statement and a use of the FLOAT function to avoid mixed mode arithmetic in a little program to compute the average of some test results (see Program 2-6 named TSTAV1).

```
      PROGRAM TSTAV1
C  **  THIS PROGRAM CALCULATES A TEST SCORE AVERAGE

      INTEGER COUNT
      DATA TEST1, TEST2, TEST3, TEST4, TEST5/
     +     21.83, 62.41, 54.2 , 50.0 , 31.92/
     +     COUNT/ 5/

      SUM = TEST1 + TEST2 + TEST3 + TEST4 + TEST5
      WRITE ( 5, 100 ) TEST1, TEST2, TEST3, TEST4, TEST5
100      FORMAT ( ' ', 'TEST SCORES ARE' /
     +            ' ', 5F7.2 /)

C  **  FLOAT IS USED TO AVOID MIXED MODE ARITHMETIC
      AVG = SUM / FLOAT( COUNT )
      WRITE ( 5, 200 ) AVG
200      FORMAT ( ' ', 'AVERAGE IS ', F6.2 )

      END
```

**Program 2-6.** Calculate test results average.

Very often in a problem, like the test result average problem we just considered, the data itself and even the number of data items will not be known until the program is going to be in regular use, often by someone who knows nothing about our program or even programming at all. We cannot require such

```
[Begin execution]

TEST SCORES ARE
  21.83  62.41  54.20  50.00  31.92

AVERAGE IS  44.07
```

**Fig. 2-11.** Execution of Program 2-6.

a person to type a new DATA initialization statement and recompile our program for every use. Therefore, we must provide a method that enables the user of our program to easily enter sets of data during execution. It may even be unreasonable to expect such users to count the number of data items in any set of data.

### *Dummy Data*

One method for entering data sets containing differing numbers of numbers is to agree ahead of time upon a special data value to be recognized as the signal for "no more data." Thus data may be entered from the keyboard of a terminal or on cards with the agreed upon special value as the last data value to be entered. This special data value is sometimes called dummy data. For our test results, we might select "999.0" as the dummy value. In other situations "0.0" or "−1.0" might be selected. In order to incorporate the dummy data concept into our Program TSTAV1, we must provide a counter to count the number of actual data values received. We must be sure that the counting and summing takes place only if we have genuine data. Since the data values themselves will be typed at the keyboard, we needn't provide for printing those

```
      PROGRAM TSTAV2
C  **  THIS PROGRAM CALCULATES THE AVERAGE OF VALUES ENTERED
C  **  FROM THE KEYBOARD.  THE NUMBER OF VALUES IS COUNTED
C  **  BY THE PROGRAM.

      INTEGER COUNT
      REAL  SUM, RESULT, AVE

      WRITE ( 5, 102 )
102      FORMAT ( ' ', 'ENTER TEST RESULTS - ONE TO A LINE', /
     +            ' ', 'TERMINATE WITH ''999.0'''// )
      COUNT = 0
      SUM   = 0.0

110   WRITE ( 5, 112 )
112      FORMAT ( '+', 'RESULT = ? ' )
      READ ( 5, 114 ) RESULT
114      FORMAT ( F6.2 )
      IF ( RESULT .EQ. 999.0 ) GO TO 120
       COUNT = COUNT + 1
       SUM   = SUM + RESULT
       GO TO 110

120   AVE = SUM / FLOAT( COUNT )
      WRITE ( 5, 122 ) AVE
122      FORMAT ( ' ', ' AVERAGE = ', F6.2 )

      END
```

**Program 2-7.** Average test results using dummy data.

values. For card input we would want to print those values as part of the program's output (see Program 2-7 named TSTAV2).

```
[Begin execution]

ENTER TEST RESULTS - ONE TO A LINE
TERMINATE WITH '999.Ø'

RESULT = ? 93.2
RESULT = ? 91.3
RESULT = ? 67.9
RESULT = ? 7Ø.Ø
RESULT = ? 72.5
RESULT = ? 999.Ø

 AVERAGE =   78.98
```

**Fig. 2-12.** Execution of Program 2-7.

Note in Program 2-7 the use of adjacent apostrophes to get an apostrophe printed in the format statement labeled 102. Also note the use of '+' in the FORMAT statement labeled 112 to avoid printing a blank line between successive requests for numbers from the keyboard.

## Summary

The concept of program control has been introduced. The unconditional GO TO statement has been used and the logical IF statement has been used as a conditional transfer statement. We have used relational operators in the logical IF statement.

We have seen that the equals sign in the arithmetic assignment statement directs the computer to evaluate the expression on the right and save the result in the variable named on the left.

The PROGRAM statement has been introduced as a means of program identification. The type declarations INTEGER and REAL have been used to override the FORTRAN variable name first letter default convention. Apostrophe editing has been used as an alternative to H-format. We have seen the use of logical operators to test compound conditions in a logical IF statement. We have seen the value in considering the structure of the flow of control in a program for the purpose of making FORTRAN programs readable.

The DATA initialization statement has been utilized as one technique for providing data for a program to work on during execution.

## Problems for Chap. 2

1. Four test scores were 100, 86, 71, and 92. What was the average?
2. Write a program to add the odd integers from 1 to 100.
3. Write a program to add the integers from 1 to 1000. (What type variable should you use for the sum?)
4. Write a program to count the number of odd integers from 5 to 1191 inclusive.

5. Write a program to find the number of and the sum of all integers greater than 1000 and less than 2213 that are divisible by 11.
6. Three pairs of numbers follow in which the first is the base and the second is the altitude of a triangle: 10,21; 12.5,8; 289,114. Write a program to print the area for each triangle. Use dummy data.
7. A person is paid $0.01 the first day, $0.02 the second day, $0.04 the third day, and so on, doubling each day on the job for 30 days. Write a program to calculate the wages for the thirtieth day and the total for the 30 days.
8. Write a program to print the integers from 1 to 25 paired with their reciprocals.
9. A customer put in an order for four books that retail at $10.95 and carry a 25 percent discount, three records at $4.98 with a 15 percent discount, and one record player for $59.95 on which there is no discount. In addition, there is a 2 percent discount allowed on the total order for prompt payment. Write a program to compute the amount of the order.

*10. Write a program to find the amount of $100 deposited for one year in a savings account at 5 percent per year compounded four times yearly and compounded daily.

*11. In the song "The Twelve Days of Christmas," gifts are bestowed upon the singer in the following pattern: the first day she received a partridge in a pear tree; the second day two turtle doves and a partridge in a pear tree; the third day three french hens, two turtle doves, and a partridge in a pear tree. This continues for 12 days. On the twelfth day she received 12 + 11 + . . . + 2 + 1 gifts. How many gifts did she receive altogether? Another way to ask this question is to ask: If she had to return one gift each day after the first, on what day would she return the last gift?

*12. For problem 11, have the computer print the number of gifts on each of the 12 days and the total up to that day.

*13. George took tests in two courses. For the first course the scores were 83, 91, 97, 100, and 89. For the second course the scores were 65, 72, 81, and 92. Write a program that will compute both test averages. You will need two dummy data values. One value will signal the end of this set of scores and the other will signal the end of this execution of the program.

---

*An asterisk indicates that a more complex program may be required for these problems and all those that follow with that designation.

# 3

# Loops and Linear Arrays

## 3-1 Introduction to DO Loops

On a scale of 1 to 10, how well do you like FORTRAN? How about 9? We can easily write a program to display "I LIKE FORTRAN" 9 times. Program 3-1 named LIKE does exactly this.

```
      PROGRAM LIKE
C  **  WRITE 'I LIKE FORTRAN' 9 TIMES

      INTEGER INDEX

      INDEX = 1

10    WRITE ( 5, 12 ) INDEX
12       FORMAT ( ' ', 'I LIKE FORTRAN', I4 )
      INDEX = INDEX + 1
      IF ( INDEX .LE. 9 )  GO TO 10

      END
```

**Program 3-1.** Write "I LIKE FORTRAN" 9 times.

To write "I LIKE FORTRAN" 99 times, we could simply change the value that INDEX is being compared to in the logical IF statement of our program from 9 to 99. What we have here is a program that directs the computer to repeat an action 9 times. In this case, the action to be repeated is very simple. It consists of writing a message. In other situations the repeated action is more complex. We might test for some property of INDEX—is it a prime or is it a perfect square?—or we might direct the computer to carry out some detailed calculation on a set of data for an inventory item or a tax return for example.

The need to repeat an action occurs often in computer programming. In fact, repetition is one of the things that the computer is best at. This is called a *loop*. In Program LIKE, the computer writes the message, increments the variable INDEX, and then, if INDEX is less than or equal to 9, loops back to write the message again.

In Chap. 2 we constructed a program loop for the sole purpose of counting from 1 to 7. Note that if we replaced the message in Program LIKE with 'NUMBER = ' the result would be a program that counts from 1 to 9. Program 2-4, which sums up counting numbers from 1 to 10, from 1 to 100, and from 1 to 200, also contains all the ingredients of a loop.

Since looping permeates computer programming to such a great degree, FORTRAN includes the DO loop. The DO loop automatically incorporates all of the controls necessary for repetition in a single statement. The FORTRAN statement

DO label INDEX = expr-1, expr-2

is all that is required to execute all statements from the DO statement through the statement labeled "label" for all integer values of INDEX from expr-1 to expr-2 inclusive. Expr-1 is the lower limit and expr-2 is the upper limit on the value of INDEX.

Examine Program 3-2, which uses a DO loop to write "I LIKE FORTRAN" 9 times.

```
      PROGRAM DOLIKE
C  **  WRITE 'I LIKE FORTRAN' 9 TIMES WITH A DO LOOP

      INTEGER INDEX

      DO 1Ø INDEX = 1, 9
1Ø    WRITE ( 5, 12 ) INDEX
12       FORMAT ( ' ', 'I LIKE FORTRAN', I4 )

      END
```

**Program 3-2.** Using a DO loop for Program LIKE.

The single statement

DO 10 INDEX = 1, 9

from Program 3-2 replaces the three statements

INDEX = 1
INDEX = INDEX + 1
IF ( INDEX .LE. 9 ) GO TO 10

which appear in Program 3-1.

A loop consists of four parts:

1. The loop variable is initialized (INDEX = 1).
2. Some programmed activity exists (WRITE ( 5, 12 ) INDEX). This is the block of FORTRAN statements to be repeated.
3. The loop variable is incremented (INDEX = INDEX + 1).

4. The loop variable is tested against an upper limit (IF ( INDEX .LE. 9 ) GO TO 10). The result of the test determines whether or not the loop repeats or is terminated.

```
[Begin execution]

I LIKE FORTRAN   1
I LIKE FORTRAN   2
I LIKE FORTRAN   3
I LIKE FORTRAN   4
I LIKE FORTRAN   5
I LIKE FORTRAN   6
I LIKE FORTRAN   7
I LIKE FORTRAN   8
I LIKE FORTRAN   9
```

**Fig. 3-1.** Execution of Program 3-2.

We may use an additional capability of the DO statement to WRITE the odd integers from 1 to 7. A FORTRAN statement of the form

DO label INDEX = expr-1, expr-2, expr-3

causes the value of the integer variable INDEX to be incremented by the value of expr-3 until INDEX is greater than expr-2. If expr-3 is omitted, the increment is assumed to be 1. The variable INDEX is called the *index of the loop*. Program 3-3 WRITEs the odd integers in the range from 1 to 7.

```
      PROGRAM ODD
C  **  WRITING OUT ODD INTEGERS IN A DO LOOP WITH
C  **  THE INCREMENT CAPABILITY.

      INTEGER COUNT

      DO 10 COUNT = 1, 7, 2
 10   WRITE ( 5, 12 ) COUNT
 12      FORMAT ( ' ', 'NUMBER = ', I3 )

      END
[Begin execution]

NUMBER =   1
NUMBER =   3
NUMBER =   5
NUMBER =   7
```

**Program 3-3.** WRITE odd integers from 1 to 7.

In Program 3-3, the statement referenced in the DO statement is called the *terminal statement* and must be executable. The terminal statement of a DO loop must not be GO TO, STOP, or another DO.

In standard FORTRAN IV the statements within the range of the loop will be executed at least once, even if expr-1 is greater than expr-2. The index of a DO loop must be a positive integer. This restriction will make it necessary for us to do special calculations and incorporate a bias in many situations. However, that is something we will quickly get used to. If a DO loop is completed by virtue of the fact that the index has taken on a value greater than the upper limit, then the value of the index must be considered as undefined. If program execution is diverted from within the range of a DO loop through some branching statement, then the index may be considered to have the value assigned to it through execution of the DO loop. Also, we may not transfer control to statements within a DO loop unless the DO statement has been properly executed. It wouldn't be a good idea, even if it were legal. Furthermore, in FORTRAN IV expr's-1 through 3 must be integer constants or integer variables. If those expressions are integer variables, then we must not alter their value within the DO loop.

In FORTRAN 77 the index may be an integer, real, or double-precision variable. The expr's-1 through 3 may be integer, real, or double-precision expressions and their values may be altered by statements within the DO loop.

## *CONTINUE*

Let us redo Program 2-5 named SUM1 using a DO loop. In this program, the terminal statement cannot be the WRITE statement, as it was for Program ODD, since we only require output conditionally. We cannot use the FORMAT statement because FORMAT statements are not executable. In FORTRAN, the CONTINUE statement was created for just such situations.

The executable statement 100 CONTINUE does nothing but provide for the proper termination of a DO loop. Even though CONTINUE may not be required to logically solve the programming problem at hand, you should always close a DO loop with a corresponding CONTINUE statement. Your programs will be much easier to read if you do this (see Program 3-4 named SUM3).

Suppose we want to calculate interest on $2000 at 4 percent compounded quarterly. Interest rates are generally understood to mean annual rate. So 4 percent per year would mean 1 percent per quarter. While there are compact and fast formulas for making compound interest calculations, we also can calculate the interest for one year by having the computer do the four calculations—one for each quarter. We also can confirm the computer result for the previous example by doing a hand calculation, but for percentages involving several years we are not likely to attempt this. At the end of the first quarter the interest is $20.00 and the principal becomes $2020.00. At the end of the second quarter the interest is $20.20, so the principal becomes $2040.20. At the end of the third quarter the interest is $20.40, so the principal becomes $2060.60. And finally, at the end of the fourth quarter the interest is $20.61, so the principal becomes $2081.21 (see Program 3-5 named CMPD1).

```
      PROGRAM SUM3
C  **  PROGRAM SUM2 USING A DO LOOP

      INTEGER COUNT, SUM

      SUM = Ø

      DO 9Ø COUNT = 1, 2ØØ
        SUM = SUM + COUNT
        IF (( COUNT .NE. 1Ø )    .AND.
     +      ( COUNT .NE. 1ØØ )   .AND.
     +      ( COUNT .NE. 2ØØ ))     GO TO 9Ø
         WRITE ( 5, 52 ) COUNT, SUM
 52         FORMAT ( ' ', 'AT COUNT =', I4, ' THE SUM IS', I6 )
 9Ø   CONTINUE

      END
[Begin execution]

AT COUNT =  1Ø THE SUM IS    55
AT COUNT = 1ØØ THE SUM IS  5Ø5Ø
AT COUNT = 2ØØ THE SUM IS 2Ø1ØØ
```

**Program 3-4.** Program SUM2 with a DO loop.

Note that in Program CMPD1 while QARTER, the index of the DO loop, is assigned the four values 1, 2, 3, and 4 during execution, the variable QARTER has not been referred to in any other way by the program. In that program, the DO loop serves only to count the number of times the interest calculation is done. A DO loop is always just a counter.

```
      PROGRAM CMPD1
C  **  CALCULATE COMPOUND INTEREST QUARTERLY

      REAL    PRINC, INT, RATE, AMOUNT
      INTEGER QARTER

      RATE  = Ø.Ø4 / 4.Ø
      PRINC = 2ØØØ.ØØ

      DO 1ØØ QARTER = 1, 4
        INT    = PRINC * RATE
        AMOUNT = PRINC + INT
        PRINC  = AMOUNT
 1ØØ  CONTINUE

      WRITE ( 5, 112 ) AMOUNT
 112     FORMAT ( ' ', 'AMOUNT = $', F8.2 )

      END
[Begin execution]

AMOUNT = $ 2Ø81.21
```

**Program 3-5.** Calculate compound interest for one year.

It is more usual for interest rates to be fractions or decimals and for compounding to be daily. It has become feasible for banks to do these calculations since they started using computers to help with their clerical work. Typical interest rates look more like 5.75 percent and with daily compounding, we need to calculate a daily rate of (0.0575/365) and do the interest calculation 365 times. In this new problem the DO loop index variable name of QARTER would not be appropriate. DAY might be a better variable name to use. These changes will be left as an exercise.

## Summary

We see that the DO loop may be used to simplify the process of writing programs to carry out repeated operations. In some situations, the CONTINUE statement may be required to provide for an executable termination for a DO loop. Where CONTINUE is not required, you should use it anyway to make your program more readable.

## Problems for Sec. 3-1

Use DO loops for all problems in this section.

1. Add the counting numbers from 1 to 50.
2. Find the number of and the sum of all integers greater than 1000 and less than 2213, which are divisible by 11.
3. Write a program to print the integers from 1 to 25 paired with their reciprocals.
4. Write a program to print the integers from 75 to 100 paired with their reciprocals.
5. Find the sum of the reciprocals of all integers from 1 to 1000.
6. Write a program to find the sum of the integers from 900 to 1000.
7. Write a program to compute the amount of $100 on deposit for one year in a savings account at 5.75 percent, compounded daily and compounded quarterly.
8. Find the sum of the squares of the reciprocals of the integers from 1 to 1000.

*9. Solve the "Twelve Days of Christmas" problem (see problem 11 in Chap. 2) with DO loops.

## 3-2 Introduction to the Linear Array

We are accustomed to using variable names to store numeric values in the computer memory. In an earlier example we handled several test scores by naming a different variable for each score. We used TEST1, TEST2, . . . , and TEST5 in that case. That worked out well for 5 scores, but what if we get into a situation where there are 25 or 100 test scores? We can't even use the variable name TEST100 in many implementations of FORTRAN—and we don't have to. FORTRAN provides the linear array so that we may store long lists of data with a single variable name.

An *array* is simply a special kind of variable that enables us to define a whole set of elements for one variable name. Each element may be used to store a single numeric value. A specific element may be designated by an integer (called a *subscript*) enclosed within parentheses following the array name. For example, LIST(5) is the designation for the fifth element of the array named LIST. LIST(5) is usually read as "list sub five." The maximum number of elements must be declared in a DIMENSION statement or a type statement. To establish the array LIST to store 15 real values, a type statement such as

REAL LIST (15)

would be required. Arrays may be used to store hundreds or even thousands of elements in memory at once. The maximum number will depend on the amount of memory available in your computer.

The individual elements of the array may be used in program statements in exactly the same manner that simple variables may be used.

The number in parentheses is called a *subscript* and may be a variable or an expression. The subscript must be an integer. In standard FORTRAN IV, if a subscript is an expression, it must conform to one of the following forms:

A   X   X+A   X−A   A*X   A*X+B   or   A*X−B

where A and B are literal constants (such as 1, 9, or 17), and X is an integer variable. The variables used in a subscript expression must not themselves be subscripted. However, many implementations permit any integer expression as a subscript. Array names follow the same conventions as unsubscripted variable names. If we want to use the array LIST to store integer values, we may declare that fact with a DIMENSION statement.

DIMENSION LIST(6), SAVE(8)

will establish LIST as an integer array providing for six elements and SAVE as a real array providing for eight elements.

We may show some of the capabilities of arrays with a demonstration program (see Program 3-6 named ARRAY1). Note that the WRITE statement that references the FORMAT statement labeled 222 merely names the array LIST without explicitly designating subscripts. In this way we may write all of the elements of an array without having to specifically name each element separately.

The computer array provides the ability to store many numbers in the computer memory so that we may process selected elements by knowing what subscripts to use. In many cases all elements will be processed by using a DO loop to generate a subscript for each possible element in the array. The capabilities of DO loops and arrays make up a very powerful programming tool.

```
      PROGRAM ARRAY1
C  **  LINEAR ARRAY DEMONSTRATION

      DIMENSION LIST(6)
      INTEGER   INDEX, ELEMNT

C  **  REQUEST SIX ARRAY ELEMENTS FROM A KEYBOARD
      DO 100 INDEX = 1, 6
        WRITE ( 5, 12 )
 12         FORMAT ( '+', 'INTEGER ? ' )
        READ ( 5, 102 )  LIST( INDEX )
 102        FORMAT ( I5 )
 100  CONTINUE

      WRITE ( 5, 112 )  LIST( 1 ), LIST( 3 ), LIST( 5 )
 112      FORMAT ( ' ', 'ELEMENTS ONE, THREE AND FIVE' /
     +                ' ', 3I6 )

      WRITE ( 5, 122 )
 122      FORMAT ( '0', 'WRITE THE ARRAY IN REVERSE ORDER' )
      DO 200 INDEX = 1, 6
        ELEMNT = 7 - INDEX
 200      WRITE ( 5, 202 )  ELEMNT, LIST( ELEMNT )
 202        FORMAT ( ' ', 'ELEMENT', I3, ' =', I6 )

C  **  WE CAN EVEN WRITE ALL VALUES WITH
C  **  AN UNSUBSCRIPTED REFERENCE.
      WRITE ( 5, 222 ) LIST
 222      FORMAT ( ' ', /
     +                ' ', 'WRITE ( 5, 222 ) LIST' /
     +                ' ', 6I6 )

      END
```

**Program 3-6.** Demonstrate a subscripted variable.

```
[Begin execution]
INTEGER ? 123
INTEGER ? 456
INTEGER ? 789
INTEGER ? 369
INTEGER ? 852
INTEGER ? 147

ELEMENTS ONE, THREE AND FIVE
   123   789   852

WRITE THE ARRAY IN REVERSE ORDER
ELEMENT  6 =   147
ELEMENT  5 =   852
ELEMENT  4 =   369
ELEMENT  3 =   789
ELEMENT  2 =   456
ELEMENT  1 =   123

WRITE ( 5, 222 ) LIST
   123   456   789   369   852   147
```

**Fig. 3-2.** Execution of Program 3-6.

### *Largest Value*

Let us use the array concept to determine the largest value in a list of numbers. In order to save the largest number at any time, we select the variable name LARGE. Prior to any processing, the value of LARGE may simply be set to the first element of the array.

We can load our array with a DATA initialization statement. As with the WRITE statement, the DATA initialization statement may include the array name without subscripts to designate "all elements."

```
      PROGRAM LARGE
C  **  FIND THE LARGEST ELEMENT IN A LINEAR ARRAY

      REAL    STORE(15), LARGE
      INTEGER INDEX, NUMBER
      DATA STORE/     1.2,    -81.7,   999.91,    78.61,      0.0,
     +               -9.3,   9921.1,      1.0,     15.1,     32.9,
     +            -81.293, -9991.0,    61.38,   -91.03,      7.0/
     +     NUMBER/ 15/

      LARGE = STORE(1)

      DO 100 INDEX = 2, NUMBER
         IF ( STORE( INDEX ) .GT. LARGE )  LARGE = STORE( INDEX )
  100 CONTINUE

      WRITE ( 5, 102 ) LARGE
  102    FORMAT ( ' ', 'LARGEST VALUE = ', F8.2 )

      END

[Begin execution]

LARGEST VALUE =  9921.10
```

**Program 3-7.** Find largest element in an array.

With the numbers stored in an array, all that is required to find the largest element is to compare LARGE with each element in the array after the first in turn. If the element in question is greater than the largest element so far, then we must direct the computer to save this greater value in LARGE and check the next element. If this is not the case, then the next action required is to check the next element (see Program 3-7 named LARGE).

## Summary

The FORTRAN linear array has been introduced. Arrays must be named in a DIMENSION statement or in a type declaration statement. Values may be entered into the elements of an array in all of the ways that values may be entered into simple variables. All elements of an array may be implicitly referenced in DATA initialization, READ, and WRITE statements.

## Problems for Sec. 3-2

1. Fill a 10-element array with the squares of the subscripts. Write the element number and the element in order in two columns down the page.
2. Prepare a 10-element array using the following numbers: 17, 18, 281, −722, 0, −5, −16, 11, −1, and 10. Find the largest number in the list and its location in the array. Write these values. Then exchange the largest number with the first element and write the new array.
3. Do problem 2 for the smallest number.
4. Prepare an array so that the first two elements are each 1 and each element after the second is the sum of the previous two elements. Write the array. You have begun to form the sequence known as the Fibonacci numbers.
5. Form a 10-element array consisting of the first ten positive odd integers in order. Form a second array so that each element is the sum of all the numbers in the first array up to and including the element number in the second array. Write the second array.
6. Prepare one array containing: 6, 1, 3, 7, 2, and 9. Prepare a second array containing: 8, 2, 3, 9, 7, and 4. Form a third array containing the sums of the corresponding elements, i.e.,

   THIRD( INDEX ) = FIRST( INDEX ) + SECOND( INDEX )

   Write the third array.
7. Do problem 6, but enter the products in the third array.
*8. Prepare one array with the numbers 0, 6, 1, 3, 7, 2, 3, 1, 4, and 9 and another array with the numbers 0, 8, 2, 3, 9, 7, 4, 1, 2, and 4. Prepare a third array with the sums of the corresponding elements from the first two arrays. Beginning with the highest subscript, consider each element in the sum array. If it is less than 10, proceed to the next element. If it is greater than 9, subtract 10 from it and add 1 to the element with the next lower subscript. Write all three arrays on three separate lines (try 10I1 format). What have you accomplished?
9. Load an array with the following numbers: 6, −89, 200, 31, 999, −999, 0, 1, and 18. Write the array across the page in the given order first. Then rearrange the elements so that they are stored in the reverse order. Write the array across the page again.

## 3-3 Nested DO Loops

Loops may be enclosed within other loops. This will enable us to perform repetitions repetitively. We could count from 1 to 9, ten times. In a compound interest program, we could write the compound amount at the end of each year for several years. We can simply include the program logic used for one year in our previous program within a DO loop that counts the years (see Program 3-8 named CMPD2).

In Program 3-8 note that the QARTER loop is entirely within the YEAR loop. Loops written in this way are called *nested loops*. They occur often in

```
      PROGRAM CMPD2
C  **  PROGRAM TO CALCULATE COMPOUND INTEREST USING A DO LOOP

      REAL RATE, PRINC, AMOUNT, INT
      INTEGER YEAR, QARTER

C  **  ESTABLISH ANNUAL RATE, BEGINNING PRINCIPAL,
C  **  AND ADJUST RATE FOR QUARTERLY COMPOUNDING
      RATE  = 0.0575
      PRINC = 2000.00
      RATE  = RATE / 4.0

      DO 200 YEAR = 1, 9
        DO 100 QARTER = 1, 4
          INT    = PRINC * RATE
          AMOUNT = PRINC + INT
          PRINC  = AMOUNT
100     CONTINUE
        WRITE ( 5, 192 ) YEAR, AMOUNT
192       FORMAT ( ' ', 'YEAR = ', I3, ' AMOUNT = $ ', F9.2 )
200   CONTINUE

      END
```

**Program 3-8.** Calculate compound interest for several years.

```
[Begin execution]

YEAR =   1 AMOUNT = $   2117.50
YEAR =   2 AMOUNT = $   2241.91
YEAR =   3 AMOUNT = $   2373.63
YEAR =   4 AMOUNT = $   2513.08
YEAR =   5 AMOUNT = $   2660.73
YEAR =   6 AMOUNT = $   2817.05
YEAR =   7 AMOUNT = $   2982.56
YEAR =   8 AMOUNT = $   3157.79
YEAR =   9 AMOUNT = $   3343.32
```

**Fig. 3-3.** Execution of Program 3-8.

programming and provide tremendous computing power. Execution of loops must be completed from inside out. This is exactly analogous to the nesting of parentheses in an algebraic expression. Sample legal and nonlegal constructions are shown below:

*Legal*

```
      DO 40 INDEX = 1, ROW
        DO 30 STEP = 8, 19, 2
          N1 = N1 + STEP
30      CONTINUE
        DO 20 VAL1 = 2, 11
20      CONTINUE
40    CONTINUE
```

*Nonlegal*

```
      DO 40 INDEX = 1, ROW
        DO 30 STEP = 8, 19, 2
          N1 = N1 + STEP
30      CONTINUE
        DO 20 VAL1 = 2, 11
40    CONTINUE
20      CONTINUE
```

If the FORTRAN statements of DO loops are properly indented, illegal nesting (see p. 43) is easily seen and therefore avoidable. For this reason, you are encouraged to close every DO loop with its own CONTINUE statement.

Let us use DO loops to write out a table of squares. We may write such a table in rectangular form with ten numbers per row and each number in a row being the square of the sum of the column label and the row label. This is a common practice for organizing such tables. To facilitate writing across the page, we may enter ten numbers into a 10-element array for each row of the table (see Program 3-9 named SQARES).

```
      PROGRAM SQARES
C  **  WRITE A TABLE OF SQUARES

      INTEGER COLUMN, ROW, ARRAY, NUMBER, ROWØ
      DIMENSION ARRAY( 1Ø )

C  **  WRITE THE COLUMN HEADERS
      WRITE ( 5, 12 )
 12      FORMAT ( ' ', 17X, 'TABLE OF SQUARES' / )
      DO 2Ø COLUMN = 1, 1Ø
        ARRAY( COLUMN ) = COLUMN - 1
 2Ø   CONTINUE
      WRITE ( 5, 42 ) ARRAY
 42      FORMAT ( ' ', 2X, 1ØI5 )

C  **  NOW SET UP THE BODY OF THE TABLE.
      DO 1ØØ ROW = 1, 6
        DO 5Ø COLUMN = 1, 1Ø

C  **  CALCULATE THE NUMBER TO BE SQUARED AND ENTER IN AN ARRAY
          NUMBER = 1Ø * ( ROW - 1 ) + ( COLUMN - 1 )
          ARRAY( COLUMN ) = NUMBER**2
 5Ø     CONTINUE
        ROWØ = ( ROW - 1 ) * 1Ø
        WRITE ( 5, 92 ) ROWØ, ARRAY
 92        FORMAT ( 'Ø', I2, 1ØI5 )
 1ØØ  CONTINUE

      END
```

**Program 3-9.** A table of squares.

Standard FORTRAN IV requires that the index of the DO loop be a positive integer. FORTRAN 77 allows REAL and even DOUBLE PRECISION values for the index of a DO loop. In Program 3-9 note the statement

$$\text{NUMBER} = 10 * (\text{ ROW } - 1 ) + (\text{ COLUMN } - 1 )$$

To make this program run under FORTRAN IV, we have simply biased all values by 1 in the index variable and subtracted 1 for calculation purposes.

```
[Begin execution]

                    TABLE OF SQUARES

         0    1    2    3    4    5    6    7    8    9

    0    0    1    4    9   16   25   36   49   64   81

   10  100  121  144  169  196  225  256  289  324  361

   20  400  441  484  529  576  625  676  729  784  841

   30  900  961 1024 1089 1156 1225 1296 1369 1444 1521

   40 1600 1681 1764 1849 1936 2025 2116 2209 2304 2401

   50 2500 2601 2704 2809 2916 3025 3136 3249 3364 3481
```

**Fig. 3-4.** Execution of Program 3-9.

FORTRAN IV requires positive integer subscripts, while FORTRAN 77 allows a subscript to be zero or even negative. In the statement

ARRAY( COLUMN ) = NUMBER**2

we have used the DO loop index, which we have adjusted to be a positive integer, as the ARRAY subscript. We also have introduced the use of the operator "**" to indicate the operation "to the power" in FORTRAN.

## *Pythagorean Triples*

There is an interesting set of right triangles with sides whose lengths are integers. Any three integers that can represent the sides of a right triangle are referred to as a Pythagorean triple. If we have sides of a right triangle LEG1, LEG2, and HYPOT, then the Pythagorean Theorem tells us that the sum of the squares of the two legs equals the square of the hypotenuse or

LEG1*LEG1 + LEG2*LEG2 = HYPOT*HYPOT

Suppose we want to find Pythagorean triples with either leg up to 25. We may simply write a short FORTRAN program to test possible sets of three integers to determine whether or not they could be sides of a right triangle according to the formula just stated. This will take three DO loops—one each for LEG1, LEG2, and HYPOT. Consider the following three DO loops to generate sets of three integers to test:

```
DO 40 LEG1 = 1, 25
  DO 30 LEG2 = 1, 25
    DO 20 HYPOT = 1, 50
```

Surely those DO loops will generate sets of three integers related to the stated problem. However, we can make significant improvements. For example, as set up, these three DO loops would generate 4, 3, and 5 as well as 3, 4, and 5. It would be poor program design to generate each solution twice! We can eliminate duplicates by replacing the middle DO with DO 30 LEG2 = LEG1, 25. We have made two major improvements by doing this. We have corrected the design and cut the number of triples we have to test nearly in half. A similar improvement will be gained by replacing the third DO with DO 20 HYPOT = LEG2, 50.

Once we have a triple to test, there are three possible conditions:

1. The square of the hypotenuse might be greater than the sum of the squares of the legs, in which case we want to increment the LEG2 loop.
2. The square of the hypotenuse might be less than the sum of the squares of the legs, in which case we want to increment the HYPOT loop.
3. The square of the hypotenuse might be equal to the sum of the squares of the legs, in which case we want to write out the values and increment the LEG2 loop (see Program 3-10 named PYTHAG).

```
      PROGRAM PYTHAG
C  ** SEARCH FOR PYTHAGOREAN TRIPLES USING DO LOOPS

      INTEGER LEG1, LEG2, HYPOT, K1, K3

      DO 40 LEG1 = 1, 25
        DO 30 LEG2 = LEG1, 25
          DO 20 HYPOT = LEG2, 50
            K1 = LEG1*LEG1 + LEG2*LEG2
            K3 = HYPOT*HYPOT
            IF ( K3 .GT. K1 ) GO TO 30
              IF ( K3 .LT. K1 ) GO TO 20
                WRITE ( 5, 12 ) LEG1, LEG2, HYPOT
12                FORMAT ( ' ', 3I5 )
              GO TO 30
20        CONTINUE
30      CONTINUE
40    CONTINUE

      END
```

**Program 3-10.** Search for Pythagorean triples.

Note that there are other Pythagorean triples with one leg less than or equal to 25, but the other leg is greater than 25, so they are not found by this limited program.

We might want to modify Program 3-10 to request an upper limit from a keyboard or from a card reader.

```
[Begin execution]

  3   4   5
  5  12  13
  6   8  10
  7  24  25
  8  15  17
  9  12  15
 10  24  26
 12  16  20
 15  20  25
 18  24  30
 20  21  29
```

**Fig. 3-5.** Execution of Program 3-10.

## Summary

Loops may be nested inside other loops as long as we see to it that operations are done from the inside out, in much the same way we deal with parentheses in algebraic expressions. The limits of one loop may be set by the values of the indices of other loops as long as we do not alter the indices of loops that are still active.

## Problems for Sec. 3-3

1. Prepare one array with the numbers 6, 4, 11, 51, and 17 and another with 51, 12, 11, and 16. Now write all possible pairs using one number from each array.
2. Do problem 1, but do not print a pair if the numbers are equal.
3. Prepare an array with the numbers 13, 31, −73, 91, and 11. Write all possible pairs of numbers from this list.
4. Enter the numbers 1, 6, 11, 71, 32, 89, and 21 in one array and 1, 26, 6, 93, 71, 2, and 7 in another. Enter into a third array only those numbers that appear in both of the first two arrays and write the third array.
5. Using the first two arrays of problem 4, create a third array consisting of all numbers that appear in either array. Allow no duplications. Write the resulting array.
6. Find some of the Pythagorean triples missing in the execution of Program PYTHAG by raising the upper limit on LEG2.
7. Prepare an array with the numbers 11, 17, 31, −82, and 22. Write all possible triples of numbers from this list without repeating any element.

## 3-4 Sorting Numbers in an Array

Suppose we have a long list of values that must be arranged in numeric order. If we look at every pair of numbers in a list and they are all in numeric order, then we are assured that the entire list is in order. Thus, one scheme for arranging such a list is to store the numbers in an array and compare all possible pairs. We should avoid comparing a number with itself, and we should avoid duplicating comparisons. For every comparison, if the numbers are in order, then proceed to the next pair, while if the pair is out of order, then exchange the numbers of the pair before proceeding to the next pair.

To identify all possible pairs, we simply use one DO loop whose index is the subscript of the first array element and a second DO loop whose index is the subscript of the second element in the array selected for comparison purposes. Let's generate all possible nonduplicated pairs by comparing the first element with the second through the last, then the second with the third through the last, then the third with the fourth through the last, and so on until we are comparing the last two elements of the array. If we allow the first index to range from one to one less than the number of numbers in the array and the second index to range from one more than the first index to the number of numbers in the array, then we will be comparing all possible pairs without comparing any pair more than once and without comparing any element with itself. These DO loops may be established with the following statements:

```
LAST = NUMBER - 1
DO 200 FIRST = 1, LAST
   BEGIN = FIRST + 1
   DO 100 SECOND = BEGIN, NUMBER
```

where NUMBER is the number of numbers in the array.

Alternatively, in FORTRAN 77 we may use the following two statements:

```
DO 200 FIRST = 1, NUMBER - 1
   DO 100 SECOND = FIRST + 1, NUMBER
```

To exchange two numbers that are out of order, we must first save one of them. The exchange requires three FORTRAN statements as follows:

```
               SAVE = ARRAY ( FIRST )
   ARRAY ( FIRST ) = ARRAY ( SECOND )
ARRAY ( SECOND ) = SAVE
```

See Program 3-11 named ARANG1.

The following two statements from Program ARANG1 bear discussion:

```
100      CONTINUE
200   CONTINUE
```

Where two DO loops logically terminate at the same point in a program, it is permissible to combine them. That is, we could replace those two CONTINUE statements with a single CONTINUE statement and the correct label references. However, having two CONTINUE statements there enables us to preserve indentation and thus to maintain good program readability. Providing two CONTINUE statements also makes it much easier to make modifications later in the program that might involve inserting new program statements between them.

```
      PROGRAM ARANG1
C  **  ARRANGE NUMBERS IN INCREASING ORDER IN AN ARRAY

      DIMENSION ARRAY(1Ø)
      INTEGER   ARRAY, LAST, NUMBER, FIRST, BEGIN, SECOND, SAVE
      DATA ARRAY/ 6, -19, 28, 2Ø, -32, 74, 19, 28, 23, 43/
     +    NUMBER/ 1Ø/

      WRITE ( 5, 12 )
 12      FORMAT ( ' ', 'ORIGINAL ORDER' )
      WRITE ( 5, 944 ) ARRAY

      WRITE ( 5, 32 )
 32      FORMAT ( ' ', 'ARRANGING IN INCREASING ORDER' )

      LAST = NUMBER - 1
      DO 2ØØ FIRST = 1, LAST
        BEGIN = FIRST + 1
        DO 1ØØ SECOND = BEGIN, NUMBER
          IF ( ARRAY( FIRST ) .LE. ARRAY( SECOND ) ) GO TO 1ØØ
           SAVE              = ARRAY( FIRST )
           ARRAY( FIRST )    = ARRAY( SECOND )
           ARRAY( SECOND )  = SAVE
           WRITE ( 5, 944 ) ARRAY
 1ØØ    CONTINUE
 2ØØ  CONTINUE

      WRITE ( 5, 3Ø2 )
 3Ø2     FORMAT ( ' ', 'THE LIST IN INCREASING ORDER' )
      WRITE ( 5, 944 ) ARRAY

 944     FORMAT ( ' ', 1ØI5 )
      END
```

**Program 3-11.** Arrange a list of numbers in order.

```
[Begin execution]

ORIGINAL ORDER
    6  -19   28   2Ø  -32   74   19   28   23   43
ARRANGING IN INCREASING ORDER
  -19    6   28   2Ø  -32   74   19   28   23   43
  -32    6   28   2Ø  -19   74   19   28   23   43
  -32  -19   28   2Ø    6   74   19   28   23   43
  -32  -19   2Ø   28    6   74   19   28   23   43
  -32  -19    6   28   2Ø   74   19   28   23   43
  -32  -19    6   2Ø   28   74   19   28   23   43
  -32  -19    6   19   28   74   2Ø   28   23   43
  -32  -19    6   19   2Ø   74   28   28   23   43
  -32  -19    6   19   2Ø   28   74   28   23   43
  -32  -19    6   19   2Ø   23   74   28   28   43
  -32  -19    6   19   2Ø   23   28   74   28   43
  -32  -19    6   19   2Ø   23   28   28   74   43
  -32  -19    6   19   2Ø   23   28   28   43   74
THE LIST IN INCREASING ORDER
  -32  -19    6   19   2Ø   23   28   28   43   74
```

**Fig. 3-6.** Execution of Program 3-11.

Note that if we later wish to work with larger arrays, we will still be able to use the format statement labeled 944. In such a case, FORTRAN will begin again at the beginning of the format statement after every multiple of ten elements.

We have included extra WRITE statements to show how the smaller values move to the low end of the array as the sorting progresses.

The algorithm we have used to arrange a list of numbers in order is commonly referred to as a BUBBLE SORT, because of the "bubbling" effect as the numbers migrate to one end of the array. There are many variations on the fundamental approach we have taken.

It turns out that sorting is one of the important applications of computers. Therefore much is known about sorting. One of the things known is that the algorithm used here is deceptively simple and very inefficient.

We could gain some improvement in efficiency by taking a slightly different approach. By comparing adjacent pairs of elements we may gain some special benefits. Note that if we make a "pass" through the entire array making adjacent comparisons and no two elements are out of order, then the entire list is in order. Using this scheme, we could select a new variable to set to zero at the beginning of a pass and set it equal to one whenever an exchange is made. At the end of any pass, if the value of the new variable is still zero, then the sort is complete and we may write the list. Another method for speeding up the bubble-type sort is to sort in both directions and test for exchanges at the end of a double pass. This will speed things up if only a small number of items are out of order.

It turns out that to sort small groups of numbers, none of these processes takes enough computer resources to matter much. Pick a method you like and use it, but for lists of many thousands of numbers, the fundamental inefficiencies of the bubble-type sort will slow things down noticeably. Most other sorting methods partition the data into segments that make it unnecessary to compare all pairs with each iteration. Such methods are generally beyond the scope of an introductory treatment.

## Summary

We have used the combination of nested loops and numbers stored in an array as a powerful tool for rearranging numbers within a program. It requires three FORTRAN program statements to exchange two values stored in two variables.

## Problems for Sec. 3-4

1. Write a program to print the following numbers in decreasing order: 300, 271, 250, −89, 76, 0, and −50. Count the number of times the computer does a comparison and the number of times the computer does an exchange of two numbers.

2. Write a program to print the following numbers in increasing order: 45, 76, −76, 45, and 98. Do not print the duplicated number, but leave it in the array.
*3. Program the computer to list the numbers from problem 1 in order by comparing elements one and two first, then elements two and three, then elements three and four, etc. Create a switch SWITCH = 0 for off and SWITCH = 1 for on. Turn the switch off, then if an exchange is required, turn the switch on. After testing the last two elements, look at the switch. If it is on, turn it off and go through the array again. If it is off, the list is in order, so print it. Count the number of comparisons and the number of exchanges.
4. Fill an array with the following numbers: 1, 92, −981, 89, −21, 0, −111, 111, 92, −929, and 1001. Arrange them in increasing order. Print the number and the original position of each number. The original position may be stored in a second array. Whenever an exchange of numbers is made to place them in increasing order, a corresponding exchange must be made in the array containing the original positions.
*5. Use the method of comparing adjacent pairs of array elements and sorting in both directions in conjunction with a switch to arrange a list in decreasing order.

# 4

# FUNCTIONs and SUBROUTINEs in FORTRAN

Good things come in small FORTRAN packages!

Suppose we find in a program that we need to average three numbers at numerous points, each with a different set of three values, or suppose we require the same intricate tax computation applied to several quantities. It is desirable to write the FORTRAN statement or statements just once and then utilize them as needed throughout the program. FORTRAN FUNCTIONs and SUBROUTINEs are included in the language for just this purpose. They provide neat packages for program statements. The computing power of these packages is at our fingertips by merely naming them as needed.

All functions require at least one value (called an *argument*) enclosed in parentheses following the function name. Values are passed to functions in the arguments and a value is returned in the function name. We have already utilized the functions FLOAT and IFIX. Remember that

```
X9 = FLOAT( NUMBER )
```

causes the computer to convert the integer representation of the value stored in the integer variable NUMBER to real representation and store that in the real variable X9. FLOAT is a FORTRAN function and NUMBER is the required argument.

FLOAT is an example of the FORTRAN-supplied or built-in function. Built-in functions we get for "free." They come with the FORTRAN implementation. IFIX is another example of the built-in function.

The statement function enables us to provide predefined calculations that can be written in a single FORTRAN statement.

The FUNCTION subprogram provides the ability to incorporate the program statements of one program unit into another. Thus the name *subpro-*

*gram*. The value of the result of the process within the function is passed back to the first program in the function name. FUNCTION subprograms are functions we can write that behave very much like built-in functions.

The SUBROUTINE subprogram also allows you to incorporate the program statements of one program unit into another. However, the SUBROUTINE name does not itself take on a value. Values are passed between program units in an argument list.

## 4-1 Built-in Functions

Every built-in FORTRAN function is called into action by incorporating the function name with appropriate argument(s) into a FORTRAN statement. They are real or integer according to the first letter of the function name.

### *Single Argument Functions*

ABS, SQRT, and AINT are three frequently utilized FORTRAN-supplied functions. Each requires a real argument and returns a real value in the function name.

ABS(A) returns the absolute value of A.

SQRT(B) returns the square root of B. It should be noted that we also could calculate the square root of B with A**.5 (remember, ** represents the instruction "to the power"), but the process of exponentiation is slower and generally subject to more computation error than the SQRT function. The argument of the SQRT function must be zero or positive. If we are applying the SQRT function to a lot of data, we might first apply the ABS function.

AINT(C) returns the largest integer less than or equal to the greatest integer in the absolute value of C times the sign of C. This is much easier to see with a couple of examples. AINT(3.61) = 3.0 and AINT(−3.61) = −3.0. FORTRAN merely "chops off" the decimal part. This process also is referred to as *truncation*.

We can illustrate the use of these functions in a demonstration program. Store six real data values in an array and write the result of calling the ABS, SQRT, and AINT functions for each of the data values with a DO loop (see Program 4-1 named FUNCT1).

Note that we have applied the ABS function before calling the SQRT function. In a problem solving program, we might test the value of the argument before calling the SQRT function. In the event that the argument is negative, we probably wish to bypass the square root function anyway.

Suppose we want to find factors of integers. If the quotient of two integers is an integer, then the denominator is a factor of the numerator. For example, 65/5 = 13 and 13 is an integer, therefore 5 is a factor of 65 and so is 13.

In a FORTRAN program we will store the quotient in a real variable using the FLOAT function so that the quotient FLOAT(65) / FLOAT(5) is stored as 13.0. Next we may apply the AINT function to the quotient to determine if

```
      PROGRAM FUNCT1
C  ** WE DEMONSTRATE A FEW BUILT-IN FUNCTIONS

      DIMENSION ARRAY(6)
      REAL      ARRAY, ROOT, ABSVAL, TRUNC
      INTEGER   INDEX
      DATA  ARRAY/ -9989.Ø, 36.31, 8392.6, .Ø39, -.Ø21, Ø.Ø/

      WRITE ( 5, 12 )
12       FORMAT ( ' ', 6X, 'DATA      ABSVAL    SQ ROOT   TRUNCATE' )
      DO 1ØØ INDEX = 1, 6
        ABSVAL = ABS  ( ARRAY(INDEX) )
        ROOT   = SQRT( ABSVAL )
        TRUNC  = AINT( ARRAY(INDEX) )
        WRITE  ( 5, 92 ) ARRAY(INDEX), ABSVAL, ROOT, TRUNC
92          FORMAT ( ' ', 4F1Ø.3 )
1ØØ   CONTINUE

      END
```

**Program 4-1.** Demonstrate ABS, SQRT, and AINT.

the quotient and the AINT of the quotient are equal. We will find that 13.0 will indeed equal 13.0, thus indicating that 5 and 13 are both factors of 65. On the other hand, FLOAT(65) / FLOAT(2) = 32.5 and AINT(32.5) = 32.0. These two values are not equal and so 2 is not a factor of 65.

```
[Begin execution]

      DATA    ABSVAL   SQ ROOT  TRUNCATE
 -9989.ØØØ 9989.ØØØ   99.945 -9989.ØØØ
    36.31Ø   36.31Ø    6.Ø26    36.ØØØ
  8392.6ØØ 8392.6ØØ   91.611  8392.ØØØ
      .Ø39     .Ø39     .197     Ø.ØØØ
     -.Ø21     .Ø21     .145     Ø.ØØØ
     Ø.ØØØ    Ø.ØØØ    Ø.ØØØ     Ø.ØØØ
```

**Fig. 4-1.** Execution of Program 4-1.

If we initialize a DO loop to index from 2 to one less than the integer in question and perform the above test on every quotient of NUMBER / INDEX, we should find a factor, if it exists. The first value of INDEX will be the smallest factor and NUMBER / INDEX will be the largest factor. This is done to find the largest factor for integers requested from the keyboard in Program 4-2 named FACTOR.

Note the use of the REAL variable FNUM in Program FACTOR. The use of functions requires certain computer resources. There is no point to repeatedly invoking the FLOAT function with the same number as the argument in this program. We were able to invoke FLOAT just once for NUMBER and save the result in the intermediate variable FNUM. Thus, for large values of NUMBER, our program will execute noticeably faster.

```
      PROGRAM FACTOR
C  **  THIS PROGRAM FINDS THE LARGEST FACTOR OF AN INTEGER

      INTEGER INDEX, NUMBER, N1, FACTOR
      REAL    DIVIDE, FNUM

C  **  REQUEST DATA FROM THE KEYBOARD
 10   WRITE ( 5, 12 )
 12      FORMAT ( ' ', 'ENTER AN INTEGER ' )
      READ ( 5, 22 ) NUMBER
 22      FORMAT ( I5 )
      IF ( NUMBER .EQ. 0 ) STOP
      FNUM = FLOAT ( NUMBER )

C  **  NOW TEST FROM TWO TO ONE LESS THAN THE INTEGER
      N1 = NUMBER - 1
      DO 100 INDEX = 2, N1
        DIVIDE = FNUM / FLOAT( INDEX )
        IF ( DIVIDE .EQ. AINT( DIVIDE ) ) GO TO 300
 100  CONTINUE

      WRITE ( 5, 112 ) NUMBER
 112     FORMAT ( '+', I5, ' IS PRIME ' / )
      GO TO 10

 300  FACTOR = IFIX( DIVIDE )
      WRITE ( 5, 312 ) NUMBER, FACTOR
 312     FORMAT ( '+', I5, ' HAS LARGEST FACTOR ', I5 / )
      GO TO 10

      END
```

**Program 4-2.** Find largest factor.

```
[Begin execution]

ENTER AN INTEGER 1949
 1949 IS PRIME

ENTER AN INTEGER 1001
 1001 HAS LARGEST FACTOR   143

ENTER AN INTEGER 0
 STOP
```

**Fig. 4-2.** Execution of Program 4-2.

If your FORTRAN compiler permits mixed mode arithmetic, then you may choose to avoid the use of the FLOAT and IFIX (or REAL and INT) functions as used in FACTOR. However, the use of FLOAT and IFIX does provide clear documentation to anyone reading your program.

While Program FACTOR got the job done, there are some aspects of the program that are of interest. For any nonprime integer the program is adequately designed, but for prime integers this program requires the computer to test many quotients unnecessarily. For large values this could require a noticeable computation time. There must be a way to test fewer quotients. There is! We can easily see that for every pair of factors of an integer, one is less than or equal to the square root of the integer and the other is greater than or equal to the square root of the integer. So we need only try divisors up to the square root. For 1949 this plan reduces the number of divisions from 1947 to 43. That is an improvement worth making in our program and is left as an exercise.

### *Multiargument Functions*

Some FORTRAN built-in functions require two or more arguments. MOD requires two arguments, while MIN0 and MAX0 allow two or more.

MOD(K1,K2) returns the value of K1 modulo K2. For example, MOD ( 9, 6 ) = 3. This also is called *remaindering*. The arguments and the function are all integer. The function AMOD(R1,R2) provides for real arguments and a real function value.

MIN0(K1,K2,...,Kn) returns the smallest of the integer values in the argument list, while MAX0(K1,K2,...Kn) returns the largest of the integer values in the argument list.

Program 4-3 named FUNCT2 illustrates the use of these functions.

For many functions we may require either integer or real values for the function and the argument(s). This implies four possible functions that carry out the same mathematical process, but which differ as to the data format type requested. Let us consider the maximum value function as an example. The four functions are shown in Table 4-1.

**Table 4-1.** Four possible functions for MAXIMUM.

| *Name* | *Argument* | *Function* |
|---|---|---|
| AMAX0 | INTEGER | REAL |
| AMAX1 | REAL | REAL |
| MAX0 | INTEGER | INTEGER |
| MAX1 | REAL | INTEGER |

The MIN function follows the same pattern as the MAX function. For some functions, it is not appropriate to provide for all four combinations. For instance, the trigonometric functions may be limited to real format (see Appendix A for a table of FORTRAN-supplied functions). You may find that your FORTRAN implementation includes some additional built-in functions of interest.

```
      PROGRAM FUNCT2
C **  WE DEMONSTRATE A FEW MULTIARGUMENT FUNCTIONS

      DIMENSION LIST1(5), LIST2(5)
      INTEGER   LIST1, LIST2, K1, MODD, MIN, MAX
      DATA LIST1/ 63, 11,  9,  Ø,  7/
     +     LIST2/ 21, 17, 58,  6,  Ø/

      WRITE ( 5, 12 )
12       FORMAT ( ' ', ' LIST1 LIST2   MOD   MIN   MAX' )

      DO 1ØØ K1 = 1, 5
         MODD = MOD  (LIST1(K1), LIST2(K1))
         MIN  = MINØ(LIST1(K1), LIST2(K1))
         MAX  = MAXØ(LIST1(K1), LIST2(K1))
1ØØ    WRITE (5, 112) LIST1(K1), LIST2(K1), MODD, MIN, MAX
112       FORMAT ( ' ', 5I6 )

      END
```

**Program 4-3.** Demonstrate MOD, MINO, and MAXO.

```
[Begin execution]

 LIST1 LIST2   MOD   MIN   MAX
    63    21     Ø    21    63
    11    17    11    11    17
     9    58     9     9    58
     Ø     6     Ø     Ø     6
     7     Ø     7     Ø     7
```

**Fig. 4-3.** Execution of Program 4-3.

## Summary

The built-in FORTRAN functions provide the programmer with easy access to the results of numerous preprogrammed packages. These functions are utilized by simply naming them along with the appropriate argument(s) in a FORTRAN program statement.

## Problems for Sec. 4-1

1. Write a program to print all pairs of factors of integers.
2. Modify Program FACTOR to utilize the concept of selecting from 2 to the square root of NUMBER for the purpose of improving execution speed. Compare execution speeds for large prime integers.
3. Write a program that will print only prime factors of integers.
4. Write a program to perform the work of the ABS function without using any built-in FORTRAN function.
5. Write a program to print all of the prime positive integers less than 100.
6. Write a program using the MOD function to convert minutes to hours and minutes.

*7. For each of the following pairs of integers find two integers so that their sum is the first number in the given pair and the product is the second number in the given pair: 3, 2; 7, 12; 11, 28; −11, 28; 3, −28; 76, 103; 7, 8; 34, 289. Note: ABS has the companion function IABS.

## 4-2 Statement Functions

We may find in a program that a particular calculation occurs often that is not provided by one of the built-in FORTRAN functions. We may use the statement function for many such situations. For example, we might be writing a program in which we need to calculate the average of three numbers in several places. The statement function

```
AVERAG( A, B, C ) = ( A + B + C ) / 3.0
```

would be entered before the first executable statement. Then, at any point in the program that the average of three numbers is required, we may simply use a statement such as one of the following:

```
Y1 = AVERAG( 6.1, 17.3, 11.91 )
Y1 = AVERAG( X1, X2, X3 )
```

and the computer will apply the formula as defined earlier in the program.

It is important to realize that the variables A, B, and C in the defining statement are in no way related to any variables named A, B, or C elsewhere in the program. These variables are placed there only to establish the relationship between the position of the variables in the argument list and the place that they occupy in the formula to the right of the equals sign. Such arguments are referred to as *dummy arguments*. Statement functions are real or integer according to the first letter in the function name. The data type of a function may be declared in a type specification statement. The rules for naming statement functions are the same as for naming variables.

### *A Rounding Function*

We might want to define a statement function to round off real values to a specified precision. A frequently used precision is hundredths, since that correlates to dollars and cents. Many FORTRAN compilers round values when they are printed using F-format, but if we wish to carry the rounded values for further calculation within the program, F-format does not help us.

To round to the nearest hundredth we can first multiply the number by 100 and then add 0.5, then truncate and divide by 100. For example, let's take 128.361 and 19.416:

| | | |
|---|---|---|
| number | 128.361 | 19.417 |
| times 100 | 12836.1 | 1941.7 |
| add 0.5 | 12836.6 | 1942.2 |
| truncate | 12836. | 1942. |
| divide by 100 | 128.36 | 19.42 |

The following statement function will perform these calculations:

```
ROUND0(X) = AINT( 100.*X + .5 ) / 100
```

An algorithm may be described as the recipe for solving a problem. We have developed an algorithm for rounding real numbers with a FORTRAN statement function, but there are correct algorithms and incorrect ones! Our goal is to always develop correct algorithms. The function ROUND0(X) will fail for negative values of X. Let's try −12.613:

| | |
|---|---|
| number | −12.613 |
| times 100 | −1261.3 |
| add 0.5 | −1260.8 |
| truncate | −1260. |
| divide by 100 | −12.60 |

We get −12.60 where we expected −12.61. This suggests that for negative numbers we should subtract 0.5. What we need is a way of determining what the sign of our number to be rounded is. Since X / ABS(X) will be +1 or −1 as X is positive or negative, we could then add

```
.5 * X / ABS(X)
```

This indicated division will cause trouble if the value of X is zero. Alternatively, we can use another FORTRAN built-in function to transfer the sign of X to 0.5. The function

```
SIGN( A1, A2 )
```

transfers the sign of A2 to A1. For our rounding problem, we would use the expression

```
SIGN( .5, X )
```

and our rounding function becomes

```
ROUND1(X) = AINT( 100. * X + SIGN( .5, X ) ) / 100
```

We demonstrate the various calculations with Program 4-4 named ROUND.

The statement function ROUND1 as written rounds to the nearest hundredth. We could easily generalize it by replacing 100.0 with a dummy variable and round to differing precisions depending on the value of this second dummy argument. This is left as an exercise.

## Summary

The statement function allows us to define a calculation to be performed upon a variable list. It must be defined once among the nonexecutable statements at the beginning of a program and may be referenced at any point in that program. A statement function is data typed according to the first letter of the function name and may be declared otherwise with a type declaration statement.

```
      PROGRAM ROUND
C  **  WE DEMONSTRATE A ROUNDING STATEMENT FUNCTION

      REAL NUMBER, A1, A2, A3
      ROUND1(X1) = AINT( 100.0 * X1 + SIGN( .5, X1 ) ) / 100.0

10    WRITE ( 5, 12 )
12       FORMAT ( ' ', 'NUMBER TO ROUND ? ' )
      READ ( 5, 112 ) NUMBER
112      FORMAT ( F10.3 )
      IF ( NUMBER .EQ. 0.0 ) GO TO 999

       A1 = .5 * NUMBER / ABS( NUMBER )
       A2 = SIGN( .5, NUMBER )
       A3 = ROUND1( NUMBER )
       WRITE ( 5, 142 ) A1, A2, A3
142         FORMAT ( '+', '.5 * NUMBER/ABS( NUMBER ) =', F10.3 /
     +                ' ', '        SIGN( .5, NUMBER ) =', F10.3 /
     +                ' ', '          ROUND1( NUMBER ) =', F10.3 / )
       GO TO 10

999   END
```

**Program 4-4.** Demonstrate rounding with a statement function.

```
[Begin execution]

NUMBER TO ROUND ? 1234.56
.5 * NUMBER/ABS( NUMBER ) =       .500
       SIGN( .5, NUMBER ) =       .500
         ROUND1( NUMBER ) =   1234.560

NUMBER TO ROUND ? 12.499
.5 * NUMBER/ABS( NUMBER ) =       .500
       SIGN( .5, NUMBER ) =       .500
         ROUND1( NUMBER ) =     12.500

NUMBER TO ROUND ? -45.5001
.5 * NUMBER/ABS( NUMBER ) =      -.500
       SIGN( .5, NUMBER ) =      -.500
         ROUND1( NUMBER ) =    -45.500

NUMBER TO ROUND ? 0.0
```

**Fig. 4-4.** Execution of Program 4-4.

## Problems for Sec. 4-2

1. Write a program with a statement function that calculates the area of a circle.
2. Write a program using a statement function that calculates the Celsius temperature from the Fahrenheit temperature. Note:

$$C = (5/9)(F - 32)$$

3. Write a program using a statement function that calculates the Fahrenheit temperature from the Celsius temperature. Note:

$$F = (9/5)(C + 32)$$

4. Define a function for Y = −3X**2 + 7X − 3. Print pairs of values of X and Y for X = −4 to 5.
5. Define a function for Y = 3X + 4. Print pairs of values of X and Y for X = −5 to 5.
6. Define a function for Y = 2X**2 + 8X − 1. Print pairs of values of X and Y for X = −6 to 2.

## 4-3 FUNCTION Subprograms

Many of the common mathematical functions are so routinely used in FORTRAN programming that they are built-in functions in FORTRAN as we saw in Sec. 4-1. However, there are other functions we might have frequent use for that do not appear as built-in functions and that cannot be provided by the statement function.

We may create a program unit to satisfy our specialized requirements and compile it as an independent entity. The FUNCTION subprogram is one method for doing this. FUNCTION subprograms are linked to other programs through the FUNCTION subprogram name. Values are passed into the FUNCTION subprogram through an argument list and a single value is returned in the function name. The rules for naming FUNCTION subprograms are the same as for naming variables.

When the FUNCTION subprogram is used in a program, it is named in the same way as a built-in function. This means that the function name with arguments enclosed within parentheses is referenced in a FORTRAN expression and the single value is returned to the program statement in which the function reference appears.

For demonstration purposes, let us write a FUNCTION subprogram that will return the absolute value of a real number without using the ABS function. Every FUNCTION subprogram must begin with the FUNCTION statement that names the function and specifies the number of arguments required by placing a dummy argument list in parentheses.

FUNCTION ABSVAL( X1 ) names the FUNCTION ABSVAL and requires one argument from the calling program. Every FUNCTION subprogram must contain at least one statement that assigns a value to the function name. Every FUNCTION subprogram must have a RETURN statement that is the last statement to be processed as part of the FUNCTION subprogram before the computer returns to continue processing the statements of the program that referenced the FUNCTION subprogram in the first place. The form of the RETURN statement is simply

```
RETURN
```

Every FUNCTION subprogram must have as its last statement the FORTRAN END statement (see Program 4-5 named ABSVAL).

While there are some restrictions on what you may do with a FUNCTION subprogram, fundamentally we may think of it as a group of FORTRAN statements that is accessible to other FORTRAN programs. Now that we have different kinds of programs, we note that FORTRAN programs of the kind we have been writing until now are referred to as MAIN programs.

```
      FUNCTION ABSVAL( X1 )
C  **  THIS IS A FUNCTION SUBPROGRAM.
C  **  WE ARE FINDING THE ABSOLUTE VALUE WITHOUT THE USE OF
C  **  THE ABS BUILT-IN FUNCTION.

      REAL  X1

      IF ( X1 .LT. Ø.Ø ) ABSVAL = -1 * X1
      IF ( X1 .GE. Ø.Ø ) ABSVAL = X1
      RETURN

      END
```

**Program 4-5.** FUNCTION subprogram returns absolute value.

FUNCTION subprograms may be compiled and saved (on disk for example) for future use by any MAIN program. This makes it possible to write subprograms just once to solve often encountered problems. We do not have to reinvent program code every time a particular need reappears. To make things easier, the variables that are named in a FUNCTION subprogram are completely independent of variables named in any MAIN program that references it. That is, variables like COUNT, INDEX, and TAXES in a subprogram do not interact in any way with the variables COUNT, INDEX, or TAXES that might appear in the MAIN program that calls it. They are referred to as *local variables*. All that we have to account for in the referencing program is that the variables in the variable list are real or integer according to the requirements of the FUNCTION subprogram. The FUNCTION subprogram is typed according to the first letter of the FUNCTION name, unless we state otherwise in a type declaration statement. For example,

REAL FUNCTION NUMBER( X1, X2, X3 )

will declare the FUNCTION NUMBER as a REAL function. However, since FUNCTION subprograms will be referenced in future programs, it is desirable to select function names with a first letter that conforms to the FORTRAN default convention as has been done with the FORTRAN-supplied functions.

Now that we have a FUNCTION subprogram, let us prepare a MAIN program to reference it. We can write a short program that simply prints some data values and the ABSVAL for those data values (see Program 4-6 named TSTABS).

Let us write a FUNCTION subprogram that will return the smallest prime factor of an integer. When we write a FUNCTION subprogram that is likely to be used for later programs, it makes sense to invest some effort to utilize the power available to us in the interest of improving efficiency. There

```
      PROGRAM TSTABS
C  **  THIS MAIN PROGRAM INVOKES FUNCTION SUBPROGRAM ABSVAL

      REAL    ARRAY(5), NUMB1, NUMB2
      INTEGER INDEX
      DATA ARRAY/ -1.56, 45.Ø9, -31.72, Ø.Ø, -18.32/

      WRITE ( 5, 12 )
12       FORMAT ( ' ', 'ORIGINAL  ABSVAL' )

      DO 1ØØ INDEX = 1, 5
        NUMB1 =  ARRAY( INDEX )
        NUMB2 = ABSVAL( NUMB1 )
        WRITE ( 5, 52 ) NUMB1, NUMB2
52         FORMAT ( ' ', 2F8.2 )
1ØØ   CONTINUE

      END
```

**Program 4-6.** MAIN program to check subprogram ABSVAL.

```
[Begin execution]

ORIGINAL  ABSVAL
   -1.56    1.56
   45.Ø9   45.Ø9
  -31.72   31.72
    Ø.ØØ    Ø.ØØ
  -18.32   18.32
```

**Fig. 4-5.** Execution of Program 4-6.

are several techniques that we may use to improve on the efficiency of our earlier factoring routine. We may first check to see if our number is divisible by two. If it is, we have found the smallest prime factor; if it is not, then we need check only odd divisors. If we do not find a factor up to the square root of the number, then it is prime and we must assign the original number to the function name.

We could improve execution speed by replacing the two statements

DIVIDE = FNUM / FLOAT( INDEX )
IF ( DIVIDE .EQ. AINT( DIVIDE ) ) GO TO 300

with

FACTOR = NUMBER / INDEX
IF ( FACTOR * INDEX .EQ. NUMBER ) GO TO 300

utilizing integer division. We can do even better by using the MOD function (see Program 4-7 named IPRIME).

In Program 4-7 we have a FUNCTION subprogram that we may reference in any future programs that require finding the smallest prime factor of an integer. Note that we can easily reference FUNCTION IPRIME repeatedly

```
      FUNCTION IPRIME( N1 )
C **  THIS FUNCTION SUBPROGRAM FINDS THE SMALLEST PRIME FACTOR

      INTEGER N1, LAST

      IPRIME = 2
      IF ( MOD( N1, 2 )  .EQ.  Ø )  GO TO 999

       LAST = INT( SQRT(FLOAT(N1)) )
       DO 1ØØ IPRIME = 3, LAST, 2
         IF ( MOD( N1, IPRIME )  .EQ. Ø )  GO TO 999
1ØØ    CONTINUE

       IPRIME = N1
999   RETURN

      END
```

**Program 4-7.** FUNCTION subprogram finds smallest prime factor.

in order to find all prime factors of an integer. And now we will write a short MAIN program to check out the FUNCTION subprogram IPRIME (see Program 4-8 named TSTPRM).

```
      PROGRAM TSTPRM
C **  THIS PROGRAM TESTS FUNCTION SUBPROGRAM IPRIME

      INTEGER NUMBER, SPF

1Ø    WRITE ( 5, 12 )
12       FORMAT ( 'Ø', 'ENTER AN INTEGER ? ' )
      READ ( 5, 22 ) NUMBER
22       FORMAT ( I6 )
      IF ( NUMBER .EQ. Ø )          GO TO 999

C **  NOW REFERENCE FUNCTION SUBPROGRAM IPRIME
      SPF = IPRIME( NUMBER )
      WRITE ( 5, 122 ) SPF
122      FORMAT ( '+', 'SMALLEST PRIME FACTOR = ', I6 )
      GO TO 1Ø

999   END
```

**Program 4-8.** MAIN program to check FUNCTION IPRIME.

```
[Begin execution]


ENTER AN INTEGER ? 1ØØ1
SMALLEST PRIME FACTOR =      7

ENTER AN INTEGER ? 4999
SMALLEST PRIME FACTOR =   4999

ENTER AN INTEGER ? Ø
```

**Fig. 4-6.** Execution of Program 4-8.

FUNCTION subprograms are important for a number of reasons. They obviously are useful as a way of providing the same calculation at several points in the same program and in several programs. In either case, the program code needs to be written and tested only once.

When we are reading a program, the ability to associate a single function name with a whole set of FORTRAN program statements is invaluable. The use of FUNCTION subprograms makes it possible to write much shorter MAIN programs. Short programs are easier to read than long ones. We can mentally associate the function reference with the process without the need to think about the program statements themselves.

## Summary

FUNCTION subprograms are compiled separately and, once stored and accessible to the computer, may be referenced by any MAIN program. A value will be returned to the MAIN program in the FUNCTION name of a FUNCTION subprogram. So the FUNCTION name must be assigned a value at least once in any FUNCTION subprogram. At least one RETURN statement must appear in the subprogram. Every subprogram must have as its final statement, the FORTRAN END statement. FUNCTION subprograms may be declared as integer or real; it is recommended that you use names that agree with the FORTRAN default convention.

## Problems for Sec. 4-3

1. Write a FUNCTION subprogram to return the factorial of the argument. A factorial is the product of all of the integers from 1 to the number and is defined as 1 for factorial 0 (zero). Also write a MAIN program to test your FUNCTION subprogram.
2. Write a program that finds all prime factors of an integer by repeatedly referencing the FUNCTION IPRIME of this section.
3. Write a FUNCTION subprogram to apply Hero's Formula to find the area of a triangle, given the lengths of the three sides. Hero's Formula:

   A = SQRT(s(s − a) (s − b) (s − c) )

   where a, b, and c are the lengths of the three sides and

   s = (a + b + c) / 2

4. Find the greatest common factor in a subprogram.
5. Find the lowest common multiple in a subprogram.

## 4-4 SUBROUTINE Subprograms

Unlike FUNCTION subprograms, SUBROUTINE subprograms do not associate a value with the subprogram name for return to the MAIN program.

SUBROUTINE subprograms are referenced with a new FORTRAN statement.

CALL XAMPLE( A1, A2, A3 )

causes the computer to execute the statements of the SUBROUTINE subprogram named XAMPLE. Thus FORTRAN SUBROUTINE subprograms are referred to as CALLable SUBROUTINEs. The SUBROUTINE may use any of the arguments in the calling statement. Furthermore, the SUBROUTINE may return values to the MAIN program in any of the arguments in the calling statement. It is this ability to return multiple values to the calling program that gives the SUBROUTINE tremendous power. Take care that you don't change the value of any of the elements in the variable list that you don't want to change for subsequent use in the CALLing program.

```
      SUBROUTINE CVT1( IN1, FT, IN2, M1 )
C **  THIS SUBROUTINE CONVERTS INCHES TO
C **  FEET AND INCHES AND TO METERS.

      INTEGER IN1, FT, IN2
      REAL    M1

C **  WE USE INTEGER DIVISION FOR FEET
      FT     = IN1 / 12
      IN2    = MOD( IN1, 12 )
      M1     = FLOAT( IN1 ) * Ø.Ø254
      RETURN

      END
```

**Program 4-9.** SUBROUTINE converts inches.

The SUBROUTINE must have a statement designating it as a SUBROUTINE. Thus

SUBROUTINE XAMPLE( X1, X2, X3 )

must be the first statement of the SUBROUTINE called above. Note that since no value will be returned in the name XAMPLE, SUBROUTINEs are not typed as integer or real; however, the values passed through the dummy arguments must be coordinated between the two program units.

While the FUNCTION subprogram requires at least one argument, the SUBROUTINE subprogram does not. So

CALL XPLE

will execute the program statements of SUBROUTINE XPLE without passing any values between the two program units. (There may be an exception to this that we will not discuss at this time.) A specific example of such a SUBROUTINE is

CALL EXIT

```
      PROGRAM TSTCVT
C **   MAIN PROGRAM TO TEST INCHES CONVERSION SUBROUTINE

      INTEGER INCH, FEET, INCHES
      REAL    METERS

 1Ø   WRITE ( 5, 12 )
 12      FORMAT ( 'Ø', 'INCHES ? ' )
      READ ( 5, 22 ) INCHES
 22      FORMAT ( I6 )
      IF ( INCHES .EQ. Ø )  STOP

C **   CALL THE CONVERSION SUBROUTINE
      CALL CVT1( INCHES, FEET, INCH, METERS )

C **   WRITE THE RESULTS
      WRITE ( 5, 1Ø2 ) FEET, INCH, METERS
 1Ø2     FORMAT ( '+', I3, ' FEET ', I3, ' INCHES',
     +            '     CONVERTS TO ', F5.2, ' METERS' )
      GO TO 1Ø

      END
```

**Program 4-10.** Program to call SUBROUTINE CVT1.

```
[Begin execution]


INCHES ? 125
 1Ø FEET    5 INCHES     CONVERTS TO  3.17 METERS

INCHES ? 2ØØ
 16 FEET    8 INCHES     CONVERTS TO  5.Ø8 METERS

INCHES ? 5Ø
  4 FEET    2 INCHES     CONVERTS TO  1.27 METERS

INCHES ? Ø
 STOP
```

**Fig. 4-7.** Execution of Program 4-10.

which is a SUBROUTINE call required by many computer installations (as we mentioned in Chap. 1). The SUBROUTINE EXIT is a program unit that performs the necessary operations to finish up one program and prepare the machine to begin the next job in line. This is the usual case for a batch machine

SUBROUTINE subprograms must have at least one RETURN statement and they must have END as the last statement of the program unit.

Let us write a SUBROUTINE subprogram that will convert measurements in inches to feet and inches, and to meters (see Program 4-9 named CVT1); and a short program to CALL the SUBROUTINE subprogram CVT1 (see Program 4-10 named TSTCVT).

SUBROUTINE subprograms have all of the same desirable features that FUNCTION subprograms have. They enable us to incorporate the same set of calculations at several points in the same program and in several different programs. They help improve the readability of programs by associating a process with a single FORTRAN statement. In addition, we have the ability to return multiple values to the calling program. In the world of commercial computing many subprograms have been written and are for sale for significantly less than the cost of writing and testing them from scratch.

## Summary

SUBROUTINE subprograms are compiled separately and, once stored and accessible to the computer, they may be referenced by any MAIN program. Values may be returned in any variable named in the argument list of SUBROUTINE subprograms. At least one RETURN statement must appear in the subprogram. Every subprogram must have as its final statement, the FORTRAN END statement. SUBROUTINE subprogram names are not data typed and no value is returned in the subprogram name.

## Problems for Sec. 4-4

1. Write a SUBROUTINE subprogram that exchanges the two values stored in two variables. Such a SUBROUTINE will allow us to replace the three statements

```
SAVE               = ARRAY( FIRST )
ARRAY( FIRST )     = ARRAY( SECOND )
ARRAY( SECOND )    = SAVE
```

   with the statement

```
CALL XCHANG( ARRAY( FIRST ), ARRAY( SECOND ) )
```

   Write a short MAIN program to test your SUBROUTINE.
2. Write a SUBROUTINE to convert numbers of cents less than a dollar to the fewest possible number of coins.
3. Write a SUBROUTINE subprogram that accepts a, b, c, and d and returns A, B, and C in

```
AX**2 + BX + C = (aX + b)(cX + d)
```

# 5

# Miscellaneous FORTRAN Features and Techniques

At this point we have acquired a good basis for writing a wide variety of significant programs in FORTRAN. However, there are many FORTRAN capabilities that greatly enhance what we can do. Some features merely enable us to achieve desired results with reduced programming effort or in some more elegant way. Others truly extend our ability to solve problems through computer programs.

## 5-1 Additional Variable Types

We have used the INTEGER and REAL variable types in all of our work. Up to three additional variable types may be available to us, depending on our particular FORTRAN implementation. They are LOGICAL, DOUBLE PRECISION, and COMPLEX. Each of these variable types may be utilized in a program by providing the appropriate type declaration statement.

```
LOGICAL L1, L2, L3
DOUBLE PRECISION NUMB1, NUMB2(5)
COMPLEX A5
```

at the beginning of a program would provide for the LOGICAL variables L1, L2, and L3, the DOUBLE PRECISION variable NUMB1, the DOUBLE PRECISION array NUMB2 to accommodate up to five double-precision elements, and the COMPLEX variable A5 to accommodate one two-part complex entry. Since all of the letters of the alphabet are allocated to either REAL or INTEGER type by the FORTRAN variable default convention, a type declaration statement is required for any of these new variable types.

## *LOGICAL*

In a standard FORTRAN implementation, LOGICAL variables are reserved for one of the two logical states, true or false. Statements such as the following may be used to assign one of the two logical states to variables that have been declared in a LOGICAL statement:

```
L1 = .TRUE.
L2 = .FALSE.
L3 = A .GT. B
L4 = A1 .GT. A2 .OR. C2 .LE. C4
```

We may then use the variables in LOGICAL IF statements such as

```
IF ( L1 .AND. L2 .OR. L3 ) GO TO 123
```

Or we might simply write out the contents of a logical variable using the L-format, which will result in an F or a T being printed for false or true, respectively. The results are printed right justified in the field width w specified by Lw in a FORMAT statement. In a FORTRAN implementation that adheres to the standard, a LOGICAL variable occupies the same amount of memory as an INTEGER or a REAL variable.

Some FORTRAN implementations, especially for microcomputers, extend the definition of LOGICAL variables to permit their use as a special kind of integer. In such an implementation a LOGICAL variable is defined to occupy typically one quarter as much memory as a REAL variable. Thus the permissible range of values may be −128 to +127. This type of variable makes it possible to work with larger arrays in memory, provided that the data to be stored in the arrays falls within the permissible range. One should use LOGICAL variables on such a system in this way only if such use permits solving a problem not otherwise solvable and then only with great care. Be sure to clearly document exactly how such data types are used in your program.

The fact that the LOGICAL variable may be used to process integer data does not mean that a LOGICAL variable may be substituted for an INTEGER variable indiscriminately. The FORTRAN-supplied functions that call for INTEGER arguments will produce surprising and incorrect results if a LOGICAL variable is used as an argument. So be careful.

## *DOUBLE PRECISION*

DOUBLE PRECISION variables enable us to obtain numeric results to much greater precision than REAL variables without having to write special extended precision calculation routines within our program. The precision is not necessarily exactly double the number of digits obtained with REAL variables. It is fairly typical for an implementation that provides 7-digit precision for REAL variables to provide 16-digit precision for DOUBLE PRECISION variables. Other representative figures are 6 and 12, 10 and 25, and 11 and 19.

DOUBLE PRECISION variables occupy more memory than REAL variables and special calculation routines are called into play. Since double precision requires more memory and program execution is slower, we should not use DOUBLE PRECISION variables where REAL variables are adequate for the job.

Along with DOUBLE PRECISION variables goes a set of DOUBLE PRECISION built-in functions. Most REAL function names become DOUBLE PRECISION function names by inserting a D in front of the REAL function name. For example, to calculate the double-precision square root use DSQRT ( NUMBER ) where NUMBER is a DOUBLE PRECISION variable. You should determine exactly what DOUBLE PRECISION functions are available before trying to use them.

Two additional FORTRAN-supplied functions are provided. SNGL ( DNUMB ) converts the value of the double-precision number DNUMB into single precision or real storage representation. Conversely DBLE( RNUMB ) converts the value of the real number RNUMB into double-precision storage representation.

Double-precision values may be printed using F-format by providing sufficient field width to accommodate the desired number of digits.

An additional format type is provided for use with double-precision values. D-format specifies that a double-precision number is to be expressed in exponential format. Thus 164389286 will be written as 1.64389286D+08 (meaning 1.64389286 times 10 to the 8th power) using D15.8. The D signifies that the value is in double-precision storage representation. The number is to be printed in a field width of fifteen spaces including the decimal point, one for the leading sign, and four for D+xx. And the 8 calls for eight digits to the right of the decimal point.

Some implementations differentiate between real and double-precision constants according to the number of digits that appear in the FORTRAN statement. Others require that all double-precision constants be entered in D-format. All will accept double-precision constants entered in D-format.

```
DOUBLE PRECISION Y
Y = 3.1415926535897932D0
```

will set Y equal to a double-precision approximation of pi; and 1.0D-4, 40.0D1, and 16D0 may be used to represent the constants 0.0004, 400, and 16 respectively.

Let's write a simple program to demonstrate precision limits on the Cromemco computer being used to develop the programs in this book. The precision claimed for FORTRAN on this machine is 6+ digits for REAL and 16+ for DOUBLE PRECISION. What we require to demonstrate precision is a program to print predictable results. We simply select quotients of integers that produce nicely repeating decimal values (see Program 5-1 named DOUBLE).

```
      PROGRAM DOUBLE
C  **  THIS PROGRAM DEMONSTRATES THE POINT AT WHICH DIGITS EXCEED
C  **  THE PRECISON OF A FORTRAN IMPLEMENTATION.

      DOUBLE PRECISION D1, D2, D3
      REAL R1, R2, R3
      INTEGER INDEX
      DATA D3/ 7.ØDØ/ R3/ 7.Ø/

      WRITE ( 5, 12 )
12       FORMAT ( ' ', 13X, '1234567890123456', 9X, '123456' )
      DO 1ØØ INDEX = 1, 7
        R1 = FLOAT( INDEX )
        D1 = DBLE( R1 )
        D2 = D1 / D3
        R2 = R1 / R3
        WRITE ( 5, 42 ) R1, D3, D2, R2
42         FORMAT ( ' ', F3.Ø, ' /', F3.Ø, ' =', F22.19, F15.9 )
1ØØ   CONTINUE

      END
```

**Program 5-1.** Demonstrate precision limits.

```
[Begin execution]

                1234567890123456         123456
1. / 7. =  .1428571428571428600     .142857149
2. / 7. =  .2857142857142857100     .285714298
3. / 7. =  .4285714285714285700     .428571433
4. / 7. =  .5714285714285714200     .571428597
5. / 7. =  .7142857142857142700     .714285731
6. / 7. =  .8571428571428571400     .857142866
7. / 7. = 1.0000000000000000000    1.000000000
```

**Fig. 5-1.** Execution of Program 5-1.

This program does yield results to the expected precision. The pattern of digits for the various sevenths is in itself a curious phenomenon. It is important to note that this demonstration does not imply that all final results will be accurate to the same precision. It simply demonstrates that for this single calculation, we may count on the specified precision. Many programs will construct successive calculations that result in less accurate final numeric values.

## *COMPLEX*

Some FORTRAN implementations provide variables capable of storing and working with complex numbers. Complex numbers consist of two parts, one real and one imaginary. Such applications are particularly suited to electrical engineering and abstract mathematics. It is suggested that you refer to your system documentation for the use of complex variables.

So we find that we may have up to five variable types in FORTRAN In addition to the five names we have used, some implementations may provide for additional variable types. The general use of these additional types is to be avoided unless the requirements of the program cannot otherwise be met. The primary reason for mentioning them here is to inform the reader so that the additional types will be recognizable in other programs. Not all systems support these additional variable types. Programs that use them may not be movable from one computer to another.

BYTE, INTEGER*1, and LOGICAL*1 all behave much like a LOGICAL variable. However, on a computer that otherwise assigns the same amount of storage to a LOGICAL as to a REAL, the storage is declared as one byte.

INTEGER*2 and LOGICAL*2 each behave similarly to INTEGER variables, except that storage is declared to be two bytes.

REAL*4 and REAL are equivalent, as are REAL*8 and DOUBLE PRECISION.

Again, we note that these additional designations are presented so that the reader will recognize them in other peoples' programs and not to encourage their widespread use.

## 5-2 Implied DO Loops

How can we write out only the first three elements of a 10-element array? That is easy. We simply put an appropriate WRITE statement in a DO loop as follows:

```
      DO 100 K1 = 1, 3
         WRITE ( 5, 82 ) ARRAY( K1 )
82          FORMAT ( ‘ ’, I6 )
100   CONTINUE
```

But suppose we don't want the three numbers on three separate lines? We could try using '+' for printer carriage control, but then the three numbers would be written on top of each other. Or we would have to use three separate FORMAT statements. We could first transfer the first three elements of ARRAY into a 3-element array. But then suppose the next time we want the first four elements written out. Clearly this is not the way to approach writing out parts of arrays, but there is a much better way.

FORTRAN provides the implied DO for just such problems. The implied DO enables us to define ranges of integer variables within the WRITE statement itself. To write out the first three elements of ARRAY, we could use the following WRITE statement:

```
WRITE ( 5, 82 ) (ARRAY(K1), K1 = 1, 3)
```

In this case,

```
(<. . .>, K1 = 1, 3)
```

and

```
      DO 100 K1 = 1, 3
         <. . .>
100   CONTINUE
```

are functionally equivalent: <. . .> stands for ARRAY(K1) here in both program fragments. Note that the leading comma in the implied DO is required. The difference between the implied DO loop and the explicit DO loop is that for the implied DO loop, the WRITE statement is executed only once and therefore there is only one line of output, whereas, for the explicit DO loop, the WRITE statement is executed three times and has to deal with carriage control three times.

Implied DO loops are exactly analogous to explicit DO loops. The three loop parameters may be integer constants and/or integer variables.

Implied DO loops may be nested as explicit DO loops are nested. They are executed from the inside out.

```
      DO 200 K1 = 1, 15
         DO 100 K2 = 1, 9
            <. . .>
100      CONTINUE
200   CONTINUE
```

and

```
((<. . .>,K2 = 1, 9), K1 = 1, 15)
```

are conceptually identical. Implied DO loops are governed by all of the same rules that govern explicit DO loops. For example,

```
((<. . .>, K2 = K1, N1, 3), K1 = 3, 15, 2)
```

is a perfectly valid implied DO loop. Notice that the value of K1 that is established in the outer loop may be used as a parameter of the inner loop. This kind of flexibility gives us tremendous control over the way in which printed output appears on the page.

The implied DO feature is available in READ and WRITE statements. Some FORTRAN implementations permit implied DOs in DATA initialization statements as well, though this is not part of standard FORTRAN IV.

Let's write a program to demonstrate what we can accomplish with implied DO loops. We simply enter the integers from 1 to 15 into a linear array and then write out the elements in a variety of patterns (see Program 5-2 named IMPDO1).

Let's examine the four implied DO applications in this program that produce four different arrangements of printed output from the same array.

```
(STORE(K1), K1 = 1, 15)
```

will write out all 15 elements of STORE in order.

```
      PROGRAM IMPDO1
C  **  THIS PROGRAM DEMONSTRATES THE IMPLIED DO

      INTEGER STORE(15), K1, K2

      DATA STORE/ 1,2,3,4,5,6,7,8,9,10,11,12,13,14,15/

      WRITE ( 5, 12 ) (STORE(K1), K1 = 1, 15)
12       FORMAT ( ' ', 'CONTENTS OF STORE() AS ENTERED' /
     +               ' ', 15I3 )

      WRITE ( 5, 22 ) (STORE(K1), K1 = 1, 15, 3)
22       FORMAT ( '0', 'EVERY THIRD VALUE' /
     +               ' ', 5I3 )

      WRITE ( 5, 32 ) ((STORE(K1), K1 = K2, 15, 3), K2 = 1, 3)
32       FORMAT ( '0', '((STORE(K1), K1 = K2, 15, 3), K2 = 1, 3)'
     +         3( / ' ', 5I3 ) )

      WRITE ( 5, 42 ) ((STORE(K1),K1 = K2, 15, 5 ), K2 = 1, 5)
42       FORMAT ( '0','((STORE(K1),K1 = K2, 15, 5 ), K2 = 1, 5)'
     +         5( / ' ', 3I3 ) )

      END
```

**Program 5-2.** Demonstrate implied DOs.

(STORE(K1), K1 = 1, 15, 3)

will write out every third element beginning with the first and ending with the thirteenth.

(STORE(K1), K1 = K2, 15, 3), K2 = 1, 3)

uses nested implied DO loops to write out the elements of the array in the order: 1, 4, 7, 10, 13, 2, 5, 8, 11, 14, 3, 6, 9, 12, and 15. And finally,

```
[Begin execution]

CONTENTS OF STORE() AS ENTERED
  1  2  3  4  5  6  7  8  9 10 11 12 13 14 15

EVERY THIRD VALUE
  1  4  7 10 13

((STORE(K1), K1 = K2, 15, 3), K2 = 1, 3)
  1  4  7 10 13
  2  5  8 11 14
  3  6  9 12 15

((STORE(K1),K1 = K2, 15, 5 ), K2 = 1, 5)
  1  6 11
  2  7 12
  3  8 13
  4  9 14
  5 10 15
```

**Fig. 5-2.** Execution of Program 5-2.

(STORE(K1), K1 = K2, 15, 5), K2 = 1, 5)

uses nested implied DO loops to write out the elements of the array in the order: 1, 6, 11, 2, 7, 12, 3, 8, 13, 4, 9, 14, 5, 10, and 15.

Note the combination of the use of implied DOs and format specifications. The implied DOs determine the order in which the elements are printed, while the formats determine the form of the output. It is the 5( / ' ', 5I3 ) that causes the computer to print five integers per line in the first rectangular pattern and the 5( / ' ', 3I3 ) that causes the computer to print three integers per line in the second rectangular pattern. We explicitly write out a blank character after each new line generated by a slash so that each I-format will occupy the same number of columns on the printed output. It is not a good idea to bury this blank as the first character of some other field.

We may want to use an explicit DO loop to establish parameters for an implied DO loop. This greatly enhances what we can do (see Program 5-3 named IMPDO2).

```
      PROGRAM IMPDO2
C  **  THIS PROGRAM COMBINES EXPLICIT AND IMPLIED DO'S

      INTEGER STORE(15), K1, K2, K3, INDEX
      DATA STORE/ 1,2,3,4,5,6,7,8,9,10,11,12,13,14,15/

      WRITE ( 5, 12 ) (STORE(K1), K1 = 1, 15)
12       FORMAT ( ' ', 'CONTENTS OF STORE() AS ENTERED' /
     +            ' ', 15I3 )

      WRITE ( 5, 22 )
22       FORMAT ( '0', 'THIS IS DONE COMBINING EXPLICIT ',
     +            'AND IMPLIED DO LOOPS' )
      K3 = 0
      DO 60 INDEX = 1, 5
        K2 = K3 + 1
        K3 = K3 + INDEX
        WRITE ( 5, 42 ) (STORE(K1), K1 = K2, K3 )
42         FORMAT ( ' ', 5I3 )
60    CONTINUE

      END
```

**Program 5-3.** Combining implied DOs with explicit DOs.

## 5-3 Multidimensional Arrays

So far we have been able to store numbers only in a simple variable or a linear array. There are often situations when we would like to arrange data in a two-dimensional pattern. And so FORTRAN does provide two-dimensional arrays. ARRAY( COLUMN, ROW ) contains the value stored in the two-dimensional array named ARRAY at column COLUMN and row ROW. Just as it took one subscript to name an element of a linear array, it requires two subscripts to name an element of a two-dimensional array.

```
[Begin execution]

CONTENTS OF STORE() AS ENTERED
  1  2  3  4  5  6  7  8  9 10 11 12 13 14 15

THIS IS DONE COMBINING EXPLICIT AND IMPLIED DO LOOPS
  1
  2  3
  4  5  6
  7  8  9 10
 11 12 13 14 15
```

**Fig. 5-3.** Execution of Program 5-3.

## *Two-Dimensional Arrays*

The structure of a two-dimensional array is shown in Table 5-1.

**Table 5-1.** The subscript pattern in a two-dimensional array.

| | | | | |
|---|---|---|---|---|
| 1. (1, 1) | 4. (1, 2) | 7. (1, 3) | 10. (1, 4) | 13. (1, 5) |
| 2. (2, 1) | 5. (2, 2) | 8. (2, 3) | 11. (2, 4) | 14. (2, 5) |
| 3. (3, 1) | 6. (3, 2) | 9. (3, 3) | 12. (3, 4) | 15. (3, 5) |

It is important to know how FORTRAN stores the elements of a two-dimensional array in memory. The elements are actually stored in one linear pattern with the first subscript varying faster than the second subscript. So the elements of Table 5-1 are stored in the order: (1,1), (2,1), (3,1), (1,2), (2,2), (3,2), . . . (3,4), (1,5), (2,5), and finally the last number stored will be (3,5) as shown by the numbers 1 through 15 that precede the parenthesized subscripts. We must be aware of this order in any situation where we instruct the computer to handle the array as an entity.

Let us demonstrate with a program the order in which FORTRAN reads numbers in a DATA initialization statement.

The implied DO loop is essential to certain types of printing. As we saw in the previous section, we could not easily print out an array in a rectangular pattern without at least one implied DO loop. We could in fact first enter all elements of one row of our two-dimensional array into a linear array and then print the linear array with an appropriate FORMAT statement. We would then have to load the linear array with the next row and repeat the process until the entire rectangular array has been printed. However, all of that data manipulation is peripheral to the actual printing of the contents of the array and diverts our attention from the real problem solving process. Implied DO loops are definitely the preferred method. We are able to print our entire rectangular array with a single WRITE statement. It will be desirable to use nested implied DOs, with the column numbers moving faster than the row numbers. Therefore, the inner DO variable will be the column subscript and the outer DO variable will be the row subscript, as follows:

WRITE ( 5, 42 ) ((ARRAY(K1,K2), K2 = 1, 5), K1 = 1, 3)

See Program 5-4 named ARRAY.

```
      PROGRAM ARRAY
C  **  THIS PROGRAM DEMONSTRATES THE ORGANIZATION AND ORDERING OF
C  **  THE SUBSCRIPTS WITHIN A TWO DIMENSIONAL ARRAY IN FORTRAN.

      INTEGER  ARRAY(3,5), K1, K2
      DATA  ARRAY/ 1,2,3,4,5,6,7,8,9,10,11,12,13,14,15/

      WRITE ( 5, 42 ) ((ARRAY(K1,K2), K2 = 1, 5), K1 = 1, 3)
 42      FORMAT ( ' ', 'TWO DIMENSIONAL ARRAY STORAGE SEQUENCE'
     +         3( / ' ', 5I5 ) )

      END
```

**Program 5-4.** Demonstrating the subscript order in FORTRAN two-dimensional arrays.

```
[Begin execution]

TWO DIMENSIONAL ARRAY STORAGE SEQUENCE
    1    4    7   10   13
    2    5    8   11   14
    3    6    9   12   15
```

**Fig. 5-4.** Execution of Program 5-4.

Standard FORTRAN specifies that arrays shall permit up to seven subscripts. There are some implementations that place no limit on the number of subscripts, except as limited by available computer memory. Generally up to three subscripts will be available. For three-dimensional arrays we may think in terms of rows, columns, and planes. However, for four and more dimensions, the concepts of plane geometry break down. You will quickly realize that memory is gobbled up by multidimensional arrays. A 10 by 10 by 10 by 10 array requires storage for 10,000 elements, for example.

## *Warning: No Out of Bounds Checking Done Here*

Most implementations of FORTRAN do not check to see if the subscript that we use is within the bounds stated in a DIMENSION statement or a type declaration statement. So if we dimension an array to be 20 by 30 and we write a program statement that tries to store a number at subscript position (50,50), the results may be unpredictable. We might alter some memory location in the operating system and shut down the computer or send it into some strange loop, printing a system error message that appears to have nothing to do with anything in our program. It is the programmer's responsibility to provide valid subscripts.

Let us look at one case of a ''bad subscript'' in a FORTRAN program. Suppose we have the following program fragment:

```
INTEGER    ARRAY(10,9), NUMBER
NUMBER = -1
ARRAY( 11, 9 ) = 50
```

Since the two-dimensional variable ARRAY is 10 by 9, it should contain no more than 90 elements. However, we have specified a pair of subscripts that comes out to the 91st element in the array. But that is the first location beyond the end of ARRAY and has been allocated to the integer variable NUMBER. At this point, all we have done is to set the value of NUMBER to 50. Having set the value of NUMBER to −1 earlier, won't we be surprised at some strange value later on in the program? That program bug will be hard enough to find. But consider the difficulty of finding the error when the subscripts are variables, which is the more usual case. Forewarned is forearmed!

The uses for multidimensional arrays are unlimited. One gets to a point where it is difficult to write a program without using arrays for something. Arrays are used for tic-tac-toe, chess, to tabulate data, to keep track of lines at a supermarket check out, to store tax tables, to record the current state of an iterative process, and so on.

## Summary

We may now use a powerful extension of the linear array: the multidimensional array. A two-dimensional array may be thought of as an arrangement of numbers in which there are rows and columns. Numbers in a two-dimensional array may be accessed by a double subscript such as NUMBS( 3, 8 ) for the number in array named NUMBS, which is located in the row numbered 3 and the column numbered 8. We have seen that the elements of a two-dimensional array are stored column by column in one contiguous linear collection. We have been warned that FORTRAN may not check to see if the subscripts yield valid elements and that unpredictable and undesirable results will occur for out of range subscripts.

## Problems for Sec. 5-3

1. Fill an array having three rows and six columns with zeros. Write it out.
2. Fill an array having three rows and six columns with ones. Write it out.
3. Fill the addresses along the top left to bottom right diagonal of a square 7 by 7 array with ones and all other locations with zeros. Write out the results.
4. Enter the integers 0 through 20 into a 3 by 7 array. Write it out. Multiply each entry by the sum of the row and column number and write out the resulting array.
5. Fill a 12 by 12 array with the addition table and write it out.
6. Fill a 12 by 12 array with the multiplication table and write it out.
7. Fill a 5 by 5 array with the addition table mod 5 and write it out.
8. Fill a 5 by 5 array with the multiplication table mod 5 and write it out.

## 5-4 Program Control

We have been using the logical IF and the GO TO statements to control the sequence in which the statements of our programs have been executed. We may gain greater flexibility through the use of two additional control statements.

### *Arithmetic IF*

The FORTRAN arithmetic IF statement provides a three-way branch depending on the value of a FORTRAN expression. The statement

IF ( NUMBER ) 100, 200, 300

in a FORTRAN program will pass control to one of the three statements labeled 100, 200, or 300. If the value of NUMBER is negative, then control passes to the statement labeled 100. If the value of NUMBER is zero, then control passes to the statement labeled 200. And if the value of NUMBER is positive, then control passes to the statement labeled 300. Any legal FORTRAN arithmetic expression may be enclosed within the parentheses of an arithmetic IF statement.

### *Computed GO TO*

The branching provided by the computed GO TO is determined by the value of an INTEGER variable. The statement

GO TO ( al, a2, . . . , an ), i

will branch to the statement labeled a1 if the value of i is one, to the statement labeled a2 if the value of i is two and to the statement a*n* if the value of i is n. If the value of i is less than one or greater than n, the computed GO TO is ignored and control passes to the next statement in the program.

## 5-5 Character Handling

Most of our work has dealt with numbers and calculations. However, we have used H-format and apostrophe format to write out labels to describe program results. We also can treat letters and other characters as data in FORTRAN programs. This might be in the form of names and addresses, brand names, or part names in inventory. We may even wish to use digits in data without associating the symbol for a digit with its numeric value. Such data is referred to as *alphanumeric*.

### *A-format*

A-format is used to store and write alphanumeric data. The form is rAw, where r is the repeat factor and w is the field width. This is exactly analogous to rIw as applied to I-format. We can store alphanumeric data in numeric variables; that is, we can get the computer to store numeric represen-

```
      PROGRAM ALPHA
C **  HERE WE DEMONSTRATE READING THE ALPHABET INTO AN INTEGER
C **  ARRAY AND WRITING IT BACK OUT WITH SEVERAL DIFFERENT
C **  A-FORMATS

      INTEGER ALPBET(26), K1
      DATA  ALPBET/ 'A','B','C','D','E','F','G','H','I',
     +              'J','K','L','M','N','O','P','Q','R',
     +              'S','T','U','V','W','X','Y','Z'/

      WRITE ( 5, 12 ) ALPBET
12       FORMAT ( ' ', 'FULL ALPHABET 26A1 FORMAT' /
     +              ' ', 26A1 )

      WRITE ( 5, 22 ) ALPBET
22       FORMAT ( 'Ø', 'FULL ALPHABET 26A2 FORMAT' /
     +              ' ', 26A2 )

      WRITE ( 5, 32 ) (ALPBET(K1),K1 = 1, 26, 3)
32       FORMAT ( 'Ø', '(ALPBET(K1),K1 = 1, 26, 3) 26A2 FORMAT' /
     +              ' ', 26A2 )

      END
```

**Program 5-5.** Processing the alphabet in an integer array.

tations of alphanumeric characters in numeric variables. The numeric representations are determined by a conversion code. One such code in common use is the ASCII code that equates "1" and 49, "A" and 65, "B" and 66, and "Z" and 90. Another such code is the EBCDIC code that equates "1" and −3776, "A" and −16064, "B" and −15808, and "Z" and −5824. The manuals for your implementation should reveal which code is used. You could write a simple little program to enter alphanumeric data using A-format in a READ statement and then write the data out as a numeric value using I-format in a WRITE statement to determine the code used by your implementation.

It is typical to be able to store two characters in an integer variable, four characters in a real variable, and eight characters in a double-precision variable. As an example, let's write a little FORTRAN program to store the alphabet in a 26-element array and write out the contents of the array in a couple of different forms. We will load the alphabet into an integer array using DATA initialization (see Program 5-5 named ALPHA).

```
[Begin execution]

FULL ALPHABET 26A1 FORMAT
ABCDEFGHIJKLMNOPQRSTUVWXYZ

FULL ALPHABET 26A2 FORMAT
A B C D E F G H I J K L M N O P Q R S T U V W X Y Z

(ALPBET(K1),K1 = 1, 26, 3) 26A2 FORMAT
A D G J M P S V Y
```

**Fig. 5-5.** Execution of Program 5-5.

We can store labels in elements of an array and then select a label to be printed by specifying which element of the array to print. To demonstrate how this might work, let's store abbreviations of the names of the days of the week in a real array and simply write them out again (see Program 5-6 named WEEK).

```
      PROGRAM WEEK
C  **  WE DEMONSTRATE A USE OF A-FORMAT IN A REAL ARRAY
C  **  STORE THE DAYS OF THE WEEK IN A 7 ELEMENT ARRAY.

      REAL  WEEK(7)
      INTEGER INDEX
      DATA  WEEK/ 'SUN','MON','TUE','WED','THU','FRI','SAT'/

      WRITE ( 5, 12 ) WEEK
 12      FORMAT ( ' ', 7(A3, 2X) )
      END

[Begin execution]

SUN  MON  TUE  WED  THU  FRI  SAT
```

**Program 5-6.** Printing in A-format from a real array.

## 5-6 EQUIVALENCE

Suppose you have just written a mammoth program in which two large arrays are required at different times, but they will not both fit in memory at the same time. You might say, ''Just use the same array for both purposes.'' That is a good idea, but suppose one array is 10 by 500 and the other is 100 by 40. We would have to dimension our array 100 by 500 to do that. The FORTRAN EQUIVALENCE statement will allow us to use the same array for both purposes and provide the appropriate dimensions for each. As long as we use them at different times during the execution of the program, we will not destroy needed data. We may specify two variables to occupy the same locations in memory with the EQUIVALENCE statement. The statements

```
INTEGER WIN(10,500), LOSS(100,40)
EQUIVALENCE ( WIN(1), LOSS(1) )
```

accomplish just this for the two arrays WIN and LOSS. The EQUIVALENCE statement specifies that the first storage location occupied by WIN also must be occupied by LOSS. Furthermore, since all of the elements of arrays are stored linearly, all of the rest of the elements of the two arrays will coincide up to and including the last location of the array with the fewer elements. If we set WIN(1,1) = 18, then LOSS(1,1) also will be set to 18. Some implementations require that the two variables equivalenced must be of the same data type; others do not.

```
EQUIVALENCE ( WIN(5), LOSS(1), K1 ), ( A1, B2 )
```

would be used to require that the fifth storage location of WIN, the first storage location of LOSS, and the variable K1 all occupy the same location in memory and that A1 and B2 occupy the same location in memory.

## 5-7 Wrap-up

You have doubtless noted that we have not included problems for you to do for all sections. You are encouraged to develop your own problems. Explore and experiment. Of course, just how much exploration you can do may depend on the availability of a computer. You can maximize utilization of a hard-to-get-at computer by trying lots of concepts in a single program. This way you will get several ideas tested with a single trip to the computer. Be cautious, but be adventurous and the rewards will be tremendous.

# 6

# Elementary Data Processing

## 6-1 Introduction to Data Processing

Computers are used extensively for data processing. There doesn't seem to be a clear-cut definition for data processing that distinguishes it from other kinds of computer activity. In a sense, all computer work is data processing. However, data processing often implies that the computer is being used to sort, collate, tabulate, and/or otherwise digest data. An activity such as tabulating questionnaire responses falls in this category. The computer tirelessly adds, tabulates, orders, totals, checks and cross-checks, verifies, and prints reports for us.

### *Tabulating One Item*

Let us ask some families how many television sets they have in their homes. The answers will be one number per family. We can set up a linear array so that the first element counts the number of families with one set and the Nth element counts the number of families with N sets. Before we begin counting, there will be zero families having each number of sets. So we will have to initialize each element of the linear array at 0. Then when the number for a family is up for tabulation, we will add 1 to the element in the linear array corresponding to that number of television sets. For example, if the first family has one set, then we have the computer look at TVS(1). TVS(1) = 0 to start, and adding 1 makes TVS(1) = 1. The next time a family has one set we have the computer add 1 to TVS(1), and then TVS(1) will equal 2. This process is repeated until all of the data has been tabulated. We can use a dummy data value of −1 to signal that the last data value has been processed, so that we may write out the results after tabulation is complete.

There are several possible methods for entering the data into the computer. We could enter it from the keyboard, use cards, or incorporate it into the program in a DATA initialization statement. Let us use DATA initialization and store the data in a linear array. We will omit families with no TVs and assume a maximum of four sets (see Program 6-1 named TVS).

```
      PROGRAM TVS
C  **  THIS PROGRAM TABULATES THE NUMBER OF FAMILIES WITH
C  **  FROM 1 TO 5 TV SETS.

      INTEGER  DATA1(5Ø), TAB(5), INDEX, N

      DATA  DATA1/ 1,2,4,3,5,2,3,4,3,2,1,2,3,4,5,3,2,3,2,2,
     +             2,2,1,1,4,3,2,5,3,4,3,2,1,2,3,2,1,4,2,3,
     +             1,1,2,1,4,2,1,3,-1/
     +      TAB  / 5*Ø/

C  **  WE TABULATE THE NUMBER OF OCCURANCES OF EACH NUMBER
C  **  IN ARRAY DATA1 HERE.
C  **  A VALUE OF -1 SIGNALS THE END OF ACTUAL DATA.
      DO 1ØØ INDEX = 1, 5Ø
        N = DATA1( INDEX )
        IF ( N .LT. Ø )                                   GO TO 2ØØ
         TAB( N ) = TAB( N ) + 1
 1ØØ  CONTINUE

 2ØØ  WRITE ( 5, 2Ø2 )
 2Ø2     FORMAT ( ' ', 'NO. OF TV''S   NO. OF FAMILIES' )
      DO 21Ø INDEX = 1, 5
        WRITE ( 5, 2Ø4 ) INDEX, TAB( INDEX )
 2Ø4       FORMAT ( ' ', 1ØX, I1, 16X, I2 )
 21Ø  CONTINUE

      END
```

**Program 6-1.** Tabulating TVs per family.

A new feature of the DATA initialization statement has been introduced in Program TVS. An "*" (asterisk) may be used as a repeat factor. The line

```
+      TAB  / 5*0/
```

is equivalent to

```
+      TAB  / 0,0,0,0,0/
```

and easier to type.

```
[Begin execution]

NO. OF TV'S   NO. OF FAMILIES
          1                1Ø
          2                16
          3                12
          4                 7
          5                 3
```

**Fig. 6-1.** Execution of Program 6-1.

```
      PROGRAM COURS1
C  **  THIS PROGRAM TABULATES THE NUMBER OF STUDENTS
C  **  REQUESTING EACH OF 5 COURSES.

      INTEGER  DATA1(70), TAB(5), INDEX, INDEX1, INDEX2, N

C  **  THE DATA IS ENTERED IN GROUPS OF FIVE NUMBERS - ONE GROUP
C  **  FOR EACH STUDENT.  THE FIVE NUMBERS REPRESENT
C  **  CHEMISTRY, PHYSICS, FRENCH, SPANISH, AND CALCULUS -
C  **  IN THAT ORDER.  '1' MEANS 'REQUEST THIS COURSE'.
C  **  SO 1,0,1,1,0 IS A REQUEST FOR CHEMISTRY, FRENCH,
C  **  AND SPANISH.
      DATA  DATA1/ 1,0,1,1,0, 0,0,1,1,0, 1,1,0,1,1, 1,0,1,1,0,
     +             0,0,1,0,1, 1,0,1,1,0, 1,1,1,0,0, 1,0,1,0,1,
     +             1,0,1,1,0, 1,1,0,1,0, 1,1,0,1,1, 1,1,0,1,0,
     +             1,1,0,0,0, -1/
     +       TAB  / 5*0/

C  **  WE TABULATE THE COURSE REQUESTS HERE
C  **  A VALUE OF -1 SIGNALS THE END OF ACTUAL DATA.
      DO 100 INDEX1 = 1, 65, 5
        DO 90 INDEX2 = 1, 5
          INDEX = INDEX1 + INDEX2 - 1
          N     = DATA1( INDEX )
          IF ( N .LT. 0 )                          GO TO 200
           TAB( INDEX2 ) = TAB( INDEX2 ) + N
 90     CONTINUE
 100  CONTINUE

 200  WRITE ( 5, 202 )
 202     FORMAT ( ' ', 'CHEMISTRY  PHYSICS   FRENCH',
     +                 '  SPANISH CALCULUS' )
      WRITE ( 5, 204 ) TAB
 204     FORMAT ( ' ', 5I9 )

      END
```

**Program 6-2.** Tabulating course selections.

There are some more things we can do with Program TVS. We might have the computer count the number of families and/or count the total number of television sets. If we have the computer do both, then it would be a simple matter to calculate the average number per family.

### *Tabulating Yes-No Answers*

We are not limited to numeric quantities. We easily can list the expected answers and assign a numeric code to each of them. A simple example of this is to assign zero to the answer "no" and one to the answer "yes." Let us ask a group of students if they want to take the following courses: chemistry, physics, French, Spanish, calculus. If someone wants to take chemistry, French, and Spanish, then that person's data will be: 1,0,1,1,0. We can use one linear array to count all courses. The first element will count people who want to take chemistry, the second will count people who want to take French, etc. This is done with array TAB in Program 6-2 named COURS1. We keep track of the groups of five by using the increment parameter of the DO loop.

Note these two statements in Program 6-2:

```
INDEX = INDEX1 + INDEX2 - 1
N     = DATA1( INDEX )
```

INDEX1 keeps track of the array element at the beginning of the active student's group of data. The value of INDEX2 is which of the five courses the current tabulation is for. Thus we have to add those two values and subtract 1 to find the current response in the linear array. We will see a way to simplify this in the next section.

```
[Begin execution]

CHEMISTRY  PHYSICS    FRENCH  SPANISH CALCULUS
       11        6         8        9        4
```

**Fig. 6-2.** Execution of Program 6-2.

If we were offering a large number of courses, we might assign a course number to each course and ask students to list only those courses desired.

## Summary

We have seen linear arrays used to analyze data from questionnaire-type questions having numeric answers or answers that may be coded into numeric values.

## Problems for Sec. 6-1

1. Modify Program TVS to total the number of television sets and the number of families. Find the average number of television sets per family.
2. Modify Program COURS1 to find the number of people who want to take chemistry and physics.
3. Modify Program COURS1 to find the number of people who want to take physics but not calculus.
4. Write a program to tabulate several items. Tabulate the number of TVs, cars, and bathrooms for some number of families. Use three separate arrays to tabulate the three different items.

## 6-2 Using Two-Dimensional Arrays

In Program 6-2, we used a linear array to store data that naturally fell into groups of five numbers. Here, we will see that it is better to use a two-dimensional array to store such data. Since FORTRAN stores two-dimensional arrays in memory with the first subscript varying faster than the second subscript and we will enter the data with a DATA statement, we will use each column of the array to store the data for one student. Each row will correspond to a different course. With this format, we no longer have to do a calculation to determine the meaning of each position of the array. We may now directly address locations in our two-dimensional array.

DATA1( K2, K1 ) stores the response from the K1th student for the K2th course. For example: DATA1( 3, 5 ) is the French response for the fifth student. So we have eliminated the need for the variable INDEX and the calculation to establish its value. We will change the range on the DO loop governing K1 from 1, 65, 5 to 1, 14. And we must declare the array DATA1 to be 5 by 14. Now the value of N (which is zero for "no" and one for "yes") is simply the value of DATA1( K2, K1 ). These changes are all made to create Program 6-3 named COURS2.

```
      PROGRAM COURS2
C  **  THIS IS PROGRAM COURS1 DONE WITH A TWO DIMENSIONAL ARRAY

      INTEGER  DATA1(5,14), TAB(5), K1, K2, N

C  **  SEE PROGRAM COURS1 FOR ADDITIONAL COMMENTS
      DATA  DATA1/ 1,Ø,1,1,Ø, Ø,Ø,1,1,Ø, 1,1,Ø,1,1, 1,Ø,1,1,Ø,
     +              Ø,Ø,1,Ø,1, 1,Ø,1,1,Ø, 1,1,1,Ø,Ø, 1,Ø,1,Ø,1,
     +              1,Ø,1,1,Ø, 1,1,Ø,1,Ø, 1,1,Ø,1,1, 1,1,Ø,1,Ø,
     +              1,1,Ø,Ø,Ø, -1/
     +      TAB  / 5*Ø/

      DO 1ØØ K1 = 1, 14
        DO 9Ø K2 = 1, 5
          N = DATA1( K2, K1 )
          IF ( N .LT. Ø )                              GO TO 2ØØ
           TAB( K2 ) = TAB( K2 ) + N
9Ø      CONTINUE
1ØØ   CONTINUE

2ØØ   WRITE ( 5, 2Ø2 )
2Ø2      FORMAT ( ' ', 'CHEMISTRY  PHYSICS    FRENCH',
     +              '  SPANISH CALCULUS' )
      WRITE ( 5, 2Ø4 ) TAB
2Ø4      FORMAT ( ' ', 5I9 )

      END
```

**Program 6-3.** Tabulating course selections with a two-dimensional array.

```
[Begin execution]

CHEMISTRY  PHYSICS    FRENCH  SPANISH CALCULUS
       11        6         8        9        4
```

**Fig. 6-3.** Execution of Program 6-3.

As always, there are still aspects of this program that we could pursue further. We could easily store abbreviations of the course names in a real array so that we could be more flexible about the printed output. This is left as an exercise.

Now let's tackle a more complex analysis. Consider a questionnaire submitted to four categories of people: male (21 or over), male (under 21), female (21 or over), and female (under 21). On this questionnaire there are eight questions calling for yes-no answers. Our task is to present a tabulated summary of the data collected. We can provide sample data for say ten people for testing purposes.

There are only three things we must keep track of: (1) the category of the respondent, (2) the question number, and (3) the response.

The category of the respondent may simply be a number from 1 to 4 in exactly the order listed above. The question number may be determined by the position of the response in a column of the data array. And clearly we may use zero for "no" and one for "yes." Thus a sample data line might look like the following:

3,1,0,0,0,0,0,0,1

where the respondent is in category 3, which is female (21 or over), and the first and last questions elicited "yes" responses and questions 2 through 7 elicited "no" responses. So, rows numbered 2 through 9 within a column of the data array correspond to questions 1 through 8 on the questionnaire.

This tabulation clearly calls for four categories of totals. The best way to handle this will be with a second two-dimensional array. Let's define each column to correspond to a respondent category and each row to correspond to a question number. Thus, an array RESULT with eight rows and four columns will be required to store the tabulated results (see Program 6-4 named SURVY1).

Note the simplicity of the actual tabulation process in the following two lines from Program 6-4:

```
K2 = DATA1( 1, K1 )
   RESULT( K3, K2 ) = RESULT(K3, K2) + DATA1(K3 + 1, K1)
```

K1 is the respondent number and is used only to identify the active column of the data array. K2 simply gets the respondent category from the data array so that we know what column of the RESULT array to use for the rest of the data in this column of the data array. The K3 + 1 is required because rows 2 through 9 are used to store the responses to questions numbered 1 through 8 respectively. It is important to note that the numbers written out by this program count the number of "yes" responses. To find the number of "no" responses, we would have to subtract the number of yeses from the total number of respondents in the corresponding category.

There are many other things we might do with the data of our little survey. We could increase the number of rows in the RESULT array to nine and tabulate the total number of respondents in each of the four categories in this extra row. Armed with this figure, we could report all results as percentages of both category and of total respondents. Our program could be modified to create composite categories of respondents such as male, female, under 21, and

```
      PROGRAM SURVY1
C  **  TABULATING YES-NO ANSWERS TO 8 SURVEY QUESTIONS.

      INTEGER  DATA1(9,10), RESULT(8,4), K1, K2, K3

C  **  TYPING GUIDE  1,2,3,4,5,6,7,8     1,2,3,4,5,6,7,8
      DATA  DATA1/ 3,1,0,1,1,1,0,0,1, 3,1,0,0,0,0,1,1,0,
     +             2,1,1,1,1,0,0,1,0, 4,1,1,1,0,0,0,1,0,
     +             2,1,1,0,0,1,0,0,1, 1,1,1,0,0,1,0,1,0,
     +             1,1,0,0,1,1,0,1,1, 3,0,0,1,0,1,1,0,1,
     +             3,0,0,1,0,1,1,0,0, 2,0,1,1,1,0,0,0,1/
      DATA RESULT/ 32*0/

C  **  NOW TABULATE THE FOUR CATEGORIES
      DO 100 K1 = 1, 10
        K2 = DATA1( 1, K1 )
        DO 90 K3 = 1, 8
          RESULT( K3, K2 ) = RESULT( K3, K2 ) + DATA1(K3 + 1, K1)
 90     CONTINUE
 100  CONTINUE

 200  WRITE ( 5, 202 )
 202     FORMAT ( ' ', ' QUEST    MALE    MALE FEMALE FEMALE' /
     +            ' ', ' NUMBER     21+  UNDER     21+  UNDER' )
      WRITE ( 5, 204 ) (K1, (RESULT(K1,K2),K2 = 1, 4),K1 = 1, 8)
 204     FORMAT ( ' ', 5I7 )

      END
```

**Program 6-4.** Survey data tabulation with data in the program.

```
[Begin execution]

 QUEST   MALE   MALE FEMALE FEMALE
NUMBER    21+  UNDER    21+  UNDER
     1      2      2      2      1
     2      1      3      0      1
     3      0      2      3      1
     4      1      2      1      0
     5      2      1      3      0
     6      0      0      3      0
     7      2      1      1      1
     8      1      2      2      0
```

**Fig. 6-4.** Execution of Program 6-4.

21 or over. We could then create additional columns in our result array to accommodate these new categories and do the additional tabulation at the same point in our program that the current tabulation is being done.

## Summary

We have seen that the two-dimensional array enables us to keep track of numbers in two categories very easily by simply establishing the appropriate row and column numbers.

## Problems for Sec. 6-2

1. Modify Program COURS2 by entering abbreviations of the course names in a 5-element real array. Write the results in two columns with the course name as one column and the number of students as the other column.
2. Modify Program COURS2 to tabulate the number of people who want to take each possible pair of courses. There are ten possible pairs. An easy way to do this for our small amount of data is to use nested DOs to decide pairs and scan the data for each pair in turn. (If you store the course names in a real array as described in text, you will be able to label the pairs with the course names.)
3. In Program SURVY1 add row 9 to RESULT and tabulate the total number of respondents in each of the four original categories there.
4. In Program SURVY1 add a column and tabulate the total number of "yes" responses there.
5. Do problem 3 writing the results as percentages.
6. Modify Program SURVY1 by adding the four categories: male, female, under 21, and 21 or over.

*7. Modify Program SURVY1 to accommodate a third possible response, such as two for "other." Tabulate each of the three responses by scanning the data three times, once for each possible response, and write the results after each scan. Be sure to zero the elements of the result array before each scan.

*8. Modify Program SURVY1 to accommodate a third possible response, such as "other." Tabulate the results in a three-dimensional array by allowing three elements in the third dimension. You might use one for "no," two for "yes," and three for "other." Scan the data only once.

## 6-3 Processing External Data

The methods we have been using are fundamentally sound, with one exception. In the real world of data processing, it is never practical to provide large amounts of data with the FORTRAN DATA initialization statement. We have been doing so here to limit the number of new ideas presented in a single shot and to make the data visible for our first programs. It is usual to provide such data on punch cards or in a computer file. In many FORTRAN implementations, it may be impossible to determine from the program whether the data is on cards or in a file. It may be that the only difference is a device number in a FORMAT statement. It may be possible to change from reading a file to reading cards by changing a job control card, or by giving a command from a keyboard.

A *file* is simply an area within some computer device that is treated as data instead of as a program. In fact, a program is just a special file. A source code or text editor program treats a FORTRAN program as a file. A file may be on disk, mag tape, floppy diskette, mini floppy, or even on cassette tape.

The advantages of having data in a file are numerous. Once we have data in a file, we may write several programs to perform different processes on the same data. Thus we do not have to provide the same DATA statement in several different programs. We may write the results of one computer process out to another file so that yet another program may continue some further processing. And, of course, we may now use programs over and over again on new sets of data without having to enter the data in DATA initialization statements that would require we recompile our program for each new set of data. Processing data stored in a file is faster than reading punched cards, too. The availability of data files makes it possible to process more data than can be stored at one time in the computer's memory. The list of advantages goes on and on.

There is some variation in the specifics of file handling from one FORTRAN implementation to another, but the general principles are common. We are still using a Cromemco here. Cromemco FORTRAN is based on Microsoft FORTRAN-80.

For our first demonstration with a data file, let's write a program to create a file to contain the data from our survey of the last section. We can do this with a minimum number of changes to Program 6-4. Since the data will be external to any program that is going to READ it, we must provide dummy data to designate the end of the file. So we may add a set of nine zeros to the DATA statement. If we were going to write the data out to our terminal, we would use device number 5, because that is the way the FORTRAN used for this book is set up. For this same reason, if we were to direct output to a file, we would select any device number from 6 to 10. If we use the statement

```
WRITE ( 6, 12 ) DATA1
```

the output of our program will go to device number 6. In this case, device number 6 is a file named, appropriately enough, FORT06.DAT. Devices 7–10 are named FORT07.DAT-FORT10.DAT. That file will automatically be created on a disk and the contents of our array DATA1 will be written to the file in exactly the same physical layout as though it were printed out on paper. The physical layout will be determined by the FORMAT statement labeled 12. Since we want nine numbers in each data set, the following format statement might be used:

```
12   FORMAT ( ' ', 9I3 )
```

Note that we have provided for the same leading space that we have been using to send output to a printer or our terminal. Formatting is done this way so that output may be selected during program execution to be either paper or file without having to provide different FORMAT statements. We could use the WRITE statement

```
WRITE ( N, 12 ) DATA1
```

and assign N according to the purpose of this particular execution of the program.

The subject of computing with data files is very extensive. The intent of the current discussion is merely to introduce a few data file handling concepts. There simply isn't room in this book to cover the subject thoroughly.

The previously mentioned changes to Program 6-4 have been made to create Program 6-5 named FWRITE.

```
      PROGRAM FWRITE
C  **  WRITE DATA TO THE DATA FILE AT DEVICE #6
C  **  THIS IS THE DATA OF THE YES-NO SURVEY

      INTEGER  DATA1(9,11)

C  **  TYPING GUIDE  1,2,3,4,5,6,7,8    1,2,3,4,5,6,7,8
      DATA  DATA1/ 3,1,Ø,1,1,1,Ø,Ø,1, 3,1,Ø,Ø,Ø,Ø,1,1,Ø,
     +             2,1,1,1,1,Ø,Ø,1,Ø, 4,1,1,1,Ø,Ø,Ø,1,Ø,
     +             2,1,1,Ø,Ø,1,Ø,Ø,1, 1,1,1,Ø,Ø,1,Ø,1,Ø,
     +             1,1,Ø,Ø,1,1,Ø,1,1, 3,Ø,Ø,1,Ø,1,1,Ø,1,
     +             3,Ø,Ø,1,Ø,1,1,Ø,Ø, 2,Ø,1,1,1,Ø,Ø,Ø,1,
     +             Ø,Ø,Ø,Ø,Ø,Ø,Ø,Ø,Ø/

      WRITE ( 6, 12 ) DATA1
 12      FORMAT ( ' ', 9I3 )

      END
```

**Program 6-5.** Write data to an external data file.

Since there is no visible output produced by this program, there is no point in trying to show an execution. However, we may now write a very short program to read the data from device 6 and write it out on paper by writing out to device 5 (see Program 6-6 named FREAD).

Note in this program that the data was read from the file with I3 format and written out to paper with I6 format. There is no connection between the two formats. Once the data is in the memory of the computer, the fact that it was once in a file is insignificant. Since the data was originally defined to be

```
      PROGRAM FREAD
C  **  READ THE DATA STORED IN FILE 'FORTØ6.DAT' AT DEVICE #6

      INTEGER  DATA1(9)

C  **  READ 9 INTEGERS INTO ARRAY DATA1 FROM DEVICE #6
 1Ø   READ ( 6, 12 ) DATA1
 12      FORMAT ( 9I3 )
      IF ( DATA1( 1 ) .EQ. Ø )                GO TO 2ØØ

C  **  WRITE OUT THE CONTENTS OF DATA1 TO DEVICE #5
       WRITE ( 5, 22 ) DATA1
 22       FORMAT ( ' ', 9I6 )
       GO TO 1Ø

 2ØØ  END
```

**Program 6-6.** Read a data file and write the data on paper.

all one-digit integers, we could have written the data to the file with I1 format, thereby taking less disk space for the file. This can be very important for large amounts of data. The only restriction on file formatting is that the data must be read from the file with exactly the same format that was used to write it to obtain exactly the same data.

```
[Begin execution]

      3     1     Ø     1     1     1     Ø     Ø     1
      3     1     Ø     Ø     Ø     Ø     1     1     Ø
      2     1     1     1     1     Ø     Ø     1     Ø
      4     1     1     1     Ø     Ø     Ø     1     Ø
      2     1     1     Ø     Ø     1     Ø     Ø     1
      1     1     1     Ø     Ø     1     Ø     1     Ø
      1     1     Ø     Ø     1     1     Ø     1     1
      3     Ø     Ø     1     Ø     1     1     Ø     1
      3     Ø     Ø     1     Ø     1     1     Ø     Ø
      2     Ø     1     1     1     Ø     Ø     Ø     1
```

**Fig. 6-5.** Execution of Program 6-6.

Alternatively we may create a data file using the same editing program we use to create our FORTRAN source programs. We may select our own file names or use the FORTXX.DAT names. If we select our own file names, then we must "attach" the file to the program in some way. In the FORTRAN used for these examples a SUBROUTINE has been provided for this purpose. A file named SURVEY.DAT would be attached to a program containing the statement

CALL OPEN( 7, 'SURVEY   DAT', 0 )

where 7 is the device number that must be used for any READ or WRITE statements accessing the file named SURVEY.DAT, within the current program, and the 0 designates the floppy disk drive on which the file exists. Zero specifies that the file is on the current drive, while 1 to 4 may be used to specify other drives. In the file name, spaces must be inserted to fill out 11 characters and the dot (.) is not used. We may restart reading at the beginning of the file by using the statement

REWIND 7

The file may be detached from the program with the statement

ENDFILE 7

The first READ statement that applies to a particular file begins at the beginning of the file. The first WRITE statement that applies to a particular file begins at the beginning of the file. Such a WRITE statement causes any data previously in the file to be lost.

Now we are ready to modify Program SURVY1 to use file FORT06.DAT as the source of data. Clearly, we should eliminate the question-

```
      PROGRAM SURVY2
C  **  READ YES-NO SURVEY DATA FROM A DATA FLE

      INTEGER  DATA1(8), RESULT(8,4), K1, K2, K3
      DATA  RESULT/ 32*Ø/

C  **  READ DATA FROM DEVICE #6 (FORTØ6.DAT)
C  **  AND TABULATE AS BEFORE
 1Ø   READ ( 6, 12 ) K2, DATA1
 12      FORMAT ( 9I3 )
      IF ( K2 .EQ. Ø )      GO TO 2ØØ
       DO 9Ø K3 = 1, 8
         RESULT( K3, K2 ) = RESULT( K3, K2 ) + DATA1( K3 )
 9Ø    CONTINUE
       GO TO 1Ø

 2ØØ  WRITE ( 5, 2Ø2 )
 2Ø2     FORMAT ( ' ', '  QUEST    MALE    MALE FEMALE FEMALE' /
     +            ' ', ' NUMBER     21+  UNDER     21+  UNDER' )
      WRITE ( 5, 2Ø4 ) (K1, (RESULT(K1,K2),K2 = 1, 4),K1 = 1, 8)
 2Ø4     FORMAT ( ' ', 5I7 )

      END
```

**Program 6-7.** Survey data tabulation with external data.

```
[Begin execution]

 QUEST    MALE    MALE FEMALE FEMALE
NUMBER     21+  UNDER     21+  UNDER
     1       2      2       2      1
     2       1      3       Ø      1
     3       Ø      2       3      1
     4       1      2       1      Ø
     5       2      1       3      Ø
     6       Ø      Ø       3      Ø
     7       2      1       1      1
     8       1      2       2      Ø
```

**Fig. 6-6.** Execution of Program 6-7.

naire data from the program. Now it is not necessary to read all of the data into memory at once. So we may reduce the size of our data array to eight elements and read the respondent category with a separate variable in the READ statement

10 READ ( 6, 12 ) K2, DATA1

and now we may replace the reference to DATA1(K3 + 1, K1) with a reference to DATA1( K3 ). The resulting program is much shorter and produces the same results (see Program 6-7 named SURVY2).

## Summary

We can gain tremendous flexibility for data processing by providing data in files instead of in DATA statements of programs. Data may be replaced for subsequent executions of the same program. A data set may be processed by several programs. Data files are treated as devices by FORTRAN and so are accessible to programs by simply naming the appropriate device number in READ or WRITE statements.

## Problems for Sec. 6-3

1. In Program SURVY2 add a ninth row to RESULT and tabulate the total number of respondents in each of the four original categories there.
2. In Program SURVY2 add a fifth column to RESULT and tabulate the total number of "yes" responses there.
3. Modify Program SURVY2 by adding the four categories: male, female, under 21, and 21 or over.

*4. Modify Program SURVY2 to accommodate a third possible response, such as two for "other." Tabulate each of the three responses by scanning the data three times, once for each possible response, and write the results after each scan. Be sure to zero the elements of the result array before each scan.

*5. Modify Program SURVY2 to accommodate a third possible response, such as "other." Tabulate the results in a three-dimensional array by allowing three elements in the third dimension. You might use one for "no," two for "yes," and three for "other." Scan the data only once.

# 7

# Using What We Know: Miscellaneous Applications

## 7-1 Looking at Integers One Digit at a Time

In general, the more detailed the control we have over a number in the computer, the more complex the problems we might expect to be able to handle. We also will find that, as we learn more about what goes on inside the computer, we will be able to apply more elegant solutions to problems. So for the purpose of learning to control a number in the computer digit by digit, let's write a program to separate the digits of an integer and print them one at a time.

Consider the number 8394. The 8 means 8000, which may be written 8 * 10**3; the 3 means 300, which may be written 3 * 10**2; the 9 means 90, which may be written 9 * 10**1; and the 4 means 4, which may be written 4 * 10**0. Let's look at the detail of what happens as we "peel off" the digits of 8394 one at a time from left to right.

```
8394 = 8 * 10**3 + 394
 394 = 3 * 10**2 +  94
  94 = 9 * 10**1 +   4
   4 = 4 * 10**0 +   0
```

This is an example of the general relationship

N = D * 10**E + R

where R is the remainder, D is the digit (an integer) found by

D = N/10**E

and an iterative process whereby the new N is the old R and the value of E (the power of 10) is decreased by 1 for each iteration. Solving for R we get

R = N − D * 10**E

For five-digit integers, the value of the exponent on 10 will range from 4 to 0. For this demonstration, we will enter each digit into a separate element of a 5-

```
      PROGRAM DIGIT1
C  **  THIS PROGRAM SEPARATES THE DIGITS OF AN INTEGER

      INTEGER DIGITS(5), INDEX, INTEGR, EXP, DIGIT, REMAIN

C  **  REQUEST DATA ENTRY
 10   WRITE ( 5, 12 )
 12      FORMAT ( 'Ø', 'ENTER AN INTEGER ' )
      READ ( 5, 22 ) INTEGR
 22      FORMAT ( I6 )
      IF ( INTEGR .EQ. Ø ) STOP

C  **  ENTER THE DIGITS IN ARRAY DIGITS
      DO 1ØØ INDEX = 1, 5
        EXP                = 5 - INDEX
        DIGIT              = INTEGR / 1Ø**EXP
        DIGITS( INDEX )    = DIGIT
        REMAIN             = INTEGR - DIGIT * 1Ø**EXP
        INTEGR             = REMAIN
 1ØØ  CONTINUE

      WRITE ( 5, 1Ø2 ) DIGITS
 1Ø2     FORMAT ( '+', 5( 1X, I2 ) )
      GO TO 1Ø

      END
```

**Program 7-1.** Print numeric digits separately.

element array and format the results with a space between digits to prove that we have indeed isolated the individual digits as we intended (see Program 7-1 named DIGIT1).

```
[Begin execution]


ENTER AN INTEGER 1635
  Ø  1  6  3  5

ENTER AN INTEGER 32199
  3  2  1  9  9

ENTER AN INTEGER Ø
 STOP
```

**Fig. 7-1.** Execution of Program 7-1.

There are a number of areas in which we could improve or extend our program. As written, Program DIGIT1 will accept negative integers, but it will print each digit as a negative digit. We could determine if the entered integer is positive or negative and then take the absolute value for processing. If we get a negative number, we could write out a single minus sign. Note that we get leading zeros printed; we could eliminate them. These considerations are left as exercises.

```
      SUBROUTINE IENTER( N1 )
C  **  THIS SUBROUTINE REQUESTS ONE INTEGER FROM DEVICE #5

      INTEGER N1

 10   WRITE ( 5, 12 )
 12      FORMAT ( '0', 'ENTER AN INTEGER ' )
      READ ( 5, 22 ) N1
 22      FORMAT ( I6 )
      IF ( N1 .EQ. 0 ) STOP
      RETURN

      END
```

**Program 7-2.** A SUBROUTINE to request an integer.

We might well want to consider a rather different scheme for "peeling off" digits of an integer. What is the value of MOD( 12345, 10 )? How about MOD( 4323, 10 )? And what about MOD( xxxxd, 10 )? Is it clear that using the MOD function with 10 as the modulus will always return the unit's digit for numbers expressed in base ten? We may simply find the unit's digit and then divide our number by ten. If the remaining number is zero, then we print the results. If the remaining number is not zero, we have the computer use the MOD function, repeating the whole process. This, too, is left as an exercise.

We are going to be repeating "ENTER AN INTEGER" from time to time in our work. Note that the program statements to request data in Program 7-1 take more than 20 percent of the total program statements with COMMENTS and nearly 30 percent not counting COMMENTS. Let's write a SUBROUTINE so that we can "ENTER AN INTEGER" with a single CALL statement (see Program 7-2 named IENTER).

```
      PROGRAM DIGIT2
C  **  THIS PROGRAM SEPARATES THE DIGITS OF AN INTEGER

      INTEGER DIGITS(5), INDEX, INTEGR, EXP, DIGIT, REMAIN

C  **  REQUEST DATA ENTRY - USING A SUBROUTINE CALL
 10   CALL IENTER( INTEGR )

C  **  ENTER THE DIGITS IN ARRAY DIGITS
      DO 100 INDEX = 1, 5
        EXP               = 5 - INDEX
        DIGIT             = INTEGR / 10**EXP
        DIGITS( INDEX )   = DIGIT
        REMAIN            = INTEGR - DIGIT * 10**EXP
        INTEGR            = REMAIN
 100  CONTINUE

      WRITE ( 5, 102 ) DIGITS
 102     FORMAT ( '+', 5( 1X, I2 ) )
      GO TO 10

      END
```

**Program 7-3.** Program 7-1 with SUBROUTINE CALL to IENTER.

All we have done in Program 7-2 is to extract the five program statements from Program DIGIT1 that request an integer from the keyboard and add the statements required to make it into a subroutine. Now we may request an integer from the keyboard with a single CALL statement. We present Program 7-1 with the subroutine CALL to IENTER as Program 7-3 named DIGIT2 (see p. 99).

```
[Begin execution]

ENTER AN INTEGER 12345
  1  2  3  4  5

ENTER AN INTEGER 32168
  3  2  1  6  8

ENTER AN INTEGER Ø
 STOP
```

**Fig. 7-2.** Execution of Program 7-3.

## Summary

We have seen that we have the ability to examine and treat the digits of integers one at a time. We can get at the individual digits either from left to right or from right to left. We have simplified a program by utilizing a subroutine call to request an integer from a keyboard. We thus avoided the need to recreate those program statements over and over again.

## Problems for Sec. 7-1

Where appropriate, use SUBROUTINE IENTER in your solution programs.

1. Modify Program DIGIT1 so that it does not print leading zeros. Be careful that you do not eliminate all zeros.
2. Modify Program DIGIT1 so that it will properly handle negative integers.
3. Write a program that will pick apart the digits of real numbers.
4. Write a program that will pick apart the digits of integers using the FORTRAN MOD function. Make your program accommodate negative integers and avoid printing leading zeros.
5. Write a program to construct an integer by reversing the digits of an entered integer. Print the result as an integer.
6. Find all three-digit integers that are prime. Form new integers by reversing the digits and see if the new number also is prime. Print a number only if it and its reverse number also are prime. There are 43 pairs of numbers, some of which appear twice. You might use a function to test for primes.

## 7-2 Change Number Base

The day to day world of business, commerce, and general communications reckons in the familiar base ten number system. The ultimate reckoning of the computer is in base two. Base two requires only the two digits "0" (zero) and "1" (one). Thus computers may represent a "1" with a positive voltage level or a magnetized state and a "0" may be represented by a zero voltage level or a demagnetized state. Therefore, it is useful to be familiar with the base two number system. The base two number system also is referred to as the *binary number system.* A number is a number is a number is a number. The number does not change by virtue of being expressed in a different number system. As we change from one base to another, we may be using different symbols to name the same number. In the binary number system, there are only two possible digits.

Addition in base two is very simple. Either there is a "carry" as the result of two 1's being added or there is not. Thus:

$$0 + 0 = 0 \qquad 0 + 1 = 1 \qquad 1 + 1 = 10$$

Multiplication also is simplified by the two possible digit structure. When multiplying by "1" the digits shift according to the position of the "1," and when multiplying by "0" the result is "0." Thus:

```
   10            11011
 * 10          *   101
 ----          -------
   00            11011
  10            00000
 ----          11011
  100          --------
               10000111
```

Of course when multiplying by "1" in the rightmost position the shift is zero.

One disadvantage of the binary number system is that it takes so many digits to represent numbers. For instance, 15 base ten is written as 1111 in binary, and 127 base ten is written 1111111 in binary.

Each digit of any integer number represents an integer power of the base. The digits in binary, from right to left, represent 1, 2, 4, 8, 16, 32, 64, 128, 256, 512, etc., in base ten. On some computers the largest integer allowed is 32767, while the smallest is −32768. That is 65536 numbers, and 65535 base ten is represented by 1111111111111111 in binary notation. That is 16 binary digits. Each binary digit is referred to as a *bit.* Bits are collected into groups of eight to form bytes. It takes two bytes to represent integers from 0 to 65535. In practice the leftmost binary bit is used to designate whether or not the integer stored in the other 15 bits is positive or negative. A "1" indicates negative, while a "0" indicates positive. Thus for two-byte storage, we are limited to the range of −32768 to +32767, as mentioned above. While for one-byte storage the limits are −128 to +127.

### *Decimal to Binary*

Let's get started by writing a program to convert decimal to binary. If the number we have is odd then the first digit on the right is a "1." If we have an even number, then the first digit on the right is a "0." Now, "to move the base two decimal point one to the left," we divide our number by 2 and truncate. Note that dividing by 2 in binary is equivalent to dividing by 10 in base ten for the purpose of locating the "point." If the truncated result is zero, then we are finished. If the truncated result is nonzero, then we repeat the process for the next binary digit. Consider the process for 53:

| | | | |
|---|---|---|---|
| | 53 | is odd | 1 |
| divide by 2 and truncate | 26 | is even | 01 |
| divide by 2 and truncate | 13 | is odd | 101 |
| divide by 2 and truncate | 6 | is even | 0101 |
| divide by 2 and truncate | 3 | is odd | 10101 |
| divide by 2 and truncate | 1 | is odd | 110101 |
| divide by 2 and truncate | 0 | we have finished and | |

53 base ten = 110101 base two

Now we simply need to work out a way to print the results and a program will be forthcoming. The method we use is to store the digits in a 16-element array as we determine them. We store the rightmost (or low order) digit in the sixteenth element, the second digit in the fifteenth element, and so forth until finished. This later could be easily expanded to accommodate larger numbers.

```
      PROGRAM DECBIN
C  **  THIS PROGRAM CONVERTS DECIMAL TO BINARY

      INTEGER DIGIT(16), BASE10, INDEX, PLACE

 10   CALL IENTER( BASE10 )
      DO 20 INDEX = 1, 16
        DIGIT( INDEX ) = 0
 20   CONTINUE

C  **  LOAD DIGIT ARRAY WITH BINARY DIGITS
      DO 50 INDEX = 1, 16
        PLACE             = 17 - INDEX
        DIGIT( PLACE )  = MOD( BASE10, 2 )
        BASE10            = BASE10 / 2
        IF ( BASE10 .EQ. 0 )              GO TO 100
 50   CONTINUE

 100  WRITE ( 5, 102 ) DIGIT
 102     FORMAT ( '+', 16I2 )
      GO TO 10

      END
```

**Program 7-4.** Convert decimal to binary.

How do we know if a number is odd or even? We can evaluate the remainder mod 2. BASE10 mod 2 is 0 if the number is even and 1 if the number is odd. This is an ideal application of the MOD function. Furthermore, while the odd vs. even comparison does not apply to other bases, the remainder mod N is the correct digit for conversion to base N. We might just as well use CALL IENTER to supply our program with data. Of course, note that the FORTRAN MOD function requires base ten arguments and returns base ten values (see Program 7-4 named DECBIN).

```
[Begin execution]


ENTER AN INTEGER 12345
 Ø Ø 1 1 Ø Ø Ø Ø Ø Ø 1 1 1 Ø Ø 1

ENTER AN INTEGER 128
 Ø Ø Ø Ø Ø Ø Ø Ø 1 Ø Ø Ø Ø Ø Ø Ø

ENTER AN INTEGER 32767
 Ø 1 1 1 1 1 1 1 1 1 1 1 1 1 1 1

ENTER AN INTEGER Ø
STOP
```

**Fig. 7-3.** Execution of Program 7-4.

Note that Program 7-4 prints all of the leading zeros. We might want to eliminate them. Since the variable PLACE holds the last position entered into the array, we could easily supply the appropriate implied DO loop in the WRITE statement. We also could easily format the digits into adjacent positions.

### *Binary to Octal*

The octal number system reckons in base eight. This allows us to convert numbers expressed in base two into more compact form. Note that it takes exactly three binary digits to form an octal digit:

```
101  100  010  111  binary
 5    4    2    7 = 5427 octal
```

### *Binary to Hexadecimal*

The hexadecimal number system reckons in base sixteen. Hex representations are more compact than octal or base ten, because hex uses 16 possible digits. The hex digits are 0, 1, 2, 3, 4, 5, 6, 7, 8, 9, A, B, C, D, E, and F. So 10 hex is 16 base ten and EF hex is 14*16 + 15*1 or 239 base ten. It takes four binary digits to form a hex digit:

```
1011  0001  0111  binary
 B     1     7 = B17 hex
```

### *Hexadecimal to Decimal*

The conversion from decimal to hex is exactly analogous to the conversion from decimal to binary, except that we have to work out how to get the extra digits A through F into the picture. Since the extra digit problem also occurs in the hex to decimal conversion, this is where we start.

Let's convert 1B3A hex to decimal:

| | | | |
|---|---|---|---|
| The digit A in the | unit's | column represents | 10 |
| The digit 3 in the | 16's | column represents | 48 |
| The digit B in the | 256's | column represents | 2816 |
| The digit 1 in the | 4096's | column represents | 4096 |
| 1B3A | hex | equals | 6970 base ten |

How we solve the problem of handling the alphabetic digits required for hex representation might depend on whether we are using FORTRAN 77 or FORTRAN IV. FORTRAN 77 allows us to analyze strings of characters one character at a time. It is not quite so direct in FORTRAN IV, but we can make it look as though we can! In FORTRAN IV we can enter characters with A-format so that each character is entered into one element of an array. It turns out that we can represent the most often required numbers with up to four hex digits. So we simply require that all four digits be entered, even leading zeros. So FF will be entered as 00FF.

```
      PROGRAM HEXIO
C  **  THIS PROGRAM DEMONSTRATES HEX I/O (INPUT/OUTPUT)

      INTEGER HEX(4), INDEX, ZERO
      DATA    ZERO/ 'Ø'/

C  **  REQUEST HEX DIGITS USING A-FORMAT
 1Ø   WRITE ( 5, 12 )
 12      FORMAT (  'Ø', 'ENTER 4 HEX DIGITS ? ' )
      READ ( 5, 22 ) HEX
 22      FORMAT ( 4A1 )

C  **  CHECK FOR ALL ZERO CHARACTERS
      DO 5Ø INDEX = 1, 4
        IF ( HEX(INDEX) .NE. ZERO ) GO TO 1ØØ
 5Ø   CONTINUE
      STOP

C  **  NOW WRITE BACK THE SAME DIGITS INSERTING SPACES
 1ØØ  WRITE ( 5, 1Ø2 ) HEX
 1Ø2     FORMAT ( '+', 4A2, 'H' )
      GO TO 1Ø

      END
```

**Program 7-5.** Demonstrate hex input/output.

Let's first demonstrate our ability to take in hex digits and write them out again (see Program 7-5 named HEXIO). Then we can concentrate our efforts on the rest of the details.

```
[Begin execution]

ENTER 4 HEX DIGITS ? ØØA5
Ø Ø A 5 H

ENTER 4 HEX DIGITS ? FFØØ
F F Ø Ø H

ENTER 4 HEX DIGITS ? C4ØØ
C 4 Ø Ø H

ENTER 4 HEX DIGITS ? ØØØØ
 STOP
```

**Fig. 7-4.** Execution of Program 7-5.

Now, how do we get the computer to "know" that an "A" is ten, a "B" is eleven, and so on? Since the digits are not numeric, we have this problem even for "0," "1," etc. One method is to enter all possible hexadecimal digits into a 16-element array. This will enable us to compare each entered digit with the digits in the array to identify the digit by its position in the 16-element array.

We can enter the 16 digits into the array with DATA initialization as follows:

```
      DATA ARRAY/ '0', '1', '2', '3', '4', '5', '6', '7',
     +            '8', '9', 'A', 'B', 'C', 'D', 'E', 'F'/
```

Alternatively, we might use H-format.

The digits that are entered may be located in the 16-element array with a DO loop. This will be nested inside a DO loop that scans the four entered digits, as follows:

```
      BASE10 = 0
      DO 80 INDEX = 1, 4
        DO 50 K1 = 1, 16
          IF ( HEX(INDEX) .EQ. ARRAY(K1) ) GO TO 70
50      CONTINUE
70    BASE10 = BASE10 + 16**(K1-1)
80    CONTINUE
```

Note that the exponent we are using on 16 is one less than the position in which we find the matching digit. This is because in the array containing the 16 possible hex digits, "0" is the array element numbered one and the "1" occupies the array element numbered two, and so on. Thus we must bias the exponent by −1. We may now put all this together into a single program (see Program 7-6 named HEXCVT).

In Program 7-6 look at the DO loop that terminates at 50 CONTINUE. Suppose we enter a character that is not a hex digit. Trouble! The program should check for this. If the program detects a bad digit, a message should be

```
      PROGRAM HEXCVT
C  **  THIS PROGRAM CONVERTS HEX TO DECIMAL

      INTEGER HEX(4), INDEX, BASE10, K1, ARRAY(16)
      DATA  ARRAY/ '0', '1', '2', '3', '4', '5', '6', '7',
     +             '8', '9', 'A', 'B', 'C', 'D', 'E', 'F'/

C  **  REQUEST HEX DIGITS
 10   WRITE ( 5, 12 )
 12      FORMAT ( '0', 'ENTER A NUMBER IN HEX ? ' )
      READ ( 5, 22 ) HEX
 22      FORMAT ( 4A1 )

C  **  CONVERT HERE
      BASE10 = 0
      DO 80 INDEX = 1, 4
        DO 50 K1 = 1, 16
          IF ( HEX(INDEX) .EQ. ARRAY(K1) ) GO TO 70
 50     CONTINUE
 70   BASE10 = BASE10 + (K1-1) * 16**(4-INDEX)
 80   CONTINUE

C  **  NOW OUTPUT THE RESULTS IN BASE10
      WRITE ( 5, 102 ) BASE10
 102     FORMAT ( '+', 'CONVERTS TO ', I5, ' BASE TEN' )
      IF ( BASE10 .NE. 0 ) GO TO 10

      END
```

**Program 7-6.** Convert hex to base ten.

```
[Begin execution]


ENTER A NUMBER IN HEX ? 7FFF
CONVERTS TO 32767 BASE TEN

ENTER A NUMBER IN HEX ? 00FF
CONVERTS TO   255 BASE TEN

ENTER A NUMBER IN HEX ? 0100
CONVERTS TO   256 BASE TEN

ENTER A NUMBER IN HEX ? 0000
CONVERTS TO     0 BASE TEN
```

**Fig. 7-5.** Execution of Program 7-6.

printed and control should pass to the statement labeled 10. Also note that the program will accept any four digits. But if we are limited to integer values from −32768 to 32767 for the value of BASE10, all those values from 32768 to 65535 will turn out to be an invalid integer. One solution to the problem is to use real representation for base ten.

## Summary

We have seen that the rationale for base two or binary is that the digits "0" and "1" can be represented as electrical states of one sort or another.

Octal has been shown to be more compact than binary, and hex is more compact even than base ten. All conversion techniques rely on determining the position of a particular digit and its actual value. Where it is not practical (possible?) to use FORTRAN numeric variables to store numbers, we use A-format to store and WRITE results as appropriate.

## Problems for Sec. 7-2

1. Modify Program HEXCVT to handle nonhex digits and hex representations of numbers larger than 32767 base ten using real variables.
2. Modify Program DECBIN so that it does not print leading zeros and so that digits are printed in adjacent spaces.
3. Write a program to convert base two to base ten.
4. Write a program to convert base two to octal.
5. Write a program to convert base two to hex.

*6. Write a program to convert hex to binary.

*7. Write a program to do hex addition. Use a subroutine for hex data input.

## 7-3 Miscellaneous Problems for Solution

We offer a few interesting projects for computer application here. You should be bringing your own problems to the computer. You will experience tremendous satisfaction when you begin to identify your own problems and write programs in FORTRAN to solve them. Be on the lookout for such problems.

1. Every positive integer may be expressed as the sum of the squares of four integers. Zero may be included as one or more of those integers to be squared. For example:

   1 = 0**2 + 0**2 + 0**2 + 1**2

   Write a program to find all sets of four such integers for a requested integer. Be careful about efficiency in this one. Test your solution with small integers before trying large ones!
2. Suppose you have to find the greatest common factor of 13398 and 7854. What would you do? Euclid would have found the remainder after dividing 13398 by 7854, which is 5544. Then he would have found the remainder after dividing 7854 by 5544, which is 2310. Then he would have found the rest of the remainders as follows:

```
13398 = 1 * 7854 + 5544
 7854 = 1 * 5544 + 2310
 5544 = 2 * 2310 +  924
 2310 = 2 *  924 +  462
  924 = 2 *  462 +    0
```

   Next, Euclid would have reasoned that since the remainder of the last division was zero, the greatest common factor must be the last divisor, in this case 462. We have an ideal application of the FORTRAN MOD function. Try it! Note that we found 462 in only five iterations. How many would it have taken using other methods?

3. The sieve of Eratosthenes is an ingenious method for generating prime integers. Write down all the integers from 2 to the desired upper limit. Now keep the first number and cross out all multiples of it. Now keep the next uncrossed out number and cross out all multiples of it. Repeat this process until there are no more numbers to cross out. The remaining numbers are prime.

   There are two areas in this algorithm that are potential pitfalls for unnecessary extra processing. First, if the first multiple in any case has already been crossed out, then so will all other multiples have been crossed out. Second, we only have to check for uncrossed out integers up to the square root of the largest number in the range.

   This algorithm can be nicely implemented in an array in FORTRAN. First, enter the integers from 2 to the upper limit into the array elements 2 through the upper limit. Next, use the stepping capability of the DO loop to access the multiple positions in the array. Set the contents of any element to be crossed out to zero. Finally, print all subscript positions for which the element is not zero.

4. Perfect numbers are integers, the sum of whose proper factors is the integer. The proper factors of 15 are 1, 3, and 5. The sum of the factors of 15 is 9. Therefore 15 is not a perfect number. The proper factors of 6 are 1, 2, and 3. The sum of the proper factors of 6 is 6. Thus 6 is called a perfect number. Write a program to find the first four perfect numbers. Since the fifth perfect number is 33,550,336, and there is a significant amount of execution associated with determining "perfectness," we would be unwise to test each integer up to that one! It turns out that there don't seem to be any odd perfect numbers, so let's test only even numbers.

5. Euclid was an active mathematician! He concluded that all possible even perfect numbers are of the form

   N = 2**(E−1) * F

   where

   F = 2**E − 1      and F is an odd prime

   Using Euclid's algorithm, write a program to calculate perfect numbers. Try a range of 2 to 12 for E.

6. There are many famous chess puzzles from antiquity that are appropriate for computer solution. A notable one is the Eight Queens problem. How many ways can eight Queens be placed on a chess board so that no Queen attacks another?

   This puzzle may be solved by using one 8-element array. Placing a Queen in a position of the array assures that no two Queens occupy the same row. A Queen may be placed in the row by entering her column number. Now we assure that no two Queens occupy the same column by avoiding duplicate column numbers in the 8-element array. Finally we check for diagonal attack by noting that for two Queens at positions (X,Y) and (X',Y'), one diagonal is shared if $X-X'=Y-Y'$, while the other diagonal is shared if $X+X'=Y+Y'$. We need to have the computer test this for each Queen in every column of one row. Write a program to print the positions of all Queens for each solution.

For more about the Eight Queens problem see the October 1978 and the February 1979 issues of *Byte* magazine.

# 8

# The Quadratic Function and Graphing

Find two numbers whose sum is 5 and whose product is 6. Quick as a flash you say 2 and 3. Now find two numbers whose sum is 19/15 and whose product is 2/5. We need an algorithm with no trial and error. Starting with the first example we have:

| | | | |
|---|---|---|---|
| | X + Y = 5 | and | X * Y = 6 |
| or | Y = 5 − X | and | X(5 − X) = 6 |
| or | 5 * X − X**2 = 6 | | |
| or | X**2 − 5*X + 6 = 0 | | **Eq. 8-1** |

Equation 8-1 is an example of a quadratic equation that is a special case of the quadratic function. The quadratic equation for the second example above is

15X**2 − 19X + 6 = 0

We define a quadratic function for the purposes of this chapter as

f(X) = AX**2 + BX + C **Eq. 8-2**

where X is real and A, B, and C are integers and A is nonzero.

## 8-1 Zeros of a Quadratic Function

Often in mathematics we would like to find the values of X that satisfy an equation like Eq. 8-1. The values of X that satisfy an equation of the form of Eq. 8-1 are called the *zeros of the function* of the form of Eq. 8-2 because they are the values of X for which f(X) = 0. The zeros also are referred to as the *X-intercepts* of the graph of the function. In addition these values also solve the quadratic equation

AX**2 + BX + C = 0

and so they also are called *roots*.

For some coefficients, we may factor the expression on the right in Eq. 8-2 and set each factor equal to zero, since, if the product of two real numbers is zero then at least one of them must be zero, if not both. So for

$$X^{**}2 - 5X + 6 = 0$$

Factoring, we get

$$(X - 2)(X - 3) = 0$$

and

$$(X - 2) = 0 \qquad \text{or} \qquad (X - 3) = 0$$

So

$$X = 2 \qquad \text{or} \qquad X = 3$$

and truth set or "answer" is $\{2, 3\}$.

However, not all quadratic expressions are factorable. For nonfactorable as well as factorable quadratic expressions on the right in Eq. 8-2, we may use the quadratic formula, which may be derived by the method of completing the square. The roots of f(X) = AX**2 + BX + C are

$$X1 = ( -B + \sqrt{B^{**}2 - 4AC}\ ) / ( 2A ) \qquad \textbf{Eq. 8-3}$$

and

$$X2 = ( -B - \sqrt{B^{**}2 - 4AC}\ ) / ( 2A ) \qquad \textbf{Eq. 8-4}$$

The expression B**2 − 4AC is called the *discriminant of the function* and contains some significant information about the function and its zeros. The square root of the discriminant must be evaluated to calculate both zeros. Therefore, for the zeros to be real numbers, the discriminant must be non-negative. That correlates nicely with the FORTRAN requirement for the argument of the SQRT function. We now have enough information to write a program to calculate the real zeros of a quadratic function (see Program 8-1 named QUAD1).

Note in this program the use of '0' for printer control in the FORMAT statement labeled 12 to provide a blank line between successive requests for data.

Let's return to the question of two numbers whose sum and product are given. We can demonstrate that the two numbers will be roots of a quadratic equation. That being the case, we need only relate X1 + X2 and X1 * X2 to the values of A, B, and C in Eq. 8-2 as follows:

$$X1 + X2 = \frac{-B + \sqrt{B^{**}2 - 4AC}}{2A} + \frac{-B - \sqrt{B^{**}2 - 4AC}}{2A}$$

$$= -2B / 2A$$

```
      PROGRAM QUAD1
C  **  CALCULATE THE REAL ZEROS OF A QUADRATIC FUNCTION

      INTEGER A, B, C
      REAL    X1, X2, S1, D1, A1, B1, C1

 1Ø   WRITE ( 5, 12 )
 12      FORMAT ( 'Ø', 'ENTER QUADRATIC COEFFICIENTS ' )
      READ ( 5, 22 ) A, B, C
 22      FORMAT ( 3I5 )
      IF ( A .EQ. Ø ) STOP

      A1 = FLOAT( A )
      B1 = FLOAT( B )
      C1 = FLOAT( C )

C  **  SAVE THE DISCRIMINANT AND TEST FOR NEGATIVE VALUE
      D1 = B1**2 - 4.Ø * A1 * C1
      IF ( D1 .GE. Ø.Ø ) GO TO 6Ø
       WRITE ( 5, 42 )
 42       FORMAT ( '+', 'NONREAL ZEROS' )
       GO TO 1Ø

 6Ø   S1 = SQRT( D1 )
C  **  NOW CALCULATE THE TWO REAL ZEROS
      X1 = (-B1 + S1) / (2.Ø * A1)
      X2 = (-B1 - S1) / (2.Ø * A1)

      WRITE ( 5, 1Ø2 ) X1, X2
 1Ø2     FORMAT ( '+', 'REAL ZEROS ARE', F6.2, ' AND', F6.2, )
      GO TO 1Ø

      END
```

**Program 8-1.** Calculate the real zeros of a quadratic.

So

$$X1 + X2 = -B / A \qquad \textbf{Eq. 8-5}$$

and

$$X1 * X2 = \frac{-B + \sqrt{B**2 - 4AC}}{2A} * \frac{-B - \sqrt{B**2 - 4AC}}{2A}$$

$$= \frac{B**2 - B**2 + 4AC}{4A**2}$$

So

$$X1 * X2 = C / A \qquad \textbf{Eq. 8-6}$$

Now for two numbers whose sum is 19/15 and whose product is 2/5, we have

$$-B / A = 19 / 15 \quad \text{and} \quad C / A = 2 / 5 \qquad \textbf{Eq. 8-7}$$

```
[Begin execution]

ENTER QUADRATIC COEFFICIENTS 1,2,3
NONREAL ZEROS

ENTER QUADRATIC COEFFICIENTS 1,-5,6
REAL ZEROS ARE  3.ØØ AND  2.ØØ

ENTER QUADRATIC COEFFICIENTS 5,12,17
NONREAL ZEROS

ENTER QUADRATIC COEFFICIENTS Ø,Ø,Ø
 STOP
```

**Fig. 8-1.** Execution of Program 8-1.

One possible set or values for A, B, and C is 15, −19, and 6. Note that 30, −38, and 12 or any other nonzero multiple also will satisfy Eq. 8-7.

## 8-2 Plotting a Graph of the Quadratic Function

We can use our terminal, console, or printer to plot a graph of a quadratic function. Note that the points at which the graph crosses the X-axis are the graph of the zeros of the function, since the value of Y or f(X) is zero everywhere on the X-axis. Once we have developed plotting for quadratic functions, we will be able to easily plot other functions as well. Since most terminals and printers cannot reverse the direction of the paper, more general plotting will require some additional design. First things first.

We may use the spaces across the carriage as one axis and lines lengthwise as the other axis. Since the line feed is automatically set on the terminal, the X-axis should run perpendicular to the carriage and the Y-axis should run across the page. This means that one line represents one unit on the X-axis and one space represents one unit on the Y-axis. This is rotated 90 degrees clockwise from the conventional rectangular coordinate system. Simply tear off the paper and turn it around. (Maybe you should turn your video terminal on its side?)

While some terminals provide 80 or even 128 columns, let's set things up for 65, so that our printouts will fit on a page of this book. All we have to do is to fill a 65-element array with spaces and WRITE as much of it as we need with an implied DO loop, followed by the plotted character. We can fill an array with spaces using DATA initialization with H-format or apostrophe editing, or we can write a DO loop to do the job. We can write each element of the array as a single character using A1 in the FORMAT statement. We demonstrate such a technique with a short program (see Program 8-2 named PLOT1).

Now it is a simple extension of Program 8-2 to plot some points of a quadratic function. Let's plot some points of the graph of

f(X) = X**2

```
      PROGRAM PLOT1
C  **  WE DEMONSTRATE PLOTTING WITH SPACES IN AN ARRAY AND
C  **  AN IMPLIED DO LOOP IN A WRITE STATEMENT.

      INTEGER SPACE(65), POINT, INDEX, I

C  **  LOAD 65 SPACES IN SPACE AND * IN POINT
      DATA  SPACE/ 65*' '/ POINT/ '*'/

C  **  NOW PLOT A FEW POINTS
      DO 100 INDEX = 1, 15, 2
      WRITE ( 5, 42 ) (SPACE(I), I = 1, INDEX), POINT
 42      FORMAT ( ' ', 65A1 )
 100  CONTINUE

      END
[Begin execution]

 *
   *
     *
       *
         *
           *
             *
               *
```

**Program 8-2.** Simple plotting demonstration.

We may use a DO loop to step through successive values of X. Note that FORTRAN executes every DO loop at least once. So in the implied DO of the WRITE statement, we will get one space even if the value of Y should be zero. Therefore, we bias the value of Y by adding 1 to the true value for all points on the graph. This will avoid an unwanted space for Y = 0. See Program 8-3 named PLOT2.

We have just graphed a parabola (see Fig. 8-2)! Now that we have a reasonable plot of a quadratic function, we might just as well put some axes in. Let's print the Y-axis at the top of the page. This will put it at the left of the

```
      PROGRAM PLOT2
C  **  PLOTTING POINTS FOR  Y = X**2    NOTE STATEMENT FUNCTION

      INTEGER SPACE(65), POINT, Y, X, K, INDEX, FUNCT
      DATA  SPACE/ 65*' '/ POINT/ '*'/
      FUNCT(X) = X**2

      DO 100 INDEX = 1, 15
        X = INDEX - 8
        Y = FUNCT( X ) + 1
        WRITE ( 5, 42 ) (SPACE(K), K = 1, Y), POINT
42         FORMAT ( ' ', 65A1 )
100   CONTINUE

      END
```

**Program 8-3.** Our first graph of a quadratic function.

**Fig. 8-2.** Execution of Program 8-3.

graph after we tear the paper off. We can print numeric labels by entering multiples of ten from 0 to 50 into an array and then printing them at appropriate intervals with

```
      DO 10 INDEX = 1, 6
        VLINE( INDEX ) = 10 * ( INDEX - 1 )
10    CONTINUE
      WRITE ( 5, 22 ) (VLINE( K1 ), K1 = 1, 6 )
22        FORMAT ( ' ', 6( 8X, I2 ) )
```

Next, we can print an axis of dashes with I's every ten spaces with

```
      DO 30 INDEX = 1, 65
        VLINE( INDEX ) = DASH
30    CONTINUE
      DO 40 INDEX = 10, 60, 10
        VLINE( INDEX ) = EYE
40    CONTINUE
      WRITE ( 5, 902 ) VLINE
902       FORMAT ( ' ', 65A1 )
```

Now that we see how easy it is to fill an array with characters and print it or a part of it, we might just as well use the same technique to print the lines with the plotted points as well. For each line printed, we want to fill VLINE with spaces and then place a "*" in the required position when we have found the value of Y. We also might add a character to indicate the position of the X-axis as well. This is done as the last half of Program 8-4 named PLOT3.

In this program note the statements

```
LIMIT = MAX0( 10, Y )
WRITE ( 5, 902 ) (VLINE( K1 ), K1 = 1, LIMIT )
```

The program outputs only as much of the array VLINE as is needed to print both the X-axis character and the plotted point using an implied DO loop.

There are a number of features that would be nice to have in our plotting program. It would be desirable to print the Y-axis where it really belongs. It would be nice to have a special character at the origin (where the X and Y axes intersect). We could mark intervals of ten on the X-axis. Note also that we have treated horizontal spaces and vertical lines as one each. On most output devices horizontal and vertical spacing are of different dimensions. We could incorporate a scaling factor to produce more accurate graphs. Some of these considerations are left as exercises.

```
      PROGRAM PLOT3
C  **  PLOTTING A GRAPH WITH AXES

      INTEGER VLINE(65), INDEX, K1, LIMIT, Y,
     +        DASH, EYE, SPACE, STAR
      DATA   DASH/ '-'/ EYE/ 'I'/ SPACE/ ' '/ STAR/ '*'/
      IFUNCT( Y ) = Y**2

C  **  SETUP PRINTING THE Y-AXIS LABELS
      DO 1Ø INDEX = 1, 6
        VLINE( INDEX ) = 1Ø * ( INDEX - 1 )
 1Ø   CONTINUE

C  **  WRITE OUT THE NUMERIC LABELS
      WRITE ( 5, 22 ) (VLINE( K1 ), K1 = 1, 6 )
 22      FORMAT ( ' ', 6( 8X, I2 ) )

C  **  SETUP Y-AXIS ITSELF
      DO 3Ø INDEX = 1, 65
        VLINE( INDEX ) = DASH
 3Ø   CONTINUE
      DO 4Ø INDEX = 1Ø, 6Ø, 1Ø
        VLINE( INDEX ) = EYE
 4Ø   CONTINUE

C  **  WRITE OUT THE Y-AXIS
      WRITE ( 5, 9Ø2 ) VLINE

C  **  NOW BEGIN PLOTTING POINTS ON THE GRAPH
      DO 6Ø INDEX = 1 , 15
        DO 5Ø K1 = 1 , 65
          VLINE( K1 ) = SPACE
 5Ø     CONTINUE
        VLINE( 1Ø ) = EYE
C  **  VLINE CONTAINS SPACES AND AN I FOR THE X-AXIS

        Y = IFUNCT( INDEX - 8 ) + 1Ø
C  **  LOAD * FOR THE PLOTTED POINT
        VLINE( Y ) = STAR
        LIMIT = MAXØ( 1Ø, Y )
        WRITE ( 5, 9Ø2 ) (VLINE( K1 ), K1 = 1, LIMIT)
 6Ø   CONTINUE

 9Ø2     FORMAT ( ' ', 65A1 )

      END
```

**Program 8-4.** Plotting with axes printed.

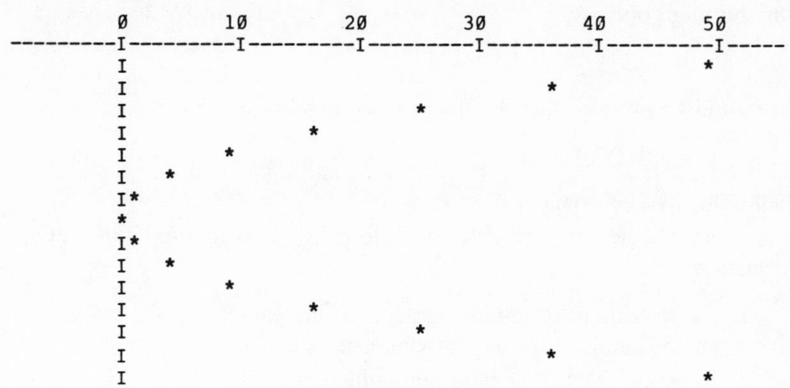

Fig. 8-3. Execution of Program 8-4.

## 8-3 Axis of Symmetry and Turning Point

The graph of a quadratic function is a parabola as we have seen. In examining a graph of a quadratic function we often want to know where the axis of symmetry is and where the turning point is. Of course we can estimate both the axis of symmetry and the turning point by examining a graph. However, we also can calculate exact values using a formula derived by completing the square on the right side of Eq. 8-2, as follows:

$$f(X) = AX{**}2 + BX + C$$

$$f(X) = A\left(X{**}2 + \frac{B}{A}X + \frac{B{**}2}{4A{**}2} - \frac{B{**}2}{4A{**}2}\right) + C$$

$$f(X) = A\left(X{**}2 + \frac{B}{A}X + \frac{B{**}2}{4A{**}2}\right) - \frac{B{**}2}{4A{**}2} + C$$

we get

$$f(X) = A\left(X + \frac{B}{2A}\right)^2 + \frac{4AC - B{**}2}{4A}$$

Now, as

$$\left(X + \frac{B}{2A}\right)$$

approaches 0, f(X) approaches a smaller or larger value depending on whether A is positive or negative. And when X + B/2A equals zero, X = −B/2A. Thus f(X) is at its maximum value for A negative and at its minimum value for A positive. And the value of f(−B/2A) is (4AC − B**2)/4A. Thus the coordinates of the turning point are

{−B/2A, (4AC − B**2)/(4A)}

You should know, too, that the line whose equation is

X = −B/2A

is called the *axis of symmetry*.

We should now be able to write a program to print three items of information:

1. The maximum or minimum status of the parabola.
2. The equation of the axis of symmetry.
3. The coordinates of the turning point.

```
          PROGRAM QUAD2
C  **     FIND PROPERTIES OF A GRAPH OF A QUADRATIC.

          INTEGER A, B, C
          REAL    X, Y, A1, B1, C1

 10       WRITE ( 5, 12 )
 12          FORMAT ( 'Ø', 'ENTER QUADRATIC COEFFICIENTS ' )
          READ ( 5, 22 ) A, B, C
 22          FORMAT ( 3I5 )
          IF ( A .EQ. Ø  .AND.  B .EQ. Ø  .AND.  C .EQ. Ø ) STOP

C  **     DETERMINE WHAT KIND OF A PARABOLA IN AN ARITHMETIC IF
          IF ( A ) 4Ø, 5Ø, 6Ø
 4Ø        WRITE ( 5, 42 )
 42           FORMAT ( '+', 'MAXIMUM PARABOLA' )
           GO TO 1ØØ
 5Ø        WRITE ( 5, 52 )
 52           FORMAT ( '+', 'NOT A PARABOLA' )
           GO TO 1Ø
 6Ø        WRITE ( 5, 62 )
 62           FORMAT ( '+', 'MINIMUM PARABOLA' )
           GO TO 1ØØ

C  **     NOW WE FIND THE AXIS OF SYMMETRY AND THE TURNING POINT
 1ØØ      A1 = FLOAT( A )
          B1 = FLOAT( B )
          C1 = FLOAT( C )

          X = -1.Ø * B1 / ( 2.Ø * A1 )
          Y = ( 4.Ø * A1 * C1 - (B1**2) ) / ( 4.Ø * A1 )

          WRITE ( 5, 112 ) X
 112         FORMAT ( ' ', 'AXIS OF SYMMETRY IS  X = ', F7.3 )
          WRITE ( 5, 122 ) X, Y
 122         FORMAT ( ' ', 'THE TURNING POINT IS ('
     +                   , F7.3, ' ,', F7.3, ' )' )
          GO TO 1Ø

          END
```

**Program 8-5.** Find properties of a graph of a quadratic.

Since a parabola is maximum, nonexistent, or minimum as A is negative, zero, or positive, we have an ideal application of the three-way branch provided by the FORTRAN arithmetic IF statement. This is done in Program 8-5 named QUAD2.

In this program note the statement

GO TO 100

immediately following the statement labeled 62 and just before the statement labeled 100. We are merely stating the obvious. Logically that statement is not required for proper execution of the program. However, placing GO TO 100 there nicely fills out the structure established by the two sets of three statements each just above it.

```
ENTER QUADRATIC COEFFICIENTS 1,2,3
MINIMUM PARABOLA
AXIS OF SYMMETRY IS  X =  -1.000
THE TURNING POINT IS ( -1.000 ,  2.000 )

ENTER QUADRATIC COEFFICIENTS 1,-5,6
MINIMUM PARABOLA
AXIS OF SYMMETRY IS  X =   2.500
THE TURNING POINT IS (  2.500 ,  -.250 )

ENTER QUADRATIC COEFFICIENTS 5,12,17
MINIMUM PARABOLA
AXIS OF SYMMETRY IS  X =  -1.200
THE TURNING POINT IS ( -1.200 ,  9.800 )

ENTER QUADRATIC COEFFICIENTS 0,0,0
 STOP
```

**Fig. 8-4.** Execution of Program 8-5.

## Summary for Secs. 8-1 to 8-3

There are several things that can be done with the quadratic function on a computer: (1) we can calculate the zeros; (2) we can plot graphs on our terminal or printer; and (3) we can get the computer to find the values of the various constants that specify the appearance of the graph. The plotting presented here can be used directly for other functions and with some additional design for other types of graphs as well.

## Problems for Secs. 8-1 to 8-3

1. Modify Program QUAD1 to print rational zeros as fractions reduced to lowest terms.
2. Modify Program QUAD1 to calculate nonreal zeros.

3. Modify Program QUAD1 to accept the coefficients as real numbers.
4. Write a program to request the sum and product of two numbers and calculate the numbers. You could request both the sum and product as two numbers each (numerator and denominator).
5. Modify Program PLOT3 to do all of the following:
   a. Print the Y-axis where it belongs.
   b. Print a "+" (plus) at the origin.
   c. Permit plotting several functions with a different character for each.
6. Modify Program PLOT3 to print "shaded" graphs by printing all periods or some other character instead of spaces either "inside" or "outside" of the graph of the parabola. Experiment!
7. Modify Program PLOT3 to print a background character everywhere and "plot" a space for the graph of the function. Experiment!

## 8-4 Graphing

As we mentioned before, any function may be graphed by methods we have discussed. However, since we could only plot a single point for any specified value of X, we could not plot nonfunction relations. For example, we could not plot circles, hyperbolas, and polar relations. Let's develop a scheme for plotting that is not so limited.

### *Plotting Points from Data in a Two-Dimensional Array*

If we simply provide for a two-dimensional array in memory that is large enough to store the full graph, then we can begin to do some really nice things. (Of course, we could do some really nice things with a plotter, too!) One of the advantages of using a two-dimensional array is that we will not have to turn the resulting graph 90 degrees counterclockwise to study the results.

Suppose we work with a 31 by 31 square array. That gives us 15 coordinate positions on either side of each axis. Thus we may plot values plus or minus 15 for both X and Y.

We need to give a little thought to the translation from coordinate positions on a graph to subscript values in an array. We would like to enter (X,Y) coordinates in the graphing array at position GRAPH(X1,Y1). To place the graph origin at (16,16) in the array we will need to add 16 to each X coordinate value to obtain the appropriate column subscript and subtract each Y coordinate value from 16 to obtain the appropriate row subscript. Statement functions will handle this very nicely.

```
XSSVAL( X ) = 16 + X
YSSVAL( Y ) = 16 - Y
```

These two statement functions will provide us with the ability to make the conversion in a highly visible way. The statement

```
      PROGRAM GRAPH1
C  **  USING A TWO DIMENSIONAL ARRAY FOR GRAPHING.

      INTEGER GRAPH(31,31), YAXIS, XAXIS, ORIGIN, POINT, SPACE,
     +        K1, K2, YSSVAL, XSSVAL, X, Y, VALUE, X1, Y1, DENSE
      DATA  YAXIS/ '!'/ XAXIS/ '-'/ ORIGIN/ '+'/ POINT/ '*'/
     +      SPACE/ ' '/

C  **  DEFINE FUNCTIONS TO CONVERT (Ø,Ø) TO (16,16)
      YSSVAL( Y ) = 16 - Y
      XSSVAL( X ) = 16 + X

 1Ø   WRITE ( 5, 12 )
 12      FORMAT ( 'Ø', 'DENSITY VALUE ?' )
      READ ( 5, 14 ) DENSE
 14      FORMAT ( I5 )
      IF ( DENSE .LT. Ø ) STOP

      DO 3Ø K1 = 1, 31
        DO 2Ø K2 = 1, 31
          GRAPH( K1, K2 ) = SPACE
 2Ø     CONTINUE
 3Ø   CONTINUE

      DO 4Ø K1 = 1, 31
        GRAPH( 16, K1 ) = YAXIS
        GRAPH( K1, 16 ) = XAXIS
 4Ø   CONTINUE
      GRAPH( 16, 16 ) = ORIGIN

C  **  LOADING POINTS TO BE PLOTTED
      DO 1ØØ K1 = 1, 31
        Y  = 16 - K1
        Y1 = YSSVAL( Y )
        DO 9Ø K2 = 1, 31
          X  = K2 - 16
          X1 = XSSVAL( X )
          VALUE = (X + 1)**2 + (Y - 2)**2 - 144
          IF ( IABS(VALUE) .LE. DENSE ) GRAPH( X1, Y1 ) = POINT
 9Ø     CONTINUE
 1ØØ  CONTINUE

      WRITE( 5, 312 ) GRAPH
 312     FORMAT ( ' ', 31A1 )
      GO TO 1Ø

      END
```

**Program 8-6.** Graphing from data in a two-dimensional array.

X1 = XSSVAL( X )

makes it clear that the value of X is being converted to an X subscript value.

First we fill the array with spaces. Next we want to enter the axes. Let's use dashes for the X-axis and exclamations for the Y-axis. It is a simple matter to place a plus sign at the origin. Note that the order in which these are done is very important. The origin has been assigned four successive values in this process. It will be labeled with a plus sign only if the plus sign is the last value that is assigned to it. Any point being plotted will, of course, replace the origin or an axis character.

In order to load the plotted points into the array we will test all coordinate pairs to see if they satisfy the equation we are graphing.

The following is the equation of a circle with a radius of 12 and center at the point (−1,2):

(X + 1)**2 + (Y − 2)**2 = 144

If we try to satisfy this equation with integer values of X and Y, only four points will be plotted. To obtain more points on our graph, we will have to use values of X and Y that make the left side approximately equal to 144. Subtracting 144 from both sides gives us

(X + 1)**2 + (Y − 2)**2 − 144 = 0

The more the left side deviates from zero, the more points will be plotted. With

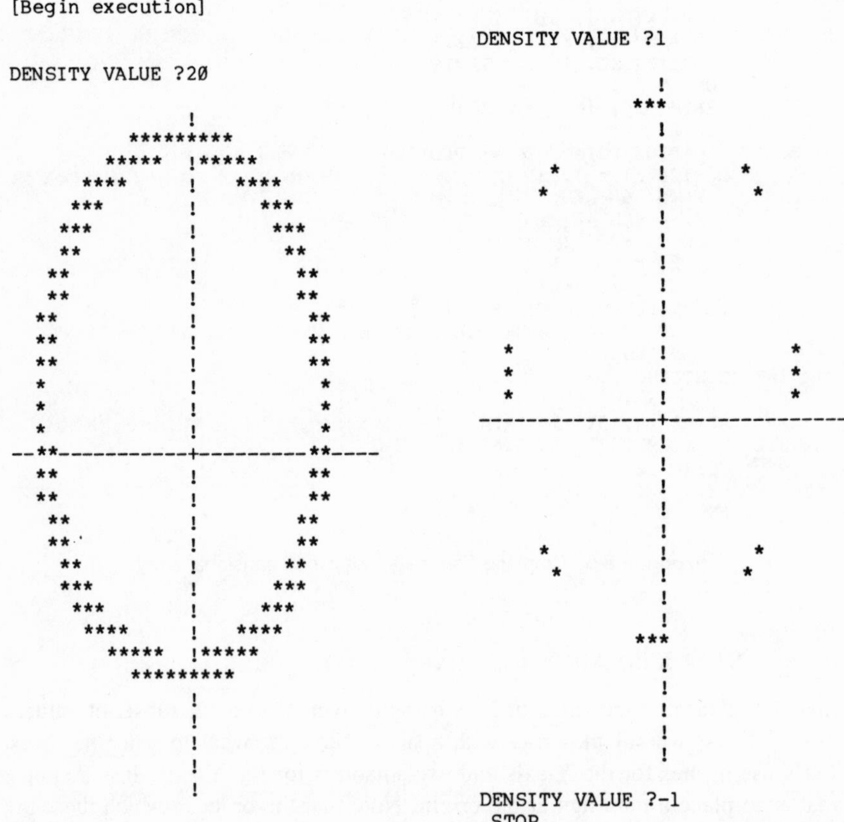


**Fig. 8-5.** Execution of Program 8-6.

a little experimenting, we can find values that give suitable graphs. The greater the deviation, the denser the graph. Thus we can request a density factor from a keyboard to facilitate experimentation. We have incorporated all of these considerations into Program 8-6 named GRAPH1 (see p. 121).

In the DO loop that terminates at line 100 (see Program 8-6) we have subtracted K1 from 16 and 16 from K2 to obtain the true values of Y and X for testing. Of course, this would not be necessary in FORTRAN 77. We include two sample density factors for the same graph here for comparison (see Fig. 8-5).

We said that we would be graphing a circle and we did just that in Fig. 8-5. The problem is with the printer! Printed characters are usually 1/10 of an inch wide and 1/6 of an inch high. Thus, to obtain a truly round circle, we will have to incorporate a scaling factor into our program. It might be nice to have a special character at +10 and −10 on the axes. If we are going to do a lot of graphing, we might replace the single line that assigns VALUE for testing with a FORTRAN function subprogram. Then we will only have to compile a very short FUNCTION for each new graph. It would be a very simple matter to incorporate the ability to plot several relations on a single graph with different symbols for each. We leave these enhancements as exercises.

## Problems for Sec. 8-4

Various problems suggested here could be combined into a single program.

1. Modify Program GRAPH1 to incorporate a scale factor. Plot a circle to test your results.
2. Modify Program GRAPH1 to accommodate two different curves on the same graph.
3. Modify Program GRAPH1 so that the origin is not restricted to the position GRAPH(16,16).
4. One way to get an interesting effect is to plot a ''shading'' character ''inside'' or''outside'' a graph.
5. Plot a ''reverse'' graph. Fill the array with stars and ''plot'' spaces.

# 9

# Trigonometry

## 9-1 Introduction to SIN(X), COS(X), and TAN(X)

We choose to define the circular functions in terms of a point (X,Y) plotted in a rectangular coordinate system. Consider the point (X,Y). It is at a distance R from the origin. We may find R from X and Y by using the Pythagorean theorem:

$$R = \sqrt{X{**}2 + Y{**}2}$$

It is conventional to use Greek letters for angles. However, since computer terminals and keypunch machines do not provide them, we may use any letters available to us. Let us use G to measure the angle whose initial side is the non-negative portion of the X-axis and whose terminal side is the ray that has its endpoint at the origin and contains the point (X,Y) (see Fig. 9-1).

From Fig. 9-1 we define three circular functions as follows:

$$\cos G = X/R$$
$$\sin G = Y/R$$
$$\tan G = Y/X$$

where cos stands for cosine, sin stands for sine, and tan stands for tangent.

FORTRAN requires that the angles be measured in radians. One radian may be defined as the central angle subtended by an arc length on the circumference of a circle equal in length to the radius. Since the circumference of a circle of radius R is $2\pi R$, we see that

$$2\pi \text{ radians} = 360 \text{ degrees}$$
$$\pi \text{ radians} = 180 \text{ degrees}$$
$$1 \text{ radian} = 180/\pi \text{ degrees}$$
$$\pi/180 \text{ radians} = 1 \text{ degree}$$

The numeric values of sin and cos may be obtained by using the FORTRAN built-in functions SIN() and COS(). The argument for these functions must be in radians. So we must be prepared to convert degrees to radians in all cases. Some implementations of FORTRAN supply the tangent function in the form TAN(), in addition to SIN() and COS(). In case the TAN() function is not available, it is a simple matter to obtain the value of tan G from SIN(G)/COS(G).

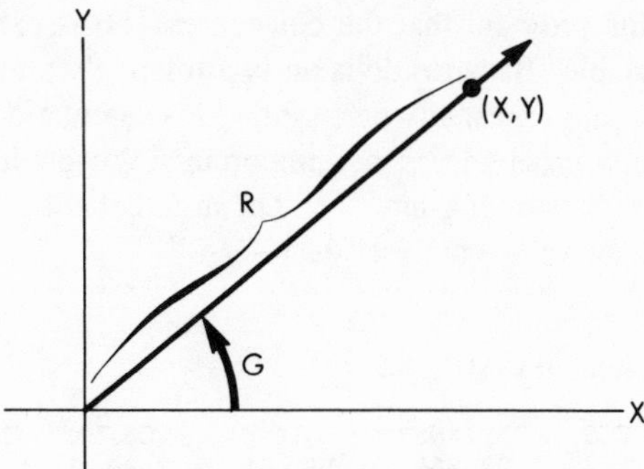


**Fig. 9-1.** Defining circular function parameters.

We need only ensure that the value of COS(G) never equals 0. We might even want to define a statement function such as

TAN(X) = SIN(X)/COS(X)

and then for the rest of the program we need not be concerned with the fact that TAN() is not a directly supplied FORTRAN function.

Let us get the computer to print a small table of values of sin, cos, and tan for 0 to 80 degrees in intervals of 10 degrees (see Program 9-1 named TRIG1).

```
      PROGRAM TRIG1
C  **  THIS IS A DEMONSTRATION OF THE USE OF THE SIN AND COS
C  **  FUNCTIONS.  WE OBTAIN THE TANGENT AS THE RATIO OF
C  **  THE SINE AND COSINE.

      REAL  RADIAN, SINE, COSINE, TAN, CONVRT
      INTEGER  DEGREE, INDEX

C  **  COMPUTE THE CONVERSION CONSTANT FOR DEGREES TO RADIANS
      CONVRT = 3.14159 / 180.

C  **  WRITE OUT COLUMN HEADINGS
      WRITE ( 5, 12 )
 12      FORMAT ( ' ', '   DEGREES   RADIANS      SINE',
     +                          '    COSINE   TANGENT' )

C  **  NOW WE WRITE THE VALUES FOR DEGREES IN THE RANGE 0 TO 80
      DO 100 INDEX = 10, 90, 10
        DEGREE = INDEX - 10
        RADIAN = DEGREE * CONVRT
        SINE   = SIN( RADIAN )
        COSINE = COS( RADIAN )
        TAN    = SINE / COSINE
        WRITE ( 5, 42 ) DEGREE, RADIAN, SINE, COSINE, TAN
 42        FORMAT ( ' ', I10, 4(F10.6) )
 100  CONTINUE

      END
```

**Program 9-1.** Demonstration program to print values of sin, cos, and tan.

Note in this program that the constant $\pi/180$ is calculated once early and stored in a variable. Because division is a relatively slow process on computers, we should avoid repeatedly performing this calculation. In this particular program, the execution saving is not important. We do it this way here to demonstrate good programming practice. The arguments of trigonometric functions and the resultant values are real data.

```
[Begin execution]

DEGREES   RADIANS      SINE      COSINE    TANGENT
      0  0.000000  0.000000  1.000000   0.000000
     10   .174533   .173648   .984808    .176327
     20   .349066   .342020   .939693    .363970
     30   .523598   .500000   .866026    .577350
     40   .698131   .642787   .766045    .839099
     50   .872664   .766044   .642788   1.191751
     60  1.047197   .866025   .500001   1.732047
     70  1.221729   .939692   .342021   2.747468
     80  1.396262   .984808   .173649   5.671242
```

**Fig. 9-2.** Execution of Program 9-1.

## 9-2 Right Triangles and Arctangent

Taking the graph of Fig. 9-1 and constructing the perpendicular from (X,Y) in the first quadrant to the X-axis, we get Fig. 9-3. In this figure we have formed a right triangle in which the length of the hypotenuse is R, the length of the base is X, and the length of the altitude is Y. Redrawing the triangle without the coordinate system, we get triangle ABC with trigonometric ratios, as shown in Fig. 9-4.

We also know from geometry that $\angle A$ and $\angle B$ are complementary angles; that is, their sum is 90 degrees or $\pi/2$ radians.

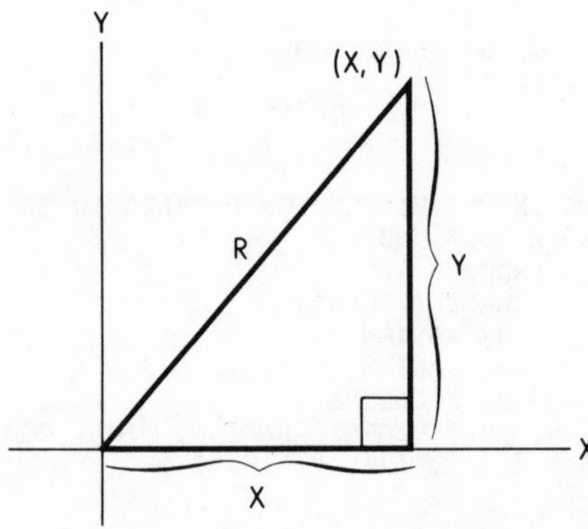


**Fig. 9-3.** Defining a right triangle in the X-Y coordinate system.

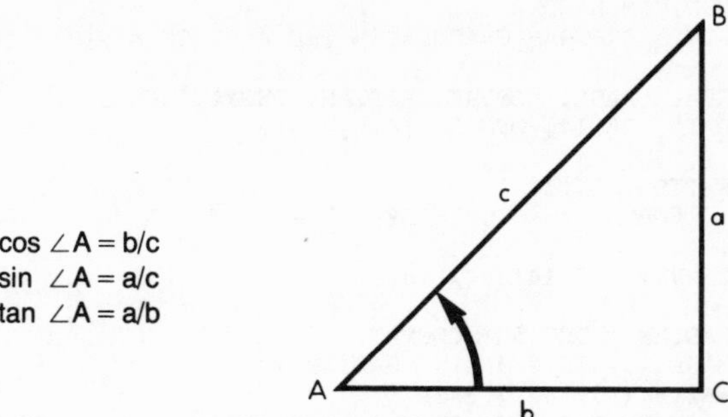


**Fig. 9-4.** Defining the trigonometric ratios for a right triangle.

Let's solve a simple problem. We have a 40-foot extension ladder and we are going to use it to paint a house that stands on level ground. We are told that the angle formed by the ladder and the side of the house should be not less than 14 degrees and not more than 15 degrees. Not being very good at judging angles, we want to know how far out from the house should we place the foot of the ladder. Note that a 40-foot ladder consists of two 20-foot sections. When a 40-foot ladder is fully extended, its length is 36 feet (see Fig. 9-5).

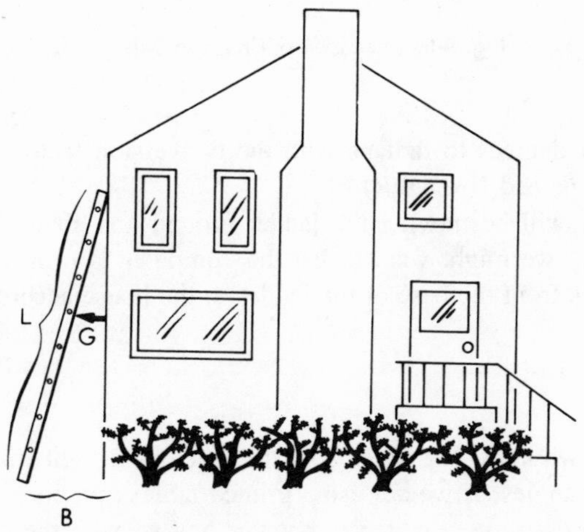


**Fig. 9-5.** We place a ladder against the side of a house.

We may use either SIN(G) = B/L or COS(90 − G) = B/L. Let's use the sin function and solve for B.

B = L * SIN(G)

```
      PROGRAM LADDER
C **  THIS PROGRAM CALCULATES THE BASE OF A RIGHT TRIANGLE

      REAL  BASE, CONVRT, RADIAN, DEG14, DEG15
      DATA  DEG14, DEG15/ 14.0, 15.0/

      WRITE ( 5, 12 )
12       FORMAT ( ' ', 'BASE DISTANCE FOR A 40'' LADDER' )

      CONVRT = 3.14159 / 180.0

      RADIAN = DEG15 * CONVRT
      BASE   = 36.0 * SIN( RADIAN )
      WRITE ( 5, 42 ) BASE
42       FORMAT ( ' ', 'NOT MORE THAN ', F5.2, ' FT.' )
      RADIAN = DEG14 * CONVRT
      BASE   = 36.0 * SIN( RADIAN )
      WRITE ( 5, 62 ) BASE
62       FORMAT ( ' ', 'NOT LESS THAN ', F5.2, ' FT.' )

      END
```

**Program 9-2.** Finding the distance between the foot of a ladder and a building.

```
[Begin execution]

BASE DISTANCE FOR A 40' LADDER
NOT MORE THAN  9.32 FT.
NOT LESS THAN  8.71 FT.
```

**Fig. 9-6.** Execution of Program 9-2.

Again we convert degrees to radians with the conversion factor, 3.14159/180 (see Program 9-2 named LADDER).

Since we will be moving the ladder around and changing the length from time to time, we might want to get the computer to print out a table of values of distances from the base of the ladder to the house according to length of ladder.

### *ATN(X)*

Suppose we know the lengths of the sides of a right triangle and we want to know the angles. If we are using printed tables in a book, we can look up the angle whose sin, cos, or tan is known. Not so with the computer. An additional FORTRAN-supplied function is required for this. ATN(X) computes the angle whose tangent is X. If

TAN(G) = X

then

ATN(X) = G

```
      PROGRAM RIGHT
C  **  THIS PROGRAM CALCULATES THE ACUTE ANGLES
C  **  OF A 3, 4, 5 RIGHT TRIANGLE

      REAL  ANGLE3, ANGLE4, RADIAN

      RADIAN = ATAN( Ø.75 )
      ANGLE3 = RADIAN * 18Ø.Ø / 3.14159
      ANGLE4 = 9Ø.Ø - ANGLE3

      WRITE ( 5, 12 ) ANGLE3, ANGLE4
 12      FORMAT ( ' ', 'GIVEN A 3, 4, 5 RIGHT TRIANGLE' /
     +      ' ', 'THE ACUTE ANGLES ARE: ', 2F8.2, '   DEGREES' )

      END
```

**Program 9-3.** A simple arctangent calculation.

where ATN stands for arctangent and G is in radians.

Suppose we want to find the angles of a 3, 4, 5 triangle. This is one of the famous triangles of Pythagoras. We know that it is a right triangle. So we can use the FORTRAN ATAN function. The smallest angle of this triangle is ATN(0.75). Since that value will be radians, we may want to convert to degrees by multiplying by $180/\pi$. We can show this with a very short program (see Program 9-3 named RIGHT).

```
[Begin execution]

GIVEN A 3, 4, 5 RIGHT TRIANGLE
THE ACUTE ANGLES ARE:    36.87   53.13   DEGREES
```

**Fig. 9-7.** Execution of Program 9-3.

## Summary

We may now apply the computer to the trigonometry of the right triangle using SIN(X) and COS(X) to find sides when angles are known and using ATN(X) to find angles when sides are known. We always must be aware of the need to use radians for the argument of the SIN(X) and COS(X) functions. The value of the ATN(G) is always in radians as well.

## Problems for Sec. 9-2

1. Print a table of approximate distances to place a ladder from the base of a house for ladder lengths from 20 to 36 feet.
2. Modify Program RIGHT to write angle values in degrees, minutes, and seconds.
3. Find the angles of a 5, 12, 13 right triangle to the nearest minute.
4. The sides of a triangle are 10, 10, and 4. Find the angles of the triangle to the nearest minute.

5. Generate a few Pythagorean triples. Write the three sides and the two acute angles in radians and degrees.
6. A right triangle has one angle 42 degrees and 25 minutes and the side opposite that angle has a length of 10.0 inches. Find the other sides of the triangle.
7. Standing 1000 feet from the base of a TV tower on level ground, the angle of elevation is 7 degrees and 30 minutes. Find the height of the TV tower.

## 9-3 Law of Sines

By drawing a triangle with each of its vertices at the origin of a rectangular coordinate system, we may compute its area in three ways. Referring to Fig. 9-8, the area is found by

Area = (1/2)b(H1) or (1/2)a(H2) or (1/2)c(H3) **Eq. 9-1**

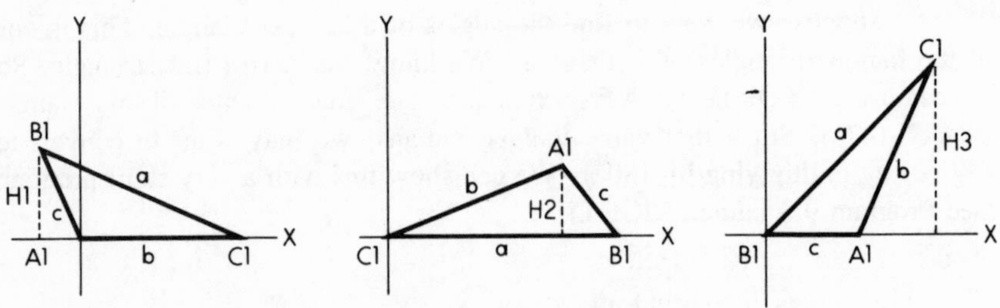


**Fig. 9-8.** Three orientations of the same triangle.

We should see that

sin C1 = H1/a
sin B1 = H2/c
sin A1 = H3/b

Solving for the heights, we get

H1 = a sin C1
H2 = c sin B1
H3 = b sin A1

Substituting in Eq. 9-1 we get

Area = (1/2)b(a sin C1) **Eq. 9-2a**
Area = (1/2)a(c sin B1) **Eq. 9-2b**
Area = (1/2)c(b sin A1) **Eq. 9-2c**

Therefore, we may find the area of any triangle by taking one-half the product of any two sides and the sine of the included angle.

Since the area of a triangle is unique, we may set the three expressions for area in Eqs. 9-2 equal to get

$$(1/2)\text{ba} \sin C1 = (1/2)\text{ac} \sin B1 = (1/2)\text{bc} \sin A1$$

By clearing of fractions and dividing through by abc, we get

$$\frac{\sin C1}{c} = \frac{\sin B1}{b} = \frac{\sin A1}{a} \qquad \textbf{Eq. 9-3}$$

Equation 9-3 is called the Law of Sines. It enables us to find all parts of a triangle if we are given any two sides and the angle opposite one of them, or if we are given any two angles and any one side (provided, of course, the triangle exists).

Let us write a program to find the remaining parts and the area of a triangle ABC given A1, B1, and a. Since the sum of the measures of the angles of a triangle is 180 degrees, we first get

$$C1 = 180 - (A1 + B1) \qquad \textbf{Eq. 9-4}$$

The Law of Sines gives us

$$\frac{\sin A1}{a} = \frac{\sin B1}{b}$$

Solving for b gives

$$b = \frac{a \sin B1}{\sin A1} \qquad \textbf{Eq. 9-5}$$

Similarly, we get

$$c = \frac{b \sin C1}{\sin B1} \qquad \textbf{Eq. 9-6}$$

And finally, the area may be found from Eq. 9-2a:

$$\text{Area} = (1/2)\text{ab} \sin C1 \qquad \textbf{Eq. 9-7}$$

All we have to do is put the last four equations into a program. We may do that almost directly from Eqs. 9-4 to 9-7 (see Program 9-4 named LAWSIN).

Note the following four statements from Program 9-4:

```
ANGLEC = 180.0 - ( ANGLEA + ANGLEB )
SIDEB  = SIDEA * SINE( ANGLEB ) / SINE( ANGLEA )
SIDEC  = SIDEB * SINE( ANGLEC ) / SINE( ANGLEB )
AREA   = .5 * SIDEA * SIDEB * SINE( ANGLEC )
```

These four statements correspond exactly to Eqs. 9-4 through 9-7 from our previous discussion.

In writing this program, we have done only slightly more work than we would do preparing to do the calculation by hand. However, we are letting the computer take the drudgery out of the actual calculation. We also have the program available to do large numbers of calculations at a later date with no additional effort. And we continue to be totally responsible for the mathematics required.

If we reflect for a moment upon the congruence of triangles, the various congruence conditions come to mind. They are angle-angle-corresponding side, side-angle-side, angle-side-angle, and side-side-side. In addition there are special cases for right triangles. With the Law of Sines, we have been able to solve the first two of the four mentioned here.

## Summary

This section has been devoted to solving triangles that may be uniquely determined. We have developed the Law of Sines into a program to solve the case of two angles and a nonincluded side. We have indicated that with small changes such a program will solve two angles and any side.

```
      PROGRAM LAWSIN
C  **  THIS PROGRAM USES THE LAW OF SINES TO SOLVE A TRIANGLE
C  **  FOR WHICH TWO ANGLES AND A NON-INCLUDED SIDE ARE GIVEN

      REAL  AREA, ANGLEA, ANGLEB, ANGLEC, SIDEA, SIDEB, SIDEC

C  **  WE USE A STATEMENT FUNCTION TO INCORPORATE THE DEGREES
C  **  TO RADIANS CONVERSION INTO THE SIN CALCULATION.
      SINE(X) = SIN( 3.14159 / 180.0 * X )

 100  WRITE ( 5, 102 )
 102     FORMAT ( ' ',
     +   'ENTER TWO ANGLES AND THE SIDE OPPOSITE THE FIRST ? ')
      READ ( 5, 112 ) ANGLEA, ANGLEB, SIDEA
 112     FORMAT ( 3F4.0 )
      IF ( ANGLEA .EQ. 0.0 )                       GO TO 9900

      ANGLEC = 180.0 - ( ANGLEA + ANGLEB )

      SIDEB  = SIDEA * SINE( ANGLEB ) / SINE( ANGLEA )
      SIDEC  = SIDEB * SINE( ANGLEC ) / SINE( ANGLEB )

      AREA   = .5 * SIDEA * SIDEB * SINE( ANGLEC )

      WRITE ( 5, 202 )
 202     FORMAT ( '+', 25X, 'A', 9X, 'B', 9X, 'C' )
      WRITE ( 5, 204 ) ANGLEA, ANGLEB, ANGLEC
 204     FORMAT ( ' ', 'THE ANGLES ARE ', 3F10.0 )
      WRITE ( 5, 206 ) SIDEA, SIDEB, SIDEC
 206     FORMAT ( ' ', 'THE SIDES ARE    ', 3F10.2 )
      WRITE ( 5, 208 ) AREA
 208     FORMAT ( ' ', ' AND THE AREA IS ', F10.2 / )

      GO TO 100

 9900 END
```

**Program 9-4.** Demonstrating the Law of Sines.

```
[Begin execution]

ENTER TWO ANGLES AND THE SIDE OPPOSITE THE FIRST ? 36,60,10
                         A          B          C
THE ANGLES ARE          36.        60.        84.
THE SIDES ARE           10.00      14.73      16.92
 AND THE AREA IS        73.26

ENTER TWO ANGLES AND THE SIDE OPPOSITE THE FIRST ? 45,45,20
                         A          B          C
THE ANGLES ARE          45.        45.        90.
THE SIDES ARE           20.00      20.00      28.28
 AND THE AREA IS       200.00

ENTER TWO ANGLES AND THE SIDE OPPOSITE THE FIRST ? 15,20,14
                         A          B          C
THE ANGLES ARE          15.        20.       145.
THE SIDES ARE           14.00      18.50      31.03
 AND THE AREA IS        74.28

ENTER TWO ANGLES AND THE SIDE OPPOSITE THE FIRST ? 0,0,0
```

**Fig. 9-9.** Execution of Program 9-4.

## Problems for Sec. 9-3

1. Modify Program LAWSIN to solve a triangle for which two angles and the included side are given.
2. Modify Program LAWSIN to handle either of the two cases: two angles and a nonincluded side or two angles and the included side. Use a data item to specify which case to solve for a particular data set.

*3. It can be shown that for any triangle A1B1C1 the following formula may be used:

$$a**2 = b**2 + c**2 - 2\ bc \cos A1$$

This is referred to as the Law of Cosines. This formula for the Law of Cosines can be solved for cos A1:

$$\cos A1 = (b**2 + c**2 - a**2)\ /\ (2bc)$$

We know that

$$\tan A1 = \sin A1\ /\ \cos A1$$

and for angles from 0 to 180 degrees

$$\sin A1 = \sqrt{1 - \cos**2\ A1}$$

Thus

$$\tan A1 = \sqrt{1 - \cos**2\ A1}\ /\ \cos A1$$

And so,

$$A1 = ATN(\sqrt{1 - \cos**2\ A1}\ /\ \cos A1)$$

and by appropriate substitutions, we are able to solve the side-side-side congruence case. Write a program to find the angles, given the three sides.

4. Project: Write a program to solve a triangle, given the data for any of the four congruence cases. Use subroutines where appropriate.

## 9-4 Polar Coordinates

Every point in a rectangular coordinate system may be named by a unique pair of real numbers. The pair is usually designated (X,Y). If we plot a point (X,Y), we find that we may determine another ordered pair of numbers, one of which is the distance from the origin and the other is an angle measured from the positive portion of the X-axis to the ray with endpoint at the origin and containing the point (X,Y). If we call the distance R and the measure of the angle G, we may designate a new ordered pair, (R,G) (see Fig. 9-1).

Ordered pairs of this kind are called *polar coordinates*. The ray consisting of the origin and the positive portion of the X-axis is called the *polar axis* and the origin is called the *pole*. Our new coordinate system appears in Fig. 9-10. Such a coordinate system is particularly adapted to plotting trigonometric functions with finite upper and lower bounds.

Note that we do not have one-to-one correspondence between ordered pairs and plotted points for the polar coordinate system. How do we designate the origin? (0,0)? How about calling it (0,10deg), or (0,1rad), or (0,−25deg)? (1,45deg) and (1,405deg) name the same point. Any particular ordered pair does name a unique point, but every point may be named by an unlimited number of ordered number pairs in this polar coordinate system.

Since the value of cos G is defined in terms of a rectangular coordinate system as X/R, it can take on negative values. So we extend the definition of R to permit this. The absolute value of R is the distance of the point from the pole and we define (−R,G) and (R,G+180deg) to name the same point.

### *Polar Equations*

Some polar equations are relatively easy to convert to rectangular form. For instance,

$$R = \cos G$$

is equivalent to

$$\sqrt{X**2 + Y**2} = \frac{2X}{\sqrt{X**2 + Y**2}}$$

which is equivalent to

$$X**2 + Y**2 - 2X = 0$$

which turns out to be a circle with radius 1 and center at the point (1,0).

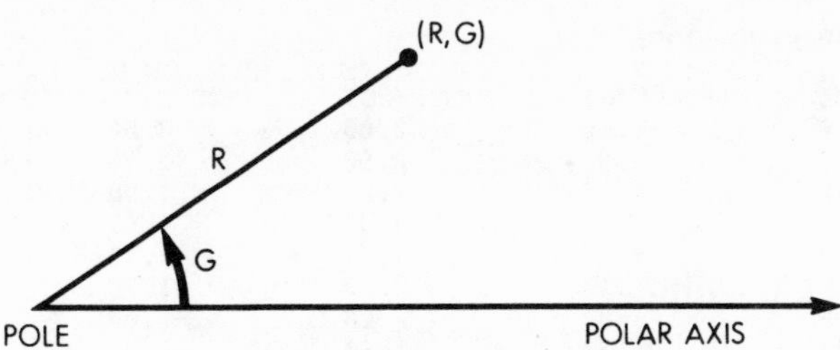


**Fig. 9-10.** Polar coordinate system.

However, other polar equations are not as easily identifiable when converted and are more appropriate to plot on a polar coordinate system. Consider

R = 1 − 2 cos G **Eq. 9-8**
R = 2 + sin 2G **Eq. 9-9**
R = 1 + 2 cos G − 3 sin**2 G **Eq. 9-10**

No matter how you approach plotting any of these, you run into a tremendous amount of calculating.

We can easily get the coordinates of the points to plot for all three of these in the same FORTRAN program (see Program 9-5 named POLAR).

In Program POLAR, we have simply calculated the value of R for each of the three polar Eqs. 9-8, 9-9, and 9-10, and set up to increment the degrees

```
      PROGRAM POLAR
C  **  THIS PROGRAM CALCULATES THE VALUES OF R IN A POLAR
C  **  COORDINATE SYSTEM FOR A RANGE OF DEGREE MEASURES.

      REAL      POLAR1, POLAR2, POLAR3, CONVRT, RADIAN
      INTEGER   INDEX, DEGREE

      CONVRT = 3.14159 / 180.0

      WRITE ( 5, 102 )
102      FORMAT ( ' ', ' ANGLE', 5X, '1-2COS(G)', 5X,
     +     '2+SIN(2G)', 5X, '1+2COS(G)-3SIN(G)**2' )

      DO 200 INDEX = 1, 361, 15
        DEGREE = INDEX - 1
        RADIAN = CONVRT * DEGREE
        POLAR1 = 1.0 - 2.0 * COS( RADIAN )
        POLAR2 = 2.0 + SIN( 2.0 * RADIAN )
        POLAR3 = 1.0 + 2.0 * COS(RADIAN) - 3.0 * SIN(RADIAN)**2
        WRITE ( 5, 104 ) DEGREE, POLAR1, POLAR2, POLAR3
104        FORMAT ( ' ', I6, 3(9X, F5.2 ) )
200   CONTINUE

      END
```

**Program 9-5.** Printing polar coordinates.

```
[Begin execution]

ANGLE     1-2COS(G)      2+SIN(2G)      1+2COS(G)-3SIN(G)**2
    0        -1.00           2.00           3.00
   15         -.93           2.50           2.73
   30         -.73           2.87           1.98
   45         -.41           3.00            .91
   60         -.00           2.87           -.25
   75          .48           2.50          -1.28
   90         1.00           2.00          -2.00
  105         1.52           1.50          -2.32
  120         2.00           1.13          -2.25
  135         2.41           1.00          -1.91
  150         2.73           1.13          -1.48
  165         2.93           1.50          -1.13
  180         3.00           2.00          -1.00
  195         2.93           2.50          -1.13
  210         2.73           2.87          -1.48
  225         2.41           3.00          -1.91
  240         2.00           2.87          -2.25
  255         1.52           2.50          -2.32
  270         1.00           2.00          -2.00
  285          .48           1.50          -1.28
  300          .00           1.13           -.25
  315         -.41           1.00            .91
  330         -.73           1.13           1.98
  345         -.93           1.50           2.73
  360        -1.00           2.00           3.00
```

**Fig. 9-11.** Execution of Program 9-5.

by 15 with a DO loop. This program may be easily changed to print coordinates for other polar equations.

## Summary

The computer may easily be used for obtaining values of ordered pairs of polar coordinates for polar equations.

## Problems for Sec. 9-4

You might want to convert Program GRAPH1 from Chap. 8 to plot graphs of some polar equations by entering points into a two-dimensional array.

1. Obtain polar coordinates for plotting any of the following polar equations. (You might want to plot the graphs as well.)

a. R = cos 2G
b. R = cos 3G
c. R = cos 4G
d. R = sin 2G
e. R = sin 3G
f. R = sin G + cos G
g. R cos G = 1
h. R = 1 + R cos G

2. Write a program to convert from polar coordinates to rectangular coordinates for any of the polar equations in problem 1.
*3. Write a program to store rectangular coordinates in an array for any of the polar equations a through f in problem 1, and then rearrange the ordered pairs in order of increasing values of X. Print the resulting set of ordered pairs. (You might want to compare the graphs here with those in problem 1.)

# 10

# Polynomials

## 10-1 Fundamental Operations

We define a real polynomial in X as an expression that can be written in the form

$$A_nX^{**}n + A_{n-1}\,X^{**}n-1 + \ldots + A_2X^{**}2 + A_1X + A_0$$

where n is a non-negative integer, X is a complex number, and the $A_n$ are constant real coefficients. The following are examples of polynomials in X:

5 X − 3 X**8 + 3X**5 − X + 1 X**2 + 3X − 4

For the polynomial 5, note that 5 = 5X**0, so that the polynomial consists of the term $A_0$, which is 5. The number 0 is considered a polynomial. All real polynomials except the zero polynomials have degree i, where $A_i$X**i is the term of the polynomial with the greatest value of i for which $A_i$ is not equal to 0. Polynomials may be used to describe many physical phenomena. For instance, the trajectory of a projectile is described by a second-degree polynomial equation.

We may perform operations on polynomials much as we perform operations on numbers themselves. You have likely had considerable experience adding and subtracting such expressions. You have probably often multiplied two binomials of the form (AX + B). One of the problems in Chap. 1 was to perform just such a multiplication by computer. We will develop a program to multiply two polynomials.

### *Multiplication*

Clearly we will perform operations on polynomials on the computer by doing calculations on the coefficients of the terms of the polynomials. As we perform the various calculations, we will have to be especially alert to line up the coefficients properly, accounting for missing terms by inserting zero coefficients where necessary. Let us begin with an example, say (2X + 7) (3X**2 + 11X − 5). By hand we get

```
         3X**2 + 11X -  5
                   2X + 7
         ----------------
        21X**2 + 77X - 35
6X**3 + 22X**2 - 10X
-------------------------
6X**3 + 43X**2 + 67X - 35
```

where all the X**n were known in advance and do not depend on the coefficients. So the problem could have been done in the following manner:

```
    3  +11  - 5
         2  + 7
   ------------
   21  +77  -35
6 +22  -10
---------------
6 +43  +67  -35
```

**Eq. 10-1**

The program can be set up by putting 3, 11, and −5 in one array, 2 and 7 in another, and making provision for putting 6, 43, 67, and −35 in a third product array. We might find the organization to be a little easier by thinking of the computation in Eq. 10-1 as being set up in columns numbered 1 to 4 from right to left.

The algorithm we used in Eq. 10-1 is well suited to hand calculation. We could devise methods to enter coefficients backwards into arrays so that the coefficients occupy the subscripts identified by the column numbers on the left in Fig. 10-1. However, we would then have to convert some of our DO loops to step in decreasing order and contrive to utilize additional arrays for writing

| *BY HAND* | | | | *FORTRAN IV* | | | |
|---|---|---|---|---|---|---|---|
| 4 | 3 | 2 | 1 | 1 | 2 | 3 | 4 |
| | 3 | +11 | − 5 | 3 | +11 | − 5 | |
| | | 2 | + 7 | 2 | + 7 | | |
| | 21 | +77 | −35 | 6 | +22 | −10 | |
| 6 | +22 | −10 | | | 21 | +77 | −35 |
| 6 | +43 | +67 | −35 | 6 | +43 | +67 | −35 |

**Fig. 10-1.** Coefficients as elements of arrays.

our results in the correct order. It seems more direct to modify the algorithm slightly as shown on the right in Fig. 10-1, so that we can do all of our calculations from left to right and all DO loops can increment in the conventional FORTRAN IV manner. (If you have access to FORTRAN 77, then none of this conversion is necessary. In fact, by using zero subscripts, you can simplify things even further.)

```
      PROGRAM  TWOX3
C  **  THIS PROGRAM MULTIPLIES A TRINOMIAL BY A BINOMIAL

      INTEGER TRI(3), BI(2), PROD(4), K2, K3, K4
      DATA   TRI/ 3, 11, -5/ BI/ 2, 7/ PROD/ 4*Ø/

C  **  CALCULATE THE COEFFICIENTS OF THE PRODUCT
      DO 1ØØ K3 = 1, 3
        DO 9Ø K2 = 1, 2
          K4          = K2 + K3 - 1
          PROD( K4 ) = PROD( K4 ) + BI( K2 ) * TRI( K3 )
 9Ø     CONTINUE
 1ØØ  CONTINUE

      WRITE ( 5, 112 ) BI, TRI, PROD
 112    FORMAT ( ' ', 2I4, '  TIMES', 3I4, '  YIELDS', 4I4 )

      END
```

**Program 10-1.** Multiply a trinomial by a binomial.

We observe that when we multiply two numbers in column 1, we put the result in column 1; when we multiply a number from column 1 by a number from column 3, we put the result in column 3; and when we multiply a number in column 2 by a number in column 3, we put the result in column 4. This suggests that multiplying a number in column K2 by a number in column K3 calls for the result to go in column (K2 + K3 − 1). [If we are able to use zero subscripts, then the result goes in column (K2 + K3).] So if we enter the two polynomials being multiplied in arrays BI and TRI and the product in an array PROD, our computer program will have an instruction to store BI(K2) * TRI(K3) in PROD( K2 + K3 − 1 ). However, for users of FORTRAN IV, an intermediate variable may have to be used to store K2 + K3 − 1, since we need that quantity as a subscript. We also must provide for subtotals, because some of the final terms are the sum of two or more terms. For example: BI(2) * TRI(1) and BI(1) * TRI(2) are added to obtain the first term in the sum polynomial. Thus we have the program statements

```
K4         = K2 + K3 − 1
PROD( K4 ) = PROD( K4 ) + BI( K2 ) * TRI( K3 )
```

where the PROD array has previously been initialized to all zeros. See Program 10-1 named TWOX3, which multiplies the two polynomials of our example. It will be left as an exercise to modify Program TWOX3 to multiply pairs of polynomials of various degrees.

```
[Begin execution]

   2   7 TIMES   3  11  -5 YIELDS   6  43  67 -35
```

**Fig. 10-2.** Execution of Program 10-1.

## *Division*

When working with polynomials, we often wish to perform the operation of division. It is especially frequent that we wish to divide by a polynomial of the form X − R, where R is an integer constant. Let us divide 2X**3 − 3X**2 − 10X + 3 by X − 3 and see what can be done to computerize the operation. As with multiplication, we will end up considering only the coefficients. First we do the division by hand:

```
          2X**2 + 3X − 1
X − 3)2X**3 − 3X**2 − 10X + 3
      2X**3 − 6X**2
      -------------
              3X**2 − 10X
              3X**2 −  9X
              -----------
                    −  X + 3
                    −  X + 3
                    --------
```

Every term in the computation that will be written twice in every problem appears in **boldface.** Now if we simply decide not to write things twice and at the same time compress the problem vertically, we get

```
         2X**2 + 3X   −   1
X − 3)2X**3 − 3X**2 − 10X + 3
            − 6X**2 −  9X + 3
            -----------------
              3X**2 −   X
```

We saw that for multiplication, as long as everything was lined up correctly, we could eliminate all of the X's. Also note that we are dividing only by binomials of the form X − R, so the coefficient of X will always be 1. Let us not even write it. Now we have the division in the following form:

```
    2 +3  −1
−3)2 −3 −10 +3
     −6 − 9 +3
     ---------
      3  −1
```

Since the coefficient of X in the divisor is always 1, the coefficient of each term in the quotient will always be the same as the coefficient of the leading term of the expression into which we divide the X term. Thus it is no accident that we see 3 −1 in the bottom row as well as in the answer. So if we agree to simply insert the leading coefficient of the polynomial into which we are dividing X − R in front of the bottom row of figures, we will always have the coefficients of the quotient polynomial in the bottom row and we will not need the top row at all. We now have reduced the problem of division for the special case of X − R as the divisor, to an iteration involving "multiply and subtract" repeatedly, and the division looks like

```
−3)2  −3  −10  +3
       −6  −9  +3
   ──────────────
   2  +3  −1
```

which we got by the following set of steps:

1. Copy down the first coefficient of the original polynomial 2.
2. Multiply 2 by −3 to get −6 and write it down under the second term of the original polynomial.
3. Subtract to get 3, multiply 3 by −3 to get −9.
4. Write it down beneath the next term to the right and subtract to get −1.
5. Multiply −1 by −3 to get +3 and write it down beneath the next term.
6. Subtract to get 0 and we have a 0 remainder.

So we see that 2 +3 −1 is interpreted as 2X**2 + 3X − 1.

Since subtracting a number may be accomplished by multiplying the number to be subtracted by −1 and adding, we may convert "multiply and subtract" to "multiply and add" if we multiply the −3 by −1 to get 3. Or for X − R we just use R. Let us complete the development of this algorithm by inserting the 0 in the last column to the right to indicate a remainder of 0.

```
3)2  −3  −10  +3
       6   +9  −3
  ──────────────
  2  +3   −1   0
```

Dividing 3X**4 − 2X**2 + 5X − 2 by X + 2 results in

```
−2)3  +0   −2   +5   −2
       −6  +12  −20  +30
   ─────────────────────
   3  −6  +10  −15  +28
```

yielding a quotient of 3X**3 − 6X**2 + 10X − 15 and a remainder of 28.

Division by the algorithm we have just developed is usually called *synthetic division*. Since this is essentially an iterative process, we should be able to get the computer to perform division in this way. We enter the original polynomial in an array POLY, and the quotient in an array QUO. We store the division constant in DIV. For every division problem of the kind we are working with here, the first coefficient of the quotient polynomial is the same as the first coefficient in the dividend polynomial. So we need a program statement such as QUO(1) = POLY(1) (see Program 10-2 named SYNDIV).

In SYNDIV (see Fig. 10-3), 2, 3, −1, 0 is to be interpreted as 2X**2 + 3X − 1 with a remainder of 0.

We should be able to easily organize the coefficients of polynomials in arrays to perform addition and subtraction.

```
      PROGRAM SYNDIV
C  **  THIS PROGRAM PERFORMS SYNTHETIC DIVISION
      INTEGER POLY(4), DIV, QUO(4), K1

C  **  ENTER COEFFICIENTS AND ZERO THE QUOTIENT ARRAY
      DATA DIV/ 3/ POLY/ 2, -3, -1Ø, 3/ QUO/ 4*Ø/

C  **  THE FIRST QUOTIENT COEFFICIENT EQUALS
C  **  THE FIRST COEFFICIENT OF THE ORIGINAL POLYNOMIAL
      QUO(1) = POLY(1)

C  **  NOW MULTIPLY AND ADD
      DO 1ØØ K1 = 2, 4
        QUO( K1 ) = POLY( K1 ) + QUO( K1 - 1 ) * DIV
 1ØØ  CONTINUE

      WRITE ( 5, 112 )
 112     FORMAT ( ' ', 'SYNTHETIC DIVISION' )
      WRITE ( 5, 122 ) POLY, DIV, QUO
 122     FORMAT ( ' ', 4I3, ' DIVIDED BY X - ', I2, ' YIELDS' /
     +            ' ', 4I3 )

      END
```

**Program 10-2.** Perform synthetic division using arrays.

```
[Begin execution]

SYNTHETIC DIVISION
  2 -3-1Ø  3 DIVIDED BY X -  3 YIELDS
  2  3 -1  Ø
```

**Fig. 10-3.** Execution of Program 10-2.

## Summary

We have written an elementary program to multiply a trinomial by a binomial by working with the coefficients of the polynomials as elements of arrays. Similarly, we have written a program to perform synthetic division.

## Problems for Sec. 10-1

1. Write a program to find the sum of two polynomials. Be sure to avoid printing leading zero coefficients when adding pairs similar to 3X**4 + 6X − 4 and −3X**4 + 5X**3 − 3X + 1.
2. Do problem 1 for subtraction.
3. Write a single program to add or subtract pairs of polynomials as determined from entered data.
4. Prepare a program to multiply two polynomials of varying degrees.
5. Write a program to multiply three polynomials. You might use part of the solution program for problem 4 as a subroutine here.

*6. Extend Program SYNDIV to divide X − R into polynomials of any degree. Have the printed result specifically identify the remainder.
*7. Write a program to print the first 11 integral powers of (X + 1).

## 10-2 Integral Zeros

It is common practice to abbreviate any polynomial by calling it $P_{(x)}$ for a polynomial in X (read as P of X). We often look at the polynomial equation

$$Y = P_{(x)}$$

and its graph. The values of X for which Y = 0 are called the *zeros of the function* and *roots of the corresponding equation.* You probably have solved many quadratic equations in which there were always two roots. Sometimes they were integral. Sometimes we need to consider real numbers or complex numbers to find zeros of a quadratic function. It can be shown that every Nth-degree polynomial equation has exactly N complex roots. There are two theorems that will be invaluable when looking for zeros of polynomial functions.

### *Remainder Theorem*

According to the *remainder theorem,* if a polynomial is divided by X − Z, then the remainder is the value of the polynomial when Z is substituted for X. Dividing $P_{(x)}$ by (X − Z) we get

$$\frac{P_{(x)}}{(X - Z)} = Q_{(x)} + \frac{R}{(X - Z)}$$

where $Q_{(x)}$ is the quotient polynomial. Multiplying both sides by (X − Z) we get

$$P_{(x)} = Q_{(x)} * (X - Z) + R$$

and we can see that if we substitute Z for X, then X − Z = 0 and

$$P_{(z)} = R \qquad \textbf{Eq. 10-2}$$

Looking at Program SYNDIV we see that substituting 3 for X in 2X**3 − 3X**2 − 10X + 3 gives 54 − 27 − 30 + 3 or 0, confirming that $P_{(3)} = 0$, which is the remainder after dividing by X − 3.

### *Factor Theorem*

The *factor theorem* states simply that if the value of R in Eq. 10-2 is 0, then X − Z is a factor of $P_{(x)}$. Looking at Program SYNDIV again, we see that X − 3 is a factor of 2X**3 − 3X**2 − 10X + 3. Now all we have to do is find a value of Z so that $P_{(z)} = 0$ and Z is a zero of the function.

### *Search for Integral Zeros*

What integers do we try for Z to test $P_{(z)}$ for 0? We have assumed that there are N complex zeros. Let us call them $Z_n, Z_{n-1}, \ldots, Z_2$, and $Z_1$. It can be shown that

$$(X - Z_n)(X - Z_{n-1}). . .(X - Z_2)(X - Z_1)$$
$$= A_nX{**}n + A_{n-1}X{**}n-1 +. . .+ A_1X + A_0$$

Multiplying the left side out we should see that the only constant term in the product is

```
      PROGRAM ROOT1
C  **  THIS PROGRAM CALCULATES INTEGRAL ROOTS
C  **  OF POLYNOMIAL EQUATIONS

      INTEGER PDATA(4,4), P(4), ANS(4), POLY,
     +        K1, K2, K3, DIV, CONST, ROOTS

      DATA PDATA/ 1, -2, -11, 12,     1,  1,  -5, -2,
     +            1, -2,   3, -4,     2, -3, -10,  3/

      POLY(K1) = P(1)*K1**3 + P(2)*K1**2 + P(3)*K1**1 + P(4)

C  **  PROCESS FOUR POLYNOMIALS
      DO 200 K1 = 1, 4
        DO 110 K2 = 1, 4
          P(K2) = PDATA( K2, K1 )
 110    CONTINUE

C  **  SEARCH FOR ROOTS AND ENTER ANY FOUND IN ANS ARRAY
        ROOTS = 0
        CONST = IABS( P(4) )
        DO 130 K3 = 1, CONST
          IF ( MOD( CONST, K3 ) .NE. 0 ) GO TO 130
          IF ( POLY( K3 ) .NE. 0 )       GO TO 120
           ROOTS = ROOTS + 1
           ANS( ROOTS ) = K3
 120       IF ( POLY( -K3 ) .NE. 0 )     GO TO 130
            ROOTS = ROOTS + 1
            ANS( ROOTS ) = -K3
 130    CONTINUE

C  **  ANY ROOTS ARE IN ANS ARRAY
C  **  THE NUMBER OF ROOTS IN VARIABLE ROOTS
        IF ( ROOTS .NE. 0 )              GO TO 180
         WRITE ( 5, 162 ) P
 162        FORMAT ( ' ', 4I4, '  NO INTEGRAL ROOTS' )
         GO TO 200

 180    WRITE ( 5, 182 ) P, (ANS(K3), K3 = 1, ROOTS )
 182       FORMAT ( ' ', 4I4, '  INTEGRAL ROOT(S):', 4I4 )

 200  CONTINUE

      END
```

**Program 10-3.** Find integral roots of a third-degree polynomial.

$$(-Z_n)(-Z_{n-1}). . .(-Z_2)(-Z_1)$$

which simplifies to

$$(-1)^{**}n * Z_n(Z_{n-1}). . .(Z_2)(Z_1)$$

and must equal the constant term in the product polynomial. That constant term is $A_0$. And so it follows that if a polynomial has any integral zeros, they must be factors of the constant term $A_0$. That is not to say that all integral factors of $A_0$ are roots of the polynomial equation. This should provide sufficient basis for writing a computer program to find the integral zeros of a polynomial function. We can define a polynomial function with a FORTRAN statement function, which we will call POLY, and test POLY(X) = 0 for all integral factors of the constant term. We continue to enter the coefficients of the polynomials in arrays. For now let's stick with third-degree polynomials. So the constant term will be P(4). One possible method for getting data for more than one polynomial into our program will be to read DATA into a two-dimensional array and load it a row at a time into our P array as we need it. If we are working with a FORTRAN that does not allow negative values for the index of a DO loop, we must use the IABS function and test for both positive and negative factors. All this is done in Program 10-3 named ROOT1 on the previous page.

```
[Begin execution]

1  -2 -11  12  INTEGRAL ROOT(S):   1  -3   4
1   1  -5  -2  INTEGRAL ROOT(S):   2
1  -2   3  -4  NO INTEGRAL ROOTS
2  -3 -10   3  INTEGRAL ROOT(S):   3
```

**Fig. 10-4.** Execution of Program 10-3.

We will be working with numerous polynomials. So let's develop some more tools.

It would be nice to be able to enter any polynomial at the time we execute a program. We can easily write a SUBROUTINE subprogram once to do this for any program we write. We can pass the maximum array size from the MAIN program, and the SUBROUTINE can pass back the number of terms actually used and their values (see Program 10-4 named PENTER).

Since we want the ability to work with polynomials having various numbers of terms, we should develop the capacity to find the value of $P_{(x)}$ with something more flexible than the statement function. We can easily write a DO loop that sums up the terms of the polynomial and utilize it as a FUNCTION subprogram. We simply pass the number of coefficients, the coefficients, and the value of X. The coefficients may be passed in an array. The value of $P_{(x)}$ will be returned in the function name. We do this with Program 10-5, which is a FUNCTION subprogram called PVALUE. Notice that we must declare PVALUE as INTEGER in both the calling program and the FUNCTION subprogram. Using a function name that fits the I-N default convention would make this declaration unnecessary.

Note that in Program 10-5 we have used NTERMS-INDEX as the exponent in the line labeled 10. Remember that we made a slight change in the multiplication algorithm so that the coefficients could be treated in increasing element number.

We simply incorporate these two subprograms into ROOT1 and present it as Program 10-6 named ROOT2.

```
      SUBROUTINE PENTER( SIZE, ARRAY, NTERMS )
C  **  THIS SUBROUTINE REQUESTS POLYNOMIAL TERMS FROM DEVICE #5

      INTEGER SIZE, ARRAY(SIZE), NTERMS, K1

100   WRITE ( 5, 102 )
102      FORMAT ( '0', 'ENTER THE NUMBER OF TERMS ' )
      READ ( 5, 104 ) NTERMS
104      FORMAT ( I5 )
      IF ( NTERMS .GT. SIZE  .OR.  NTERMS .LT. 0 ) GO TO 100
      IF ( NTERMS .EQ. 0 ) STOP

      WRITE ( 5, 106 )
106      FORMAT ( '+', 'ENTER THE TERMS ' )
      READ ( 5, 108 ) (ARRAY( K1 ), K1 = 1, NTERMS)
108      FORMAT ( 32I5 )

      RETURN

      END
```

**Program 10-4.** A SUBROUTINE to enter polynomial coefficients.

```
      INTEGER FUNCTION PVALUE( NTERMS, ARRAY, X )
C  **  THIS FUNCTION CALCULATES THE VALUE OF
C  **  A POLYNOMIAL FOR A SELECTED VALUE OF X

      INTEGER NTERMS, ARRAY( NTERMS ), X, INDEX

      PVALUE = 0
      DO 10 INDEX = 1, NTERMS
        PVALUE = PVALUE + ARRAY( INDEX ) * X**( NTERMS-INDEX )
10    CONTINUE
      RETURN

      END
```

**Program 10-5.** A FUNCTION subprogram evaluates polynomials.

## Summary

We have seen that by combining the remainder theorem, the factor theorem, and the fact that the product of all roots multiplied by (−1)**n, where N is the degree of the polynomial, gives the constant term, we are able to find

```
      PROGRAM ROOT2
C  **  THIS PROGRAM CALCULATES INTEGRAL ROOTS
C  **  USING SUBROUTINE PENTER AND INTEGER FUNCTION PVALUE

      INTEGER P(2Ø), ANS(2Ø), PVALUE,
     +         K1, K2, K3, CONST, ROOTS, SIZE, TERMS

 1Ø   SIZE = 2Ø
      CALL PENTER( SIZE, P, TERMS )

C  **  SEARCH FOR ROOTS AND ENTER ANY FOUND IN ANS ARRAY
      ROOTS = Ø
      CONST = IABS ( P(TERMS) )
      DO 9Ø K3 = 1, CONST
        IF ( MOD( CONST, K3 ) .NE. Ø )            GO TO 9Ø
         IF ( PVALUE( TERMS, P, K3 ) .NE. Ø )  GO TO 2Ø
          ROOTS          = ROOTS + 1
          ANS( ROOTS ) = K3
 2Ø      IF ( PVALUE( TERMS, P, -K3 ) .NE. Ø ) GO TO 9Ø
          ROOTS          = ROOTS + 1
          ANS( ROOTS ) = -K3
 9Ø   CONTINUE

C  **  ANY ROOTS ARE IN ANS ARRAY
C  **  THE NUMBER OF ROOTS IN VARIABLE ROOTS
      IF ( ROOTS .EQ. Ø )                         GO TO 12Ø
       WRITE ( 5, 1Ø2 ) (ANS(K3), K3 = 1, ROOTS )
 1Ø2      FORMAT ( '+', 'INTEGRAL ROOT(S):', 2ØI4 )
       GO TO 1Ø

 12Ø  WRITE ( 5, 122 )
 122     FORMAT ( '+', 'NO INTEGRAL ROOTS' )
 2ØØ  GO TO 1Ø

      END
```

**Program 10-6.** Program ROOT1 using SUBROUTINE subprogram PENTER and FUNCTION subprogram PVALUE.

```
[Begin execution]


ENTER THE NUMBER OF TERMS 3
ENTER THE TERMS 1,2,-3
INTEGRAL ROOT(S):    1  -3

ENTER THE NUMBER OF TERMS Ø
 STOP
```

**Fig. 10-5.** Execution of Program 10-6.

all integral roots. We simply test all integral factors of the constant term to see if the remainder is 0. If the remainder is 0, then we have a zero of the polynomial. If it is not 0, then we do not have a zero of the polynomial. We have evaluated polynomials for a particular value of X both by using a statement function and by summing up terms in a FUNCTION subprogram.

## Problems for Sec. 10-2

1. For each of the polynomials to follow: (a) find an integral root, (b) use synthetic division to find the resulting factor after dividing by (X − Z), and (c) search for roots of the depressed polynomial. Repeat until all integral roots are found and then print the remaining polynomial.

   10X**3 − 71X**2 − 76X + 32
   6X**8 − 32X**7 − 23X**6 − 3X**5 − 12X**4 − 36X**3 − X**2 + 8X − 12
   8X**5 − 18X**4 − 31X**2 + 2X + 3
   2X**4 + 5X**3 − 31X**2 − 21X + 45

2. It can be shown that the polynomial

   3X**4 + 2X**3 − X**2 + 4X +3

   can be written in the form

   (((3X + 2)X −1)X + 4)X + 3)

   which is called *nested form*. It also can be shown that this is a much more efficient method of evaluating such a polynomial. Write a FUNCTION subprogram to utilize this more efficient algorithm.
3. Prepare a table of ordered pairs $(X,P_{(x)})$ such as would be appropriate for plotting points. Sketch a graph on graph paper. How would you estimate nonintegral zeros from such a graph?
4. Rewrite Program SYNDIV as a SUBROUTINE subprogram so that we may CALL it for future programs.

## 10-3 Real Zeros

It can be shown that for a polynomial, if $P_{(x_1)} > 0$ and $P_{(x_2)} < 0$, then there is a value of X between $X_1$ and $X_2$ such that $P_{(x)} = 0$. This is called the *location principle*. In graphical terms, the location principle may be stated as follows: If points $(X_1,P_{(x_1)})$ and $(X_2,P_{(x_2)})$ are on opposite sides of the X-axis, then the graph must cross the X-axis between $(X_1,0)$ and $(X_2,0)$. We may now search for real roots by finding intervals in which the graph crosses the X-axis. We may anticipate more than one interval in which a root may be found, so let us enter the results into an array and use a counter to tabulate the number of intervals found. It seems reasonable to write out only the left boundary of the intervals. For our first attempt let us arbitrarily select a range from −5 to 5 and use an increment of 1. We can accomplish this with a DO loop range of 1 to 11 and a bias of −6. Again we may use our subprograms PENTER and PVALUE to enter data and to evaluate our polynomial for each increment. All of this is done in Program 10-7 named REAL1.

In our sample execution (see Fig. 10-6), we have found that the three real zeros of 12X**3 − 64X**2 + 17X + 195 lie in the intervals −2 to −1,

2 to 3, and 3 to 4. That is fine to know, but eventually we will want more precision than those intervals provide. So our program could use considerable reworking. We could even use our program as a subprogram and call it from a MAIN program that goes on to allow us to select ranges and increments from a console or terminal. One of the features that should be incorporated in such a program is the ability to identify all integral roots found while looking for intervals. We will need a subprogram that will evaluate polynomials for non-integer values of X. Some of these considerations are left as exercises.

```
          PROGRAM REAL1
C   **    THIS PROGRAM USES THE LOCATION PRINCIPLE TO FIND UNIT
C   **    INCREMENTS IN WHICH POLYNOMIAL GRAPHS CROSS THE X-AXIS

          INTEGER P(2Ø), V1, V2, PVALUE, K1, INDEX, COUNT,
     +            TERMS, ANS(2Ø), TSTVAL

 1Ø       K1     = 2Ø
          COUNT = Ø
          CALL PENTER( K1, P, TERMS )
          DO 9Ø INDEX = 1, 11
            TSTVAL = INDEX - 6
            V1 = PVALUE( TERMS, P, TSTVAL )
            V2 = PVALUE( TERMS, P, TSTVAL + 1 )
C   **    TEST FOR CHANGE IN SIGN
            IF ( (V1 .GT. Ø) .AND. (V2 .GT. Ø)   .OR.
     +           (V1 .LT. Ø) .AND. (V2 .LT. Ø) )            GO TO 9Ø
              COUNT           = COUNT + 1
              ANS( COUNT ) = TSTVAL
 9Ø       CONTINUE

          IF ( COUNT .EQ. Ø )                               GO TO 12Ø
           WRITE ( 5, 112 ) (ANS( K1 ), K1 = 1, COUNT)
 112           FORMAT ( '+', 'INTERVAL(S) BEGIN AT:' /
     +                  ' ', 2ØI4 )
           GO TO 1Ø

 12Ø      WRITE ( 5, 122 )
 122        FORMAT ( '+', 'NO INTERVALS FOUND' )
          GO TO 1Ø

          END
```

**Program 10-7.** Find intervals in which roots may be found.

```
[Begin execution]


ENTER THE NUMBER OF TERMS 4
ENTER THE TERMS 12,-64,17,195
INTERVAL(S) BEGIN AT:
   -2   2   3

ENTER THE NUMBER OF TERMS Ø
 STOP
```

**Fig. 10-6.** Execution of Program 10-7.

## Summary

We have used the location principle to find intervals within which real roots are expected to occur. It should be noted that the location principle may be applied to any continuous function and is not limited to polynomial functions.

## Problems for Sec. 10-3

1. Modify Program REAL1 to identify any integral roots found in the process of locating intervals.
2. Write a FUNCTION subprogram that will evaluate a polynomial for real values of X.
3. One of the limitations of Program REAL1 is that we cannot use large values of X, as the results of the individual calculations may quickly exceed the limitations of integer arithmetic. The limits of the program may be expanded by modifying the program to utilize the subprogram of problem 2. Do this.

*4. Project: Once we have the ability to work with real values in Program REAL1, it begins to make sense to develop a method for obtaining approximations of real zeros. One method for doing this is to simply interact with a program by making requests from a console or terminal selecting what interval to search in and what increment to use. Another method is to direct the computer to search in smaller and smaller intervals by taking half the previous interval for each iteration. If we use this second method, we need a way to direct the computer to stop searching. This may be done by selecting some reasonable accuracy, such as 0.000001. When the computer finds a value of X for which $P_{(x)}$ is within 0.000001 of zero, then consider the search finished. Write a program for either method.

# 11

# Elementary Probability and Random Simulation

## 11-1 Introduction

It is the purpose of this chapter to introduce some fundamental concepts of probability and to develop program routines for some of these applications.

Taking an intuitive approach to probability, we may think of rolling a die. The term *experiment* is used to describe a particular trial, or in the case of rolling a die, an experiment is the actual rolling of the die. The *outcome* is the number that comes up. There are six possible outcomes for rolling a die. We may say that the *probability* of the die coming up 2 is one in six or 1/6, because there is only one 2 and there are six different numbers, each of which is equally likely to come up on a single roll of the die. We refer to the outcome we are looking for as a *success* and all others as *failure*. We define probability so that the probability of success P added to the probability of failure Q is 1, or $P + Q = 1$.

Often our requirements for success permit more than one single outcome, all of which are equally likely to occur. We define probability as the quotient of the number of equally likely outcomes that constitute success and the total possible number of equally likely outcomes:

$$P = S/T$$

where P is the probability of success, S is the number of outcomes that constitute success, and T is the total number of possible outcomes. All outcomes must be equally likely to occur. One of the tasks in solving probability problems is to express the question in terms of outcomes that are equally likely.

So before we work with probability itself, we will have to develop ways of counting the numbers of outcomes of various kinds of experiments.

## 11-2 Enumeration

### *Fundamental Principle of Enumeration*

The *fundamental principle of enumeration* states that, if one choice can occur in A ways and then a second choice can occur in B ways, the total number of ways that the two choices may occur is the product of A and B, or A * B.

So if you are going to buy a car that comes in five models and seven colors, the number of cars you have to choose from is 5 * 7, or 35. The fundamental principle of enumeration may be extended to cover any number of choices. So if you are going to assemble a microcomputer system by purchasing separate components, you might choose from among six CPUs, five video terminals, five disk drives, four memories, and three printers. The total number of final systems in that case would be 6 * 5 * 5 * 4 * 3, or 1800. And that is just one of the reasons why it is so difficult to decide on a system configuration.

### *Permutations*

How many different four-letter words can be formed from the letters of the word FLAG, each used once?

Let's write a program to produce them all. Think of the letters of the word FLAG as being on each of the wheels of a four-wheel odometer in the following pattern:

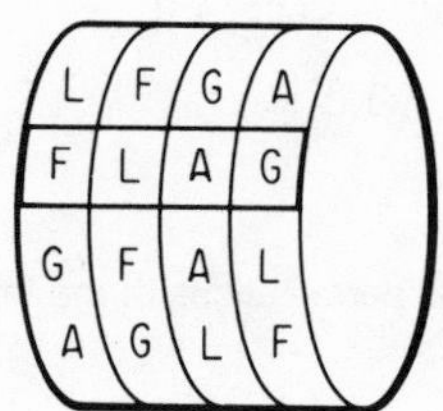


The following statements will make the odometer run:

```
      HPOS = 0
20    HPOS = HPOS + 1
      RECORD( HPOS ) = 1
30    IF ( HPOS .LT. 4 )                          GO TO 20
90    RECORD( HPOS ) = RECORD( HPOS ) + 1
      IF ( RECORD( HPOS ) .LE. 4 )                GO TO 30
       HPOS = HPOS - 1
       IF ( HPOS .GT. 0 )                          GO TO 90
```

where HPOS is the horizontal position of the wheel under consideration and RECORD is an array that keeps a record of the current numeric representation

```
      PROGRAM PERMUT
C  **  WE WRITE OUT ALL POSSIBLE PERMUTATIONS OF THE LETTERS
C  **  OF THE WORD FLAG.

      INTEGER WORD(4), PRINT(4), RECORD(4), J1, J2, J3, HPOS
      DATA  WORD/ 'F','L','A','G'/

C  **  SET UP THE RECORD ARRAY WITH THE POSITIONS FROM
C  **  WHICH THE LETTERS WILL BE TAKEN FOR OUTPUT
      HPOS = Ø
 2Ø   HPOS = HPOS + 1
      RECORD( HPOS ) = 1
 3Ø   IF ( HPOS .LT. 4 )                       GO TO 2Ø

C  **  TEST TO SEE IF WE ARE USING ANY OF THE ORIGINAL LETTERS
C  **  MORE THAN ONCE.
      DO 6Ø J1 = 1, 3
        J2 = J1 + 1
        DO 5Ø J3 = J2, 4
          IF ( RECORD( J1 ) .EQ. RECORD( J3 )) GO TO 9Ø
 5Ø     CONTINUE
 6Ø   CONTINUE

C  **  NOW LOAD PRINT AND WRITE OUT THIS PERMUTATION
      DO 8Ø J1 = 1, 4
        J2 = RECORD( J1 )
        PRINT( J1 ) = WORD( J2 )
 8Ø   CONTINUE
      WRITE ( 5, 82 ) PRINT
 82     FORMAT ( ' ', 4A1 )

C  **  NOW WE CHANGE THE LAST LETTER
 9Ø   RECORD( HPOS ) = RECORD( HPOS ) + 1
      IF ( RECORD( HPOS ) .LE. 4 )             GO TO 3Ø
       HPOS = HPOS - 1
       IF ( HPOS .GT. Ø )                      GO TO 9Ø

      END
```

**Program 11-1.** Write all permutations of the letters of the word FLAG.

of the wheels. For example, when the elements of RECORD are 1, 2, 3, and 4, the letters are F, L, A, and G.

As the wheels of our odometer turn, there are only certain points at which we wish to stop and display the current configuration. The configurations we want are those that contain no duplicate letters. So we need the following nested DO loops to determine that no letter is recorded more than once:

```
      DO 60 J1 = 1, 3
        J2 = J1 + 1
        DO 50 J3 = J2, 4
          IF ( RECORD( J1 ) .EQ. RECORD( J3 )) GO TO 90
 50     CONTINUE
 60   CONTINUE
```

where the statement labeled 90 sets up for the next turn of the odometer wheels. We simply insert this code between the previous statements labeled 30 and 90. See Program 11-1 named PERMUT.

Notice that the line labeled 90 always rotates the last wheel even if a duplicate occurs on the comparison of the first two letters. Therefore, the program will examine all 4*4*4*4 possible positions of the wheels. We can eliminate some of those if we simply set HPOS to the value of J3 in the inner DO loop of the check for duplicates. Also note that this program can be modified to handle N letters taken R at a time. These changes are left as exercises.

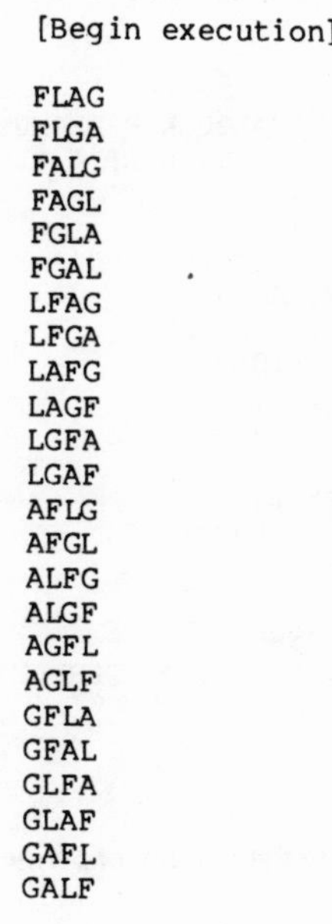

```
[Begin execution]

FLAG
FLGA
FALG
FAGL
FGLA
FGAL
LFAG
LFGA
LAFG
LAGF
LGFA
LGAF
AFLG
AFGL
ALFG
ALGF
AGFL
AGLF
GFLA
GFAL
GLFA
GLAF
GAFL
GALF
```

**Fig. 11-1.** Execution of Program 11-1.

We can easily see that the number of different arrangements is 24. Each of the arrangements is a permutation of the four letters F, L, A, and G, and is different from the others because the letters are in a different order. In other words, when we talk about permutations, order matters.

We observe that to form a four-letter word using four different letters once, we may use any one of the four letters available for our first letter. Now there are only three letters left from which to choose the second letter, two left from which to choose the third letter, and finally, we have exactly one letter for the fourth letter of the new word. Using the fundamental principle of enumeration, there are four choices. The first can occur in four ways, the second can occur in three ways, the third in two ways, and the fourth in one way. This makes 4 * 3 * 2 * 1, or 24 ways that the four choices can occur.

This kind of calculation occurs often in mathematics and so is given a special name—4 * 3 * 2 * 1 is called *4 factorial*, written as 4!. In general,

$$N! = N(N - 1)(N - 2) \ldots (2)(1)$$

where N is a positive integer. The special case of zero factorial (0!) is defined as 1. Calculation of N! is straightforward and is left as an exercise.

```
      PROGRAM NPR
C  **  CALCULATE THE NUMBER OF PERMUTATIONS OF
C  **  N THINGS TAKEN R AT A TIME.

      INTEGER N, R, INDEX, START, J1
      REAL    PERM

      WRITE ( 5, 12 )
 12      FORMAT ( ' ', 'CALCULATE PERMUTATIONS FOR N THINGS ',
     +                 'TAKEN R AT A TIME.' / )

 20   WRITE ( 5, 22 )
 22      FORMAT ( ' ', 'ENTER N AND R ? ', )
      READ ( 5, 24 ) N, R
 24      FORMAT ( 2I4 )
      IF ( N .EQ. 0 )  STOP

      PERM  = 1.0
      START = N - R + 1
      DO 40 INDEX = START, N
        J1 = START + N - INDEX
        PERM = PERM * J1
 40   CONTINUE
      WRITE ( 5, 42 ) PERM
 42      FORMAT ( '+', F20.0, '  PERMUTATIONS' / )
      GOTO 20

      END
```

**Program 11-2.** Calculate the number of permutations of N things taken R at a time.

Suppose we want to find the number of different three-letter words that can be formed from the letters of the word COMPUTER. For the first letter we may choose from among eight, for the second we may select from among the remaining seven, and for the third we may select from among the remaining six letters. Applying the fundamental principle of enumeration, we get 8 * 7 * 6, or 336 different words. Since the order is different, there are 336 different permutations. Notice that

$$8 * 7 * 6 = \frac{8 * 7 * 6 * 5 * 4 * 3 * 2 * 1}{5 * 4 * 3 * 2 * 1} = \frac{8!}{5!} = \frac{8!}{(8 - 3)\,!}$$

We should see that for the number of arrangements of R letters taken from among N different letters, we get N!/(N − R)!. This expression defines the number of permutations of N things taken R at a time and is written as

$$_{N}P_{R} = \frac{N!}{(N - R)\,!} \qquad \textbf{Eq. 11-1}$$

Expanding the right side of Eq. 11-1 as the quotient of products, we get

$$_{N}P_{R} = \frac{N(N - 1)(N - 2) \ldots (N - R + 1)(N - R)(N - R - 1) \ldots (2)(1)}{(N - R)(N - R - 1) \ldots (2)(1)}$$

which simplifies to

$$_{N}P_{R} = N(N - 1)(N - 2) \ldots (N - R + 1) \qquad \textbf{Eq. 11-2}$$

which can easily be adapted to a FORTRAN DO loop with the following:

```
START = N - R + 1
DO 40 INDEX = START, N
```

or we might prefer to more directly simulate the calculation indicated in Eq. 11-2 with the following:

```
START = N - R + 1
DO 40 INDEX = START, N
  J1 = START + N - INDEX
```

See Program 11-2 named NPR.

```
[Begin execution]

CALCULATE PERMUTATIONS FOR N THINGS TAKEN R AT A TIME.

ENTER N AND R ? 8,3
                336.   PERMUTATIONS

ENTER N AND R ? 4,4
                 24.   PERMUTATIONS

ENTER N AND R ? 8,8
              40320.   PERMUTATIONS

ENTER N AND R ? 0,0
 STOP
```

**Fig. 11-2.** Execution of Program 11-2.

### *Combinations*

The distinction between combinations and permutations is order. For combinations, order does not matter. We may think of *combinations* as selections of items while *permutations* are arrangements of selected items. The number of combinations of four letters selected from among four letters is one. The number of combinations of N different things taken R at a time is written $_{N}C_{R}$. We may find the number of combinations of N things taken R at a time by looking at the number of permutations. Each combination of R things could be arranged in R! ways. Using the fundamental principle of enumeration, the number of combinations times the number of arrangements for each combination gives the number of permutations. So

$$({}_{N}C_{R})(R!) = {}_{N}P_{R}$$

and solving for ${}_{N}C_{R}$, we get

$${}_{N}C_{R} = \frac{{}_{N}P_{R}}{R!} = \frac{N!}{(R!)\,(N - R)!}$$

Thus the number of combinations of three letters selected from among eight letters is

$${}_{8}C_{3} = \frac{8!}{(3!)\,(5!)} = 56$$

While the number of permutations is

$${}_{8}P_{3} = 336$$

Combinations pertain to such things as committees and dealing cards where order does not matter.

```
      FUNCTION COMB( N, R )
C  **  WE CALCULATE THE NUMBER OF COMBINATIONS OF
C  **  N THINGS TAKEN R AT A TIME.
C  **  THIS IS A REAL FUNCTION TO ALLOW LARGER VALUES

      INTEGER INDEX, N, R, START

      COMB  = 1.Ø
      START = N - R + 1
      IF ( START .GT. N )                       GO TO 5Ø

       DO 4Ø  INDEX = START, N
         COMB = COMB * INDEX / ( INDEX - START + 1 )
 4Ø    CONTINUE
 5Ø   RETURN

      END
```

**Program 11-3.** A FUNCTION to calculate the number of combinations of N things taken R at a time.

If we want to know the number of five-member committees that can be selected from among 20 people, we need to calculate ${}_{20}C_{5}$. One approach is to compute ${}_{20}P_{5}$ and then successively divide by the integers from 5 down to 1. That will produce the desired results in a large number of situations. However, some calculations will cause trouble. How about ${}_{50}C_{50}$? We know that ${}_{50}C_{50}$ equals 1, but what will the computer do if we first calculate ${}_{50}P_{50}$? And if your

```
      PROGRAM TCOMB
C  **  WE TEST FUNCTION COMB REQUESTING INPUT FROM A KEYBOARD.

      INTEGER N, R
      REAL    COMB1

20    WRITE ( 5, 22 )
22       FORMAT ( ' ', 'ENTER N AND R ? ', )
      READ ( 5, 24 ) N, R
24       FORMAT ( 2I4 )
      IF ( N .LT. Ø )  STOP

      COMB1 = COMB( N, R )

      WRITE ( 5, 52 ) COMB1
52       FORMAT ( '+', F8.Ø, '  COMBINATIONS' / )
      GO TO 2Ø

      END
```

**Program 11-4.** Test the combinations FUNCTION.

computer can handle 3.04E+64, try ${}_{100}P_{100}$. We will be able to accommodate a wider range of values by doing the multiplication and division in the same DO loop. Furthermore, we will obtain better accuracy by dividing by successively larger values. On the Kth iteration of the DO loop we should be dividing by K to assure that there has been an exact multiple of K used as a multiplier. The following DO loop is constructed in exactly this way.

```
   START = N − R + 1
   DO 40 INDEX = START, N
     COMB = COMB * INDEX / ( INDEX − START + 1 )
40 CONTINUE
```

Since a number of our programs will require the calculation of combinations, it seems worth developing a FUNCTION subprogram for this purpose. This is done in Program 11-3 named COMB. Since this FUNCTION will be used over and over again we should anticipate the possibility that we could invoke COMB with the value of N set at zero. Thus the IF test before the DO loop. Also note that the calculation is done in a REAL variable. This will provide a much greater range of values.

Now let's write a small program that will allow us to test the FUNCTION by entering selected values of N and R from an external device (see Program 11-4 named TCOMB).

Let's look at a program to actually produce the combinations of five things taken three at a time (see Program 11-5 named WORDS). We do this with the letters of the word GAMES. This is done by setting up an array to record what letters are in use. The execution (see Fig. 11-4) shows both what letters are in use in the RECORD array and what position in the original word each letter is from.

```
[Begin execution]

ENTER N AND R ? 8,3
     56.  COMBINATIONS

ENTER N AND R ? 4,1
      4.  COMBINATIONS

ENTER N AND R ? 1Ø,8
     45.  COMBINATIONS

ENTER N AND R ? 1Ø,5
    252.  COMBINATIONS

ENTER N AND R ? -1,-1
 STOP
```

**Fig. 11-3.** Execution of Program 11-4.

### *Permutations of Things Not All Different*

Suppose we want to know the number of arrangements possible for the letters of the word PROGRAM. Since there are two R's and we cannot tell which is which, taking 7! counts every distinguishable arrangement twice, because the R's may occupy two positions in 2! ways. Therefore, the number of words is 7!/2!. In how many ways can we arrange the letters of the word ABSENTEE? Well, if the E's were distinguishable, we would get 8!; but that counts the indistinguishable arrangements 3! times, because three E's can be arranged in three locations in 3! indistinguishable ways. So we get 8!/3!. The letters of the word SNOWSHOES can be arranged in 9!/(2!)(3!) ways, because the two O's can be arranged in 2! ways and the three S's can be arranged in 3! ways.

### *Partitioning*

In how many ways can we arrange three X's and five Y's? We get 8!/(3!)(5!). We might ask this question in the following way: In how many ways can we put eight things in two groups such that one group contains three things and the other group five if order does not matter?

In how many ways can we arrange three X's, five Y's, and six Z's? We get 14!/(3!)(5!)(6!). We could state the problem in another way. In how many ways can fourteen different items be put into three groups of three, five, and six items?

The second version of each of the last two problems are examples of partitioning. In general, if we have $R_1$, $R_2$, . . . , $R_n$ items such that $R_1 + R_2 + \ldots + R_n = T$, then the number of ways that we can place the T items into n groups of $R_1$, $R_2$, . . . , $R_n$ is

$$N = \frac{T!}{R_1!R_2! \ldots R_n!}$$

```
      PROGRAM WORDS
C  **  WE WRITE OUT ALL POSSIBLE COMBINATIONS OF GROUPS OF
C  **  THREE LETTERS FROM THE LETTERS OF THE WORD 'GAMES'

      INTEGER WORD(5), DUMMY(5), MASK(5), BLANK,
     +        PRINT(3), RECORD(3), N, R, J1, J4, INDEX

      DATA  WORD/ 'G','A','M','E','S'/
     +      DUMMY/ '1','2','3','4','5'/
     +      BLANK/ ' '/ N/ 5/ R/ 3/

      WRITE ( 5, 112 ) (DUMMY(J1), J1=1,R), WORD

C  **  SET UP THE FIRST R LETTERS FOR OUTPUT.
      DO 1Ø INDEX = 1, R
        RECORD( INDEX ) = INDEX
 1Ø   CONTINUE
      GO TO 4Ø

 2Ø   RECORD( J4 ) = RECORD( J4 ) + 1
      J4 = J4 + 1
      IF ( J4 .GT. R )                             GO TO 4Ø
       DO 3Ø J1 = J4, R
         RECORD( J1 ) = RECORD( J1 - 1 ) + 1
 3Ø    CONTINUE

 4Ø   DO 5Ø INDEX = 1, N
        MASK( INDEX ) = BLANK
 5Ø   CONTINUE

      DO 6Ø INDEX = 1, R
        J1                = RECORD( INDEX )
        PRINT( INDEX )    = WORD( J1 )
        MASK( J1 )        = DUMMY( INDEX )
 6Ø   CONTINUE
      WRITE ( 5, 112 ) PRINT, MASK

      DO 1ØØ J1 = 1, R
        J4 = 1 + R - J1
        IF ( RECORD( J4 ) .LT. N - R + J4 )    GO TO 2Ø
1ØØ   CONTINUE

112     FORMAT ( ' ', 3A1, 5X, 5A1 )
      END
```

**Program 11-5.** Display the combinations of five letters taken three at a time.

```
[Begin execution]

123     GAMES
GAM     123
GAE     12 3
GAS     12  3
GME     1 23
GMS     1 2 3
GES     1  23
AME      123
AMS      12 3
AES      1 23
MES       123
```

**Fig. 11-4.** Execution of Program 11-5.

Note that all of the problems we have treated under permutations and combinations are really special cases of partitioning. The combinations of N things taken R at a time may be thought of as partitioning into two groups of R and N − R items. The problem of arranging SNOWSHOES may be thought of as partitioning into six groups of three items for the S's, two items for the O's, and one item each for the four remaining letters N, W, H, and E. Finally, the permutations of N different items taken R at a time may be thought of as R + 1 groups of N − R in the first group and one item each for the other R groups.

## Summary

This section has been devoted to introducing the fundamental principle of enumeration and the enumeration of permutations, combinations, and partitionings of items. In counting permutations order matters. Permutations count such things as arrangements of letters in a word and books lined up on a bookshelf. When counting combinations order does not matter. Combinations count such things as the number of different committees formed from a group of people and hands dealt in a game of cards.

## Problems for Sec. 11-2

Many of the numeric results for these problems require a large number of digits. We suggest that you use E12.6 as the format for any problems that you expect to yield outsized real values. This format will provide for six significant digits and a power of ten.

1. Write a program to calculate N!. Be sure to account for 0! = 1. Use a real variable to accommodate large values of N!.
2. Generalize Program PERMUT to display all permutations of N letters taken R at a time. Incorporate the change that sets HPOS to J3 in the loop that tests for duplicates to improve execution speed. (This will make a big difference for long words.) Be careful how large your words are, unless you are using a high-speed video terminal for display.
3. (a) In how many orders can 15 people enter a room? (b) In how many different ways can 15 keys be put on a circular key ring?
4. Cars come in 18 colors, seven models, four engines, and there are 15 options such as whitewalls, outside mirror, radio, etc. How many different cars are available?
5. You have 25 different books and two bookshelves. One bookshelf will hold exactly 13 books and the other holds exactly 12 books. In how many ways can the books be arranged on the shelves?
6. In a class of 30, a six-member committee is to be selected. How many different committees are possible? If there are 15 girls in the class, how many of the committees consist of 6 girls?

7. (a) How many different five-card hands may be dealt from a 52-card deck? (b) How many different thirteen-card hands can be dealt from a 52-card deck?
8. (a) There are five people in a room. In how many ways can they all have different birthdays? (b) In how many ways can ten people have all different birthdays? Use a 365-day year and ignore Feb. 29.
9. If a state uses three letters followed by three digits for its license plates, how many different license plates can it produce?
10. (a) You have five different flags with which to form signals by arranging them all on a flagpole. How many different signals can you form? (b) You have five different flags with which to form signals by arranging up to five of them on a flagpole. How many different signals can you form?
11. You have ten different flags with which to form signals by arranging up to five of them on a flagpole. How many signals can you form?
12. You have 50 friends. You are going to have a party and can only invite 25 people. How many different guest lists could you have.
13. How many different words can be formed from the letters of the word COMPUTERS if (a) you must use all of the letters and (b) you must leave out one letter.
14. A class consists of 30 students of which seventeen are girls. In how many ways can we select a committee of four? How many will have two boys and two girls? How many will have one boy and three girls? How many will have four girls? How many will have four boys?
15. How many outcomes are possible for rolling two dice followed by drawing three cards from a 52-card deck?
16. How many different sets of two five-card hands can be dealt from a 52-card deck?
17. How many words can be formed using all of the letters of the word MISSISSIPPI?

## 11-3 Simple Probability

We defined probability in Sec. 11-1 as S/T, where S is the number of ways in which an outcome may constitute success and T is the number of possible outcomes, and all outcomes are equally likely. For flipping a coin, the probability of coming up heads is 1/2 or 0.5 (assuming a "fair" coin and omitting the possibility of standing on edge). For drawing a card from a 52-card deck, the probability of getting the ace of spades is 1/52 or about 0.0192.

Suppose you are in a group of 29 and a committee of four members is to be selected at random. What is the probability that you get on the committee? Well, the total number of committees possible is ${}_{29}C_4$. Now all we have to find is how many of those committees you would be on. We can find that out by saying in effect, "let's put you on the committee and select the other three members from the remaining 28 people." This means that you will be on ${}_{28}C_3$ of the committees, and the probability that you get on the committee is ${}_{28}C_3/{}_{29}C_4$. Let us write a program to compute this probability.

```
      PROGRAM COMITE
C  **  WE CALCULATE THE PROBABILITY THAT YOU ARE ON A COMMITTEE
C  **  OF 4 SELECTED AT RANDOM FROM AMONG 29 PEOPLE.

      INTEGER N, R
      REAL    COMB1, COMB2, PROB

      N = 28
      R = 3
      COMB1 = COMB( N, R )
      N = 29
      R = 4
      COMB2 = COMB( N, R )

      PROB = COMB1 / COMB2
      WRITE ( 5, 42 ) PROB
 42      FORMAT ( ' ',
     +              'THE PROBABILITY THAT YOU GET ON A 4 MEMBER' /
     +             ' ', 'COMMITTEE FROM A GROUP OF 29 IS ', F7.6 )

      END
```

**Program 11-6.** Calculate the probability that you are on a committee.

Since we reference FUNCTION COMB twice, our program is very short indeed (see Program 11-6 named COMITE). Notice that we could replace the first seven executable statements in Program COMITE with the single statement

PROB = COMB( 28, 3 ) / COMB( 29, 4 )

Suppose we roll a die. The probability that a 3 comes up is one in six or 1/6. Now roll the die again. Again the probability of a 3 is 1/6. We can see that if we roll the die twice, the probability of both rolls coming up 3 is (1/6)*(1/6), or 1/36. We define an *event* as a set of outcomes for a particular experiment. If we have two events A and B such that the probability of success for A is P and the probability of success for B is Q, the events A and B are said to be *independent* if the probability of success for A and B both is P * Q. This is exactly the case for rolling a 3 on each of two dice, or on two successive rolls of the same die. This enables us to arrive at probabilities without actually enumerating outcomes. Thus we have extended our definition of probability.

For rolling two dice, the events associated with the first die are independent of the events associated with the second die. The same may be said of rolling the same die twice. The outcomes of flipping two coins are independent.

```
[Begin execution]

THE PROBABILITY THAT YOU GET ON A 4 MEMBER
COMMITTEE FROM A GROUP OF 29 IS .137931
```

**Fig. 11-5.** Execution of Program 11-6.

Drawing a card from a deck is independent of rolling a die. So the probability of getting a 1 and an ace upon rolling a die and drawing a card is (1/6)*(4/52), or 1/78.

### *The Birthday Problem*

Let us look at a problem often referred to as "the birthday problem." Suppose you are in a room with twenty-nine other people. What is the probability that at least two people in the room have the same birthday? We can say that if the probability of no two people having the same birthday is P, then the probability that at least two do have the same birthday is 1 − P. The birthdays for two people are independent events, so we may multiply individual probabilities. Selecting any person first, we say that this person's probability of having

```
      PROGRAM BIRTH
C  **  WE FIND THE PROBABILITY THAT AT LEAST TWO PEOPLE SHARE
C  **  BIRTHDAYS IN A ROOM OF 30 PEOPLE SELECTED AT RANDOM.

      INTEGER INDEX
      REAL    PROB

      PROB = 1.0
      DO 40 INDEX = 336, 365
        PROB = PROB * FLOAT(INDEX) / 365.0
 40   CONTINUE
      PROB = 1.0 - PROB

      WRITE ( 5, 62 ) PROB
 62      FORMAT ( ' ',
     +            'THE PROBABILITY OF TWO OR MORE IDENTICAL' /
     +           ' ', 'BIRTHDAYS AMONG 30 PEOPLE IS ', F7.6 )

      END
```

**Program 11-7.** Find the probability of two people sharing birthdays from among thirty people.

a different birthday from those already selected is 365/365. The probability that the second person's birthday differs from the first is 364/365. We get 363/365 as the probability that the third person's birthday differs from the first two. And for the probability that the thirtieth person's birthday differs from all the others we get 336/365. So the probability that all are different is

$$P = \frac{365}{365} * \frac{364}{365} * \cdots * \frac{336}{365}$$

and the probability that at least two people have the same birthday is 1 − P. We can write a short program to compute this (see Program 11-7 named BIRTH).

We see from Fig. 11-6 that the chances are about 71 percent, which is much higher than many people estimate before analyzing the problem. Note

```
[Begin execution]

THE PROBABILITY OF TWO OR MORE IDENTICAL
BIRTHDAYS AMONG 30 PEOPLE IS .706316
```

**Fig. 11-6.** Execution of Program 11-7.

that this is not the probability that someone else in the room has the same birthday that you have. That problem is left as an exercise.

## Summary

We have initially defined probability as the quotient of the number of ways to constitute success and the total number of outcomes for equally likely outcomes. We have seen that this can easily be applied to situations where the outcomes can be enumerated. Independent events that have individual probabilities P and Q occur together with a probability of P * Q. This produces an extended definition of probability that does not require enumeration, but requires only that we know individual probabilities for successive events.

## Problems for Sec. 11-3

1. A group of 29 has 16 boys. A committee of five is selected at random. What is the probability that all five committee members are boys?
2. Ten people are to sit in a row of ten chairs. What is the probability that two particular persons sit next to each other?
3. What is the probability of being dealt the ace of spades, the three of clubs, the eight of hearts, the seven of diamonds, and the ten of clubs from a 52-card deck?
4. What is the probability of being dealt the ace, king, queen, jack, and ten of spades from a 52-card deck?
5. When flipping a coin ten times, what is the probability of the first six flips coming up heads and the last four tails?
6. What is the probability of getting all heads when flipping a coin ten times?
7. You have a list of 20 true-false questions from which 10 will be selected at random for a test. Of the 20, there are 15 you are guaranteed to get right and 5 you are guaranteed to get wrong. What is the probability that you will get exactly 8 right?
8. An experiment consists of drawing a card from a 52-card deck until the first ace appears. Find the probability of the first ace appearing on the fourth draw.
9. For the experiment of problem 8, find the probability of the first ace appearing on draws one through ten (ten separate numbers).
10. An experiment consists of rolling a die until it comes up 2. Find the probability of the first 2 coming up on the fourth roll; on the tenth roll?
11. Refer to the birthday problem (see problem 8 in Sec. 11-2). How many people must be in a room to make the probability of at least two identical birthdays be 0.5?

*12. You are in a room with 29 other people. What is the probability that at least one of them shares your birthday?

*13. How many people must be in a room for the probability of another person to have your birthday be 0.5?

## 11-4 Random Simulation

Refer to Appendix C for a discussion of random number generation and some of the options that exist for obtaining and utilizing a random number generating function.

We may use a random number generator to simulate experiments that occur at random. We can have the computer flip a coin by generating two random digits. We can roll a die by generating digits at random in the range from 1 to 6.

Let us begin by having the computer "flip a coin" 50 times. The random number generator we will be using returns a real number between 0 and 1. If we multiply by 2, we get a number between 0 and 2. Truncating produces either a 0 or a 1. Finally we can obtain a 1 or a 2 by adding 1. Thus we have the following statement to determine which way a flipped coin will fall:

COIN = INT( 2.0 * RND(4) ) + 1

where the argument of the RND function is arbitrary. Changing that argument will produce different random results. See Program 11-8 named FLIP.

```
      PROGRAM FLIP
C  **  THIS PROGRAM SIMULATES FLIPPING A COIN 50 TIMES.

      INTEGER  HT(2), INDEX, COIN, LIST(50), COUNT
      DATA  HT/ 'H','T'/

      COUNT = 0
      DO 40 INDEX = 1, 50
        COIN = INT( 2.0 * RND(4) ) + 1
        LIST( INDEX ) = HT( COIN )
        IF ( COIN .EQ. 1 )  COUNT = COUNT + 1
40    CONTINUE

      WRITE ( 5, 42 ) LIST, COUNT
42       FORMAT ( ' ', 50A1 /
     +            ' ', I3, '  HEADS OUT OF 50 FLIPS' )

      END
```

**Program 11-8.** Flip a coin 50 times.

```
[Begin execution]

HHHHTHTHHTHHTTTHHHTTTHHHHTTHHTHHHTHTHTHHTTHTTHHTHT
 29  HEADS OUT OF 50 FLIPS
```

**Fig. 11-7.** Execution of Program 11-8.

One of the intriguing things about flipping a coin many times is that we do not get heads for half of the flips for each experiment. In fact, it is theoretically possible to flip a coin 50 times and get no heads or to get all heads. Of course the probability of all heads or no heads is very small compared to the probability of half heads. We will be able to compute those probabilities in the next section. For now we are concentrating on simulation.

In many ways, flipping a coin 50 times is the same as flipping 50 coins once. Let us put the flipping logic of Program FLIP in a DO loop to perform the experiment ten times to see a range of results. This is done in Program 11-9 named FLIP1.

```
      PROGRAM FLIP1
C  **  THIS PROGRAM SIMULATES FLIPPING A COIN 5Ø TIMES.

      INTEGER  HT(2), INDEX, COIN, LIST(5Ø), COUNT, TRIAL
      DATA  HT/ 'H','T'/

      DO 1ØØ TRIAL = 1, 1Ø
        COUNT = Ø
        DO 4Ø INDEX = 1, 5Ø
          COIN          = INT( 2.Ø * RND(5) ) + 1
          LIST( INDEX ) = HT( COIN )
          IF ( COIN .EQ. 1 )  COUNT = COUNT + 1
4Ø      CONTINUE

        WRITE ( 5, 42 ) LIST, COUNT
42         FORMAT ( ' ', 5ØA1 /
     +               ' ', I3, '  HEADS OUT OF 5Ø FLIPS' )
1ØØ   CONTINUE

      END
```

**Program 11-9.** Flipping 50 coins ten times.

We get a range of 17 to 30 heads for the execution of the program, and one experiment did produce 25 heads.

One of the nice features of simulation by computer is that we can have the computer perform hundreds or thousands of trials of an experiment in a few seconds that might take days to do with physical apparatus and pencil and paper recording of results.

Let us set up an experiment to roll six dice 1000 times, counting the number of times 1 comes up for each roll of the six dice. (How long would that take with real dice?) The possibilities are from zero to six. Then let us count the number of times each of those seven numbers occurs. We can keep track of all seven totals in a 7-element linear array. We will count the number of times no 1's come up in the first element, and the number of times one 1 comes up in the second element, and so forth (see Program 11-10 named ROLL).

```
[Begin execution]

TTHTTTTTTHHTHTTTHTHHHHTTHTHHHHHHTHHTTHHTTTHTTHTTTT
 22  HEADS OUT OF 50 FLIPS
HHHTHHHHHTHTTTTHHHHTTTTTTHHHHHHHHTHHHTHTTHTHHTTHTH
 30  HEADS OUT OF 50 FLIPS
HHTTHTTTHHTTTTHHTTHHTTHTHHHHTTHHTHHHHHTHHTHTTTTTTT
 24  HEADS OUT OF 50 FLIPS
TTTTHHTTTTHHHTHTHTHTTTHHHTTTTHTTHTHTHTTHTTTTTHTTTH
 18  HEADS OUT OF 50 FLIPS
HHHHHHHHHTHTHTTHHHTHTTHTTHHHTTTTHTHTHTTTHTHTTTHTTH
 26  HEADS OUT OF 50 FLIPS
THHTTHTHTHHHTTHHHTTHTTHHTHHTTHHHTHHHHHTHHTHTTTHHTT
 28  HEADS OUT OF 50 FLIPS
HTTTTHHHHHTTHTHTTTHTTHHTHTTTTHTHTTTHHHTHHTHTHHHTHH
 25  HEADS OUT OF 50 FLIPS
TTHTTHHTTHHHTHTHHHTHTTHTTTTTTTHTTTHHHTTTHHHTHTHTTT
 21  HEADS OUT OF 50 FLIPS
TTHTTHTTTHHTTTHHHTHTTTTTTHTTHHTTHTTHTHHHTTTTTHTTTT
 17  HEADS OUT OF 50 FLIPS
TTHHHTHTHHTHHTHTHTHTHHTHHHTTHHTTTTHHHHHTHHHTTTTHHH
 29  HEADS OUT OF 50 FLIPS
```

**Fig. 11-8.** Execution of Program 11-9.

```
      PROGRAM ROLL
C  **  WE ARE COUNTING THE NUMBER OF TIMES THAT 'ONE'
C  **  APPEARS IN A ROLL OF 6 DICE.

      INTEGER  TRIAL, ROLL, COUNT, LIST(7), J1

      DO 20 J1 = 1, 7
        LIST( J1 ) = 0
 20   CONTINUE

C  **  SET UP TO PERFORM 1000 TRIALS
      DO 100 TRIAL = 1, 1000
        COUNT = 0

C  **  HERE WE PERFORM A SINGLE TRIAL OF ROLLING 6 DICE.
        DO 50 ROLL = 1, 6
          J1 = INT( 6.0 * RND( 7 ) ) + 1
          IF ( J1 .EQ. 1 )  COUNT = COUNT + 1
 50     CONTINUE
        LIST( COUNT + 1 ) = LIST( COUNT + 1 ) + 1

 100  CONTINUE

      WRITE ( 5, 202 ) LIST
 202    FORMAT ( ' ',
     +      ' NONE   ONE   TWO THREE  FOUR  FIVE   SIX' /
     +           ' ', 7I6 )

      END
```

**Program 11-10.** Roll six dice 1000 times counting the number of 1's.

```
[Begin execution]

 NONE    ONE    TWO THREE   FOUR  FIVE    SIX
  338    428    17Ø    55      9     Ø      Ø
```

**Fig. 11-9.** Execution of Program 11-10.

## Problems for Sec. 11-4

Access to a random number generator is necessary for these problems.

1. Have the computer flip six coins 1000 times and print the distribution of outcomes.
2. Sketch a graph of the distribution for problem 1 and the distribution for Program ROLL.
3. Write a program to deal five-card hands from a 52-card deck. Be sure not to deal the same card twice.
4. A company manufactures light bulbs and can openers. For light bulbs it is known that 1 in 20 is defective and for can openers 1 in 25 is defective. Write a program to select at random one light bulb and one can opener 1000 times. Total the number of times for each of the following: (a) neither was defective, (b) both were defective, (c) the light bulb was defective, and (d) the can opener was defective.
5. A regular tetrahedron has four equilateral triangles as faces. Let an experiment consist of numbering one face 1 and the remaining faces 2, and tossing the tetrahedron into the air to determine which number faces down. Write a program to "toss" the tetrahedron 500 times and count the number of times the 1 faces down.
6. Roll a die 500 times. Count the number of times the 1 or the 5 comes up.
7. Roll a die and toss the tetrahedron of problem 5 1000 times. Count the number of times both come out 1 and count the number of times both come out 2.
8. An experiment consists of rolling a die until a 1 comes up. Write a program to perform the experiment 500 times. Tabulate the number of rolls for each experiment.
9. An experiment consists of flipping a coin until it comes up heads. Write a program to perform the experiment 1500 times and tabulate the number of flips required for each. Print the distribution.
10. Roll ten dice 500 times. Tabulate the number of 1's that come up for each roll. Print the distribution.
11. Suppose 10 percent of the population is left-handed. Write a program to select groups of ten people at random. Tabulate the number of left-handed people. Print the distribution.
12. Project: Write a program to make the computer the dealer in a game of 21 (blackjack).

## 11-5 Binomial Trials

Suppose we roll two dice. What is the probability that a 1 comes up exactly once. If we use one red die and one green die, we may clearly describe the results. There are two ways that we could get exactly one 1. We could have the red die come up 1 and the green die come up not 1. The probability of this is (1/6) * (5/6). Or we could have the green die come up 1 and the red die come up not 1. The probability of this is (1/6) * (5/6). Now, if we roll the two dice, the probability that we get exactly one 1 is the sum of the above two possibilities, or (1/6) * (5/6) + (1/6) * (5/6). Or we can say that the probability of exactly one 1 is two times the probability of getting a 1 on the green die and not a 1 on the red die. That probability is 2 * (1/6) * (5/6).

```
      PROGRAM DICE
C  **  TEN DICE ARE ROLLED.  WE ARE FINDING THE PROBABILITY
C  **  THAT EXACTLY TWO DICE COME UP 1.

      INTEGER  R, N
      REAL     PROB

      N = 10
      R = 2
      PROB = COMB( N, R ) * (1.0/6.0)**R * (5.0/6.0)**(N-R)

      WRITE ( 5, 62 ) PROB
 62      FORMAT ( ' ', 'EXACTLY TWO DICE IN TEN COME UP 1 ' /
     +               ' ', 'PROBABILITY = ',  F7.6 )

      END
```

**Program 11-11.** Calculate the probability that exactly two 1's come up when rolling ten dice.

```
[Begin execution]

EXACTLY TWO DICE IN TEN COME UP 1
PROBABILITY = .290710
```

**Fig. 11-10.** Execution of Program 11-11.

Now suppose we roll four dice colored red, green, blue, and white. What is the probability that we get exactly two 1's? The probability that the red and the green dice are 1's and the blue and white are not is (1/6) * (1/6) * (5/6) * (5/6). But we might get the 1's only on the green and blue dice with the same probability, or we might get 1's only on the red and white dice with the same probability. In fact, there are ${}_4C_2$ ways that we could select two dice from the four to come up with 1's. The probability for each selection is (1/6) * (1/6) * (5/6) * (5/6). So the probability of exactly two 1's up for a roll of four dice is

$$P = {}_4C_2 * (1/6)^{**}2 * (5/6)^{**}2$$

which simplifies to 25/216, or about 0.1157. That is almost 12 percent.

Suppose we have ten dice. What is the probability that exactly two dice come up 1 when all ten are rolled? For a particular selection of two dice, we get (1/6)**2 * (5/6)**8 and we can select the two dice in ${}_{10}C_2$ ways. So

$$P = {}_{10}C_2 * (1/6)^{**}2 * (5/6)^{**}8$$

We can write a short program, using FUNCTION subprogram COMB from Sec. 11-2, to find the value of P (see Program 11-11 named DICE on the previous page).

Program DICE is for exactly two 1's. What about the other possible numbers of 1's? With just a few changes in Program DICE, we can answer that question. Instead of computing for R = 2 only, we can let R go from 0 to 10 using a DO loop. This is done in Program 11-12 named DICE1.

```
      PROGRAM DICE1
C  **  WE CALCULATE THE PROBABILITY DISTRIBUTION FOR THE NUMBER
C  **  OF 1'S WHICH COME UP WHEN ROLLING TEN DICE.

      INTEGER R, N, R1
      REAL    PROB

      WRITE ( 5, 12 )
 12      FORMAT ( ' ', ' ONES PROBABILITY' )

      N = 10
      DO 100 R1 = 1, 11
        R    = R1 - 1
        PROB = COMB( N, R ) * (1.0/6.0)**R * (5.0/6.0)**(N-R)
        WRITE ( 5, 62 ) R, PROB
62         FORMAT ( ' ', I5, 1X, F10.8 )
100   CONTINUE

      END
```

**Program 11-12.** Probabilities for 0 to 10 1's when rolling ten dice.

In Program DICE1 we have defined 11 events that cover all possible outcomes in this experiment. There can be no outcomes that do not give from 0 to 10 1's. It also is true that no two of the events have any outcomes in common. Events that do not have any outcomes in common are called *mutually exclusive events*. If we have a set of mutually exclusive events that also cover all possible outcomes, then the individual probabilities must total 1. We can verify that the sum of the probabilities in Program DICE1 is in fact 1 within the precision limits of real variables. We do have a precision problem when we try

```
[Begin execution]

ONES PROBABILITY
   Ø  .1615Ø555
   1  .323Ø1113
   2  .29Ø71ØØ3
   3  .155Ø4535
   4  .Ø5426587
   5  .Ø13Ø2381
   6  .ØØ217Ø64
   7  .ØØØ248Ø7
   8  .ØØØØ1861
   9  .ØØØØØØ83
  1Ø  .ØØØØØØØ2
```

**Fig. 11-11.** Execution of Program 11-12.

to sum the values for 9 and 10 1's. There are a couple of things we might do with this program. We might insert some code to calculate the sum of the individual probabilities, writing out the accumulated total along with each individual probability. We might rewrite it with double-precision variables to improve the precision so that we might have a more accurate sum and more accurate values for the probabilities of 8, 9, and 10 1's. These are left as exercises.

```
      PROGRAM LEFT
C  **   IF 1Ø% OF THE POPULATION IS LEFT HANDED, WE CALCULATE THE
C  **   PROBABILITY THAT 1Ø PEOPLE SELECTED AT RANDOM FROM
C  **   AMONG 1ØØ PEOPLE ARE ALL LEFT HANDED.

      INTEGER N, R
      REAL    PROB

      N = 1ØØ
      R = 1Ø
      PROB = COMB( N, R ) * (.1)**R * (.9)**(N-R)

      WRITE ( 5, 112 ) PROB
112      FORMAT ( ' ', F8.7 )

      END
```

**Program 11-13.** Calculate the probability of 10 left-handed people selected from 100.

Suppose we know that 10 percent of a certain population is left-handed. If we select 100 people at random, what is the probability that exactly 10 of them will be left-handed? The probability that a particular set of 10 people will be left-handed will be (1/10)**10 * (9/10)**90. There are ${}_{100}C_{10}$ ways that 10 people from among 100 can be left-handed. So the probability is

$$P = {}_{100}C_{10} * (1/10)^{**}10 * (9/10)^{**}90$$

See Program 11-13 named LEFT.

```
[Begin execution]

.1318649
```

**Fig. 11-12.** Execution of Program 11-13.

In general, we should see that if an outcome has probability P of success and Q of failure and we perform an experiment consisting of N trials, the probability of exactly R successes is

$$_{N}P_{R} * P{*}{*}R * Q{*}{*}(N - R)$$

Experiments that behave in this way are called *binomial experiments* because the values of $_{N}C_{R}$ * P**R * Q**(N − R) are the terms of the expansion of the binomial (P + Q) raised to the Nth power.

```
      PROGRAM PASCAL
C  **  WE WRITE OUT SOME BINOMIAL COEFFICIENTS USING FUNCTION COMB.
      INTEGER PAS(15), NØ, RØ, J1

      DO 1ØØ NØ = 1, 12
        J1 = NØ + 1
        DO 5Ø RØ = 1, J1
          PAS( RØ ) = COMB( NØ-1, RØ-1 )
 5Ø     CONTINUE

        WRITE ( 5, 62 ) (PAS(J1), J1= 1, NØ)
 62          FORMAT ( ' ', 15I5 )
 1ØØ  CONTINUE

      END
```

**Program 11-14.** Pascal's triangle from binomial coefficients.

Looking at (P + Q)**N, we should be able to see the general term in the product. (P + Q)**N means, write (P + Q) as a factor N times. So

$$(P + Q){*}{*}N = (P + Q)(P + Q)(P + Q)\ldots(P + Q)$$

When we multiply this out, we are actually taking one term from each factor in such a way that we can sum up all possible products of combinations of factors, one from each (P + Q) factor. How many factors are there in the product? There is one term that takes P as a factor N times. There is one term that takes P as a factor N − 1 times and Q as a factor once. There also is a term that takes P as a factor N − 2 times and Q as a factor twice, and so on, down to the term that takes Q as a factor N times. That makes N + 1 terms. Now, for a particular term, say P**3*Q**(N − 3), we want three P's and N minus three Q's. We can select three P's from among N terms in $_{N}C_{3}$ ways and so the value of this term is $_{N}C_{3}$ * P**3 * Q**(N − 3). For the Rth term we get $_{N}C_{R}$ * P**R * Q**(N − R), which is exactly what we get for a probability of R successes in N trials where the probability of success on a single trial is P and the probability of failure on a single trial is Q. So to find (P + Q)**N we simply evaluate ${}_NC_R$ * P**R * Q**(N − R) for all values of R from 0 to N.

Taking a look at the probability of any binomial experiment, we see that since P + Q = 1 and the sum of all ${}_NC_R$ * P**R * Q**(N − R) terms is (P + Q)**N, we get

if P + Q = 1 then (P + Q)**N = 1

which can be verified for one example by summing up the probabilities in Program DICE1.

Finally, if we look at (X + Y)**N for X and Y both equal to 1, we get the general term of the expansion to be ${}_NC_R$ * 1**N * 1**(N − R), which simplifies to ${}_NC_R$. So that the numeric coefficients of any binomial expansion are simply the corresponding values of ${}_NC_R$. In the case where X and Y are both 1, we are really finding the value of 2**N, if we sum up all of the coefficients. See Program 11-14 named PASCAL.

```
[Begin execution]

  1
  1    1
  1    2    1
  1    3    3    1
  1    4    6    4    1
  1    5   10   10    5    1
  1    6   15   20   15    6    1
  1    7   21   35   35   21    7    1
  1    8   28   56   70   56   28    8    1
  1    9   36   84  126  126   84   36    9    1
  1   10   45  120  210  252  210  120   45   10    1
  1   11   55  165  330  462  462  330  165   55   11    1
```

**Fig. 11-13.** Execution of Program 11-14.

These coefficients (see Fig. 11-13) are the numbers of Pascal's triangle, which has many other interesting properties.

## Problems for Sec. 11-5

Most of these problems could use FUNCTION subprogram COMB.

1. Modify Program PASCAL to sum up the coefficients. Write the values of N in ${}_NC_R$ and the sum of the coefficients without the coefficients.
2. Modify Program DICE1 to sum up the individual probabilities.
3. Modify Program DICE1 to calculate probabilities using double-precision variables.
4. It is known that 1 percent of the population has a certain type of blood. In a group of twenty-five people, what is the probability that exactly two people have this blood type?

5. A company makes bolts. It is known that 1 in 1000 is defective. You buy a box of one hundred bolts. What is the probability of getting exactly one defective bolt?
6. For the company of problem 5, what is the probability of getting at least one defective bolt.
7. For the company of problem 5, what is the probability of getting less than five defective bolts?
8. For the company of problem 5, what is the probability of getting exactly ten defective bolts?
9. Write a program to produce all of the information requested in problems 5 through 8.
10. Find the probabilities of getting zero through six 1's when rolling six dice.
11. What is the probability of getting more heads than tails when flipping ten coins.
12. What is the probability of getting zero through ten heads when flipping ten coins.
13. A test consists of 25 true-false questions. You know that your probability of guessing right on any given question is 75 percent. Find the probability of getting 76 percent on the test, if you guess on all questions. Find your probability of getting 76 percent or better.

*14. An experiment consists of flipping a coin until it comes up heads. Find the probability of success for one to ten flips.

*15. An experiment consists of rolling a die until it comes up 1. Find the probability of success for one to ten rolls. Find the probability that success will require more than ten rolls; more than twenty rolls.

# Appendix A
# Table of FORTRAN-Supplied Functions

| Name | Function | Definition | Data Type | |
|---|---|---|---|---|
| | | | *Argument* | *Function* |
| IFIX | Type conversion | Conversion from Real to Integer | Real | Integer |
| FLOAT | | Conversion from Integer to Real | Integer | Real |
| SNGLE | | Conversion from Double to Real | Double | Real |
| DBLE | | Conversion from Real to Double | Real | Double |
| AINT | Truncation | Sign of a times | Real | Real |
| INT | | largest of integer | Real | Integer |
| IDINT | | <= \|a\| | Double | Integer |
| ABS | Absolute | \|a\| | Real | Real |
| IABS | value | | Integer | Integer |
| DABS | | | Double | Double |
| AMOD | Remaindering | a1 (mod a2) | Real | Real |
| MOD | | | Integer | Integer |
| DMOD | | | Double | Double |
| SIGN | Transfer | Sign of a2 times | Real | Real |
| ISIGN | of sign | \|a1\| | Integer | Integer |
| DSIGN | | | Double | Double |
| DIM | Positive | a1 − Min(a1,a2) | Real | Real |
| IDIM | difference | | Integer | Integer |
| AMAX0 | Choosing | Max( a1, a2,...) | Integer | Real |
| AMAX1 | largest | | Real | Real |
| MAX0 | value | | Integer | Integer |
| MAX1 | | | Real | Integer |
| DMAX1 | | | Double | Double |

| Name | Function | Definition | Data Type Argument | Data Type Function |
|---|---|---|---|---|
| AMIN0 | Choosing | Min( a1, a2,...) | Integer | Real |
| AMIN1 | smallest | | Real | Real |
| MIN0 | value | | Integer | Integer |
| MIN1 | | | Real | Integer |
| DMIN1 | | | Double | Double |
| SQRT | Square root | (a)**1/2 | Real | Real |
| DSQRT | | | Double | Double |
| EXP | Exponential | e**a | Real | Real |
| DEXP | | | Double | Double |
| ALOG | Natural | ln( a ) | Real | Real |
| DLOG | logarithm | | Double | Double |
| ALOG10 | Common | $\log_{10}$( a ) | Real | Real |
| DLOG10 | logarithm | | Double | Double |
| SIN | Sine | sin( a ) | Real | Real |
| DSIN | | | Double | Double |
| COS | Cosine | cos( a ) | Real | Real |
| DCOS | | | Double | Double |
| ATAN | Arctangent | arctan( a ) | Real | Real |
| DATAN | | | Double | Double |
| ATAN2 | | arctan( a1/a2 ) | Real | Real |
| DATAN2 | | | Double | Double |
| TANH | Hyperbolic tangent | tanh( a ) | Real | Real |

# Appendix B
# Index of Programs in Text

| *Program* | *Name* | *Description* |
|---|---|---|
| 1-1 | | My first FORTRAN program |
| 1-2 | | Writing a numeric value |
| 1-3 | | Introduce the READ statement |
| 1-4 | | Demonstrate repeat and slash in FORMAT |
| 1-5 | | Calculate a paycheck |
| 2-1 | | Directing the computer to count |
| 2-2 | | Counting from 1 to 7 |
| 4-5 | ABSVAL | FUNCTION subprogram returns absolute value |
| 5-5 | ALPHA | Processing the alphabet in an integer array |
| 3-11 | ARANG1 | Arrange a list of numbers in order |
| 5-4 | ARRAY | Demonstrating the subscript order in FORTRAN two-dimensional arrays |
| 3-6 | ARRAY1 | Demonstrate a subscripted variable |
| 11-7 | BIRTH | Find the probability of two people sharing birthdays from among thirty people |
| 3-5 | CMPD1 | Calculate compound interest for one year |
| 3-8 | CMPD2 | Calculate compound interest for several years |
| 11-3 | COMB | A FUNCTION to calculate the number of combinations of N things taken R at a time |
| 11-6 | COMITE | Calculate the probability that you are on a committee |
| 2-3 | COUNT1 | Counting with new features |
| 6-2 | COURS1 | Tabulating course selections |
| 6-3 | COURS2 | Tabulating course selections with two-dimensional array |
| 4-9 | CVT1 | SUBROUTINE converts inches |
| 7-4 | DECBIN | Convert decimal to binary |
| 11-11 | DICE | Calculate the probability that exactly two 1's come up when rolling ten dice |
| 11-12 | DICE1 | Probabilities for 0 to 10 1's when rolling ten dice |
| 7-1 | DIGIT1 | Print numeric digits separately |
| 7-3 | DIGIT2 | Program 7-1 with SUBROUTINE CALL to IENTER |

| *Program* | *Name* | *Description* |
|---|---|---|
| 3-2 | DOLIKE | Using a DO loop for Program LIKE |
| 5-1 | DOUBLE | Demonstrate precision limits |
| 4-2 | FACTOR | Find largest factor |
| 11-8 | FLIP | Flip a coin 50 times |
| 11-9 | FLIP1 | Flipping 50 coins ten times |
| 6-6 | FREAD | Read a data file and write the data on paper |
| 4-1 | FUNCT1 | Demonstrate ABS, SQRT, and AINT |
| 4-3 | FUNCT2 | Demonstrate MOD, MIN0, and MAX0 |
| 6-5 | FWRITE | Write data to an external data file |
| 8-6 | GRAPH1 | Graphing from data in a two-dimensional array |
| 7-6 | HEXCVT | Convert hex to base ten |
| 7-5 | HEXIO | Demonstrate hex input/output |
| 7-2 | IENTER | A SUBROUTINE to request an integer |
| 5-2 | IMPDO1 | Demonstrate implied DOs |
| 5-3 | IMPDO2 | Combining implied DOs with explicit DOs |
| 4-7 | IPRIME | FUNCTION subprogram finds smallest prime factor |
| 9-2 | LADDER | Finding the distance between the foot of a ladder and a building |
| 3-7 | LARGE | Find largest element in an array |
| 9-4 | LAWSIN | Demonstrating the Law of Sines |
| 11-13 | LEFT | Calculate the probability of 10 left-handed people selected from 100 |
| 3-1 | LIKE | Write "I LIKE FORTRAN" 9 times |
| 11-2 | NPR | Calculate the number of permutations of N things taken R at a time |
| 3-3 | ODD | WRITE odd integers from 1 to 7 |
| 11-14 | PASCAL | Pascal's triangle from binomial coefficients |
| 10-4 | PENTER | A SUBROUTINE to enter polynomial coefficients |
| 11-1 | PERMUT | Write all permutations of the letters of the word FLAG |
| 8-2 | PLOT1 | Simple plotting demonstration |
| 8-3 | PLOT2 | Our first graph of a quadratic function |
| 8-4 | PLOT3 | Plotting with axes printed |
| 9-5 | POLAR | Printing polar coordinates |
| 10-5 | PVALUE | A FUNCTION subprogram evaluates polynomials |
| 3-10 | PYTHAG | Search for Pythagorean triples |
| 10-3 | ROOT1 | Find integral roots of a third-degree polynomial |
| 10-6 | ROOT2 | Program ROOT1 using SUBROUTINE subprogram PENTER and FUNCTION subprogram PVALUE |

# Appendix C
# Z80 Random Number Function

While many computer programming language facilities include the ability to generate random numbers, most FORTRANs do not. You may be using a FORTRAN that does supply a random number generating function, in which case you need only determine how it is to be applied. There are several other ways you can provide yourself with a source of random numbers. If you are working on a computer with a BASIC language that has a random number generator, you may be able to write a couple of thousand random numbers to an external data file, which you can read in any FORTRAN program that requires random numbers. You might write an assembly language function to generate random numbers and call it from FORTRAN programs. Or you might use an assembly language function that someone else has written.

One such function has been written by Alan R. Miller, New Mexico Tech, Socorro, NM 87801, for an 8080 CPU. That function has been translated for a Z80 CPU and is included here for your convenience.[1] You must produce relocatable binary code according to the method used by your computer. In any case, computer generated random numbers are not truly random and so are referred to as *pseudo random numbers*. Most computer routines for generating random numbers will generate the same set of random numbers for successive identical executions of the same program. Imagine playing the same game of Star Wars over and over again. Various methods may be used to overcome this.

The random number function written by Alan R. Miller requires an argument that specifies how many random numbers to skip before returning a value to the calling program. This random number function is invoked in a FORTRAN program with a statement such as

X = RND( K1 )

where K1 is the number of selections the function will pass over before returning a real value between 0 and 1 to the calling program. To produce a different sequence of random numbers on successive executions, simply request some data value in the calling program from an external source that may be used to establish the argument of the function.

---

[1] Alan R. Miller, "Microsoft Fortran for CP/M," *Interface Age,* March 1979, Volume 4, Issue 3, p. 176. Reprinted by permission of *Interface Age* magazine.)

```
CROMEMCO CDOS Z8Ø ASSEMBLER version Ø2.15                PAGE ØØØ1

              ;RND: A FORTRAN-CALLABLE FUNCTION
              ;      TO GENERATE A RANDOM
              ;      NUMBER FROM Ø TO 1
              ;
              ; METHOD: ELECTRONICS, OCT. 12, 1978
              ; USAGE:  X = RND(NPASS)
              ;  NPASS IS THE NUMBER OF TIMES TO SKIP
              ;
              ; PROGRAMMED BY ALAN R. MILLER
              ; NEW MEXICO TECH, SOCORRO 878Ø1
              ;
              ; TRANSLATED FROM 8Ø8Ø MNEMONICS
              ;                TO Z8Ø  MNEMONICS
              ; USING CROMEMCO'S PROGRAM TRANSLAT
              ;
```

```
CROMEMCO CDOS Z8Ø ASSEMBLER version Ø2.15                PAGE ØØØ2
RANDOM-NUMBER GENERATOR

              ;
                       EXT     $AC,$MA,$SA
                       ENTRY   RND
              ;
ØØØØ' Ø6Ø1    RND:     LD      B,1          ;SET FOR ONE PASS
ØØØ2' 7E               LD      A,(HL)       ;GET ARGUMENT
ØØØ3' E6ØF             AND     ØFH          ;TAKE 4 BITS
ØØØ5' CAØ9ØØ'          JP      Z,NEXTN      ;CHANGE Ø TO 1
ØØØ8' 47               LD      B,A
ØØØ9' 2A49ØØ' NEXTN:   LD      HL,(WORD2)   ;HIGH 2 BYTES
ØØØC' EB               EX      DE,HL        ;PUT IN D,E
ØØØD' 2A47ØØ'          LD      HL,(WORD1)   ;LOW 2 BYTES
ØØ1Ø' 29               ADD     HL,HL        ;SHIFT LEFT
ØØ11' 7B               LD      A,E
ØØ12' 17               RLA                  ;SHIFT LEFT
ØØ13' 5F               LD      E,A
ØØ14' AD               XOR     L            ;FEEDBACK
ØØ15' F219ØØ'          JP      P,SKIP
ØØ18' 23               INC     HL
ØØ19' 2247ØØ' SKIP:    LD      (WORD1),HL   ;HIGH 1 BYTES
ØØ1C' EB               EX      DE,HL
ØØ1D' 2249ØØ'          LD      (WORD2),HL   ;HIGH 2 BYTES
ØØ2Ø' Ø5               DEC     B            ;COUNT
ØØ21' C2Ø9ØØ'          JP      NZ,NEXTN     ;DO IT AGAIN
ØØ24' 21ØØØØ#          LD      HL,$AC       ;POINT TO FAC
ØØ27' 3A47ØØ'          LD      A,(B1)       ;LOW BYTE
ØØ2A' 77               LD      (HL),A       ;PUT IN FAC
ØØ2B' 23               INC     HL
ØØ2C' 3A48ØØ'          LD      A,(B2)       ;SECOND BYTE
ØØ2F' 77               LD      (HL),A
ØØ3Ø' 23               INC     HL
ØØ31' 3A49ØØ'          LD      A,(B3)
ØØ34' E67F             AND     7FH          ;BIT 7 PLUS
ØØ36' 77               LD      (HL),A       ;PUT INTO FAC
ØØ37' 23               INC     HL
ØØ38' 368Ø             LD      (HL),8ØH     ;SET EXPONENT
ØØ3A' 21Ø2ØØ           LD      HL,2
ØØ3D' CDØØØØ#          CALL    $MA          ;TIMES 2
```

```
ØØ4Ø' 21Ø1ØØ                  LD      HL,1
ØØ43' CDØØØØ#                 CALL    $SA         ;SUBTR 1
ØØ46' C9                      RET
                    ;
                    WORD1:
ØØ47' ØD            B1:       DEFB    ØDH
ØØ48' B1            B2:       DEFB    ØB1H
                    WORD2:
ØØ49' 9B            B3:       DEFB    9BH
ØØ4A' 8Ø            B4:       DEFB    8ØH
ØØ4B' (ØØØØ)                  END

Errors              Ø

Program Length  ØØ4B (75)
```

# Appendix D
# Answers to
# Even-Numbered Problems

# Appendix D
# Answers to Even-Numbered Problems

Each two-page spread should be read from top to bottom as one individual page.

**Chap. 1**

***Problem No. 2***

```
      KSUM = 1 + 2 + 3 + 4 + 5 + 6 + 7 + 8 + 9 + 10

      WRITE ( 5, 12 ) KSUM
12       FORMAT ( 37H THE SUM OF INTEGERS FROM 1 TO 10 IS , I5 )

      END
```

***Problem No. 4***

```
      PRODCT = 1.0 * 2.0 * 3.0 * 4.0 * 5.0 *
     +         6.0 * 7.0 * 8.0 * 9.0 * 10.0

      WRITE ( 5, 12 ) PRODCT
12       FORMAT ( 41H THE PRODUCT OF INTEGERS FROM 1 TO 10 IS , F8.0 )

      END

[BEGIN EXECUTION]

THE PRODUCT OF INTEGERS FROM 1 TO 10 IS 3628800.
```

***Problem No. 6***

```
C  **  CALCULATE GAS 'KILOMETERAGE'

      DIST   = 129.0
      GASAHL = 20.0
```

```
      INUM = N1 * ID2  +  N2 * ID1
      IDEN = ID1 * ID2

      WRITE ( 5, 42 ) INUM, IDEN
42       FORMAT ( 12H THE SUM IS , I7, 3H / , I7 )

922   FORMAT ( 2I5 )

      END

[BEGIN EXECUTION]

ADDING TWO FRACTIONS

 FIRST FRACTION: NUM, DENOM ? 1,2
SECOND FRACTION: NUM, DENOM ? 3,4

THE SUM IS      10 /      8
```

***Problem No. 12***

```
C  **  PRINTING TRINOMIAL COEFFICIENTS FROM
C  **    BINOMIAL COEFFICIENTS

10    WRITE ( 5, 12 )
12       FORMAT ( 31H ENTER BINOMIAL COEFFICIENTS ? , )
      READ ( 5, 22 ) IA, IB, IC, ID
```

```
      PRICE  = 31.9

      RATE = DIST / GASAHL
      WRITE ( 5, 12 ) RATE
12       FORMAT ( 1H , F5.2, 21H KILOMETERS PER LITER )

      COST = PRICE / RATE
      WRITE ( 5, 22 ) COST
22       FORMAT ( 1H , F5.2, 20H CENTS PER KILOMETER )

      END
```

```
[BEGIN EXECUTION]

 6.45 KILOMETERS PER LITER
 4.95 CENTS PER KILOMETER
```

***Problem No. 8***

```
C  **  LOOKING AT REAL AND INTEGER DIVISION

      DIVSON = 2.0 / 3.0
      IDIVDE =   2 / 3

      WRITE ( 5, 12 ) DIVSON
12       FORMAT ( 33H    REAL DIVISION:  2.0 / 3.0 IS , F8.6 )

      WRITE ( 5, 14 ) IDIVDE
14       FORMAT ( 33H INTEGER DIVISION:    2 / 3   IS , I8 )

      END
```

```
[BEGIN EXECUTION]

   REAL DIVISION:  2.0 / 3.0 IS  .666667
INTEGER DIVISION:    2 / 3   IS        0
```

***Problem No. 10***

```
      WRITE ( 5, 12 )
12       FORMAT ( 21H ADDING TWO FRACTIONS )

      WRITE ( 5, 22 )
22       FORMAT ( 31H0 FIRST FRACTION: NUM, DENOM ? )
      READ ( 5, 922 ) N1, ID1
      WRITE ( 5, 32 )
32       FORMAT ( 31H+SECOND FRACTION: NUM, DENOM ? )
      READ ( 5, 922 ) N2, ID2
22       FORMAT ( 4I5 )

      ICOEFA = IA * IC
      ICOEFB = IA * ID  +  IB * IC
      ICOEFC = IB * ID

      WRITE ( 5, 32 ) ICOEFA, ICOEFB, ICOEFC
32       FORMAT ( 21H TRINOMIAL PRODUCT = , 3I6 )

      END
```

## Chap. 2

***Problem No. 2***

```
C  **  WE FIND THE SUM OF THE ODD INTEGERS FROM 1 TO 100

      INTEGER ODD, SUM

      SUM = 0
      ODD = 1

20    SUM = SUM + ODD
      ODD = ODD + 2
      IF ( ODD .LE. 100 ) GO TO 20

40    WRITE ( 5, 42 ) SUM
42       FORMAT ( ' ', 'THE SUM IS', I6 )

      END
```

```
[BEGIN EXECUTION]

THE SUM IS  2500
```

***Problem No. 4***

```
C  **  FIND THE NUMBER OF ODD INTEGERS FROM 5 TO 1191 INCLUSIVE

      INTEGER COUNT, ODD

      COUNT = 0
      ODD   = 5

20    COUNT = COUNT + 1
      ODD   = ODD + 2
      IF ( ODD .LE. 1191 )  GOTO 20

40    WRITE ( 5, 42 ) COUNT
```

**Chap. 2 (*Problem No. 4 cont'd*)**

```
 42      FORMAT ( ' ', 'ODD INTEGERS FROM 5 TO 1191 NUMBER', I4 )

      END
```

```
[BEGIN EXECUTION]

ODD INTEGERS FROM 5 TO 1191 NUMBER 594
```

***Problem No. 6***

```
C  **  CALCULATE AREA OF TRIANGLES.

      REAL ALTUDE, BASE

 1Ø   WRITE ( 5, 12 )
 12      FORMAT ( ' ', 'ENTER ALTITUDE AND BASE OF A TRIANGLE' /
     +            ' ', 'ENTER ''Ø.Ø,Ø.Ø'' TO QUIT' / )

 11Ø  WRITE ( 5, 112 )
 112     FORMAT ( 'Ø', 'ALTITUDE, BASE ? ' )
      READ ( 5, 114 ) ALTUDE, BASE
 114     FORMAT ( 2F6.2 )
      IF ( ALTUDE .EQ. Ø.Ø )  GO TO  999

       AREA = ALTUDE * BASE / 2.Ø

       WRITE ( 5, 212 ) AREA
 212      FORMAT ( '+', 'AREA = ', F8.2 )
       GO TO 11Ø

 999  END
```

```
[BEGIN EXECUTION]

ENTER ALTITUDE AND BASE OF A TRIANGLE
ENTER 'Ø.Ø,Ø.Ø' TO QUIT


ALTITUDE, BASE ? 1Ø.Ø,21.Ø
AREA =   1Ø5.ØØ

ALTITUDE, BASE ? 12.5,8.Ø
AREA =    5Ø.ØØ

ALTITUDE, BASE ? 289.Ø,114.Ø
```

***Problem No. 10***

```
C  **  COMPOUND INTEREST DAILY AND QUARTERLY

      INTEGER DAY, QUARTR
      REAL  AMOUNT, RATE

      WRITE ( 5, 12 )
 12      FORMAT ( ' ', 'CALCULATE INTEREST ON $1ØØ.ØØ',
     +                 ' AT 5% PER YEAR.' / )

C  **  DO QUARTERLY INTEREST
      RATE   = Ø.Ø5 / 4.Ø
      AMOUNT = 1ØØ.Ø
      QUARTR = 1

 2Ø   AMOUNT = AMOUNT + RATE * AMOUNT
      QUARTR = QUARTR + 1
      IF ( QUARTR .LE. 4 ) GO TO 2Ø

 4Ø   WRITE ( 5, 42 ) AMOUNT
 42      FORMAT ( ' ', 'COMPOUNDED QUARTERLY YIELDS $', F8.2 )

C  **  DO DAILY INTEREST
      RATE   = Ø.Ø5 / 365.Ø
      AMOUNT = 1ØØ.Ø
      DAY    = 1

 6Ø   AMOUNT = AMOUNT + RATE * AMOUNT
      DAY    = DAY + 1
      IF ( DAY .LE. 365 ) GO TO 6Ø

 8Ø   WRITE ( 5, 82 ) AMOUNT
 82      FORMAT ( ' ', '    COMPOUNDED DAILY YIELDS $', F8.2 )

      END
```

```
[BEGIN EXECUTION]

CALCULATE INTEREST ON $1ØØ.ØØ AT 5% PER YEAR.

COMPOUNDED QUARTERLY YIELDS $  1Ø5.Ø9
    COMPOUNDED DAILY YIELDS $  1Ø5.13
```

***Problem No. 12***

```
     INTEGER DAY, GIFTS, TODAY, SUBTOT

     WRITE ( 5, 92 )
```

```
AREA = 16473.ØØ

ALTITUDE, BASE ? Ø.Ø,Ø.Ø
```

***Problem No. 8***

```
C  **  PRINTING INTEGERS AND THEIR RECIPROCALS

      INTEGER  INTGER
      REAL     INVERS

      INTGER = 1

 3Ø   INVERS = 1.Ø / FLOAT( INTGER )
      WRITE ( 5, 32 ) INTGER, INVERS
 32      FORMAT ( ' ', I4, F9.6 )
      INTGER = INTGER + 1
      IF ( INTGER .LE. 25 ) GO TO 3Ø

      END

[BEGIN EXECUTION]

   1 1.ØØØØØØ
   2  .5ØØØØØ
   3  .333333
   4  .25ØØØØ
   5  .2ØØØØØ
   6  .166667
   7  .142857
   8  .125ØØØ
   9  .111111
  1Ø  .1ØØØØØ
  11  .Ø9Ø9Ø9
  12  .Ø83333
  13  .Ø76923
  14  .Ø71429
  15  .Ø66667
  16  .Ø625ØØ
  17  .Ø58824
  18  .Ø55556
  19  .Ø52632
  2Ø  .Ø5ØØØØ
  21  .Ø47619
  22  .Ø45455
  23  .Ø43478
  24  .Ø41667
  25  .Ø4ØØØØ
```



```
92       FORMAT ( ' ', '      DAY   TODAY TO DATE' )
      GIFTS  = Ø
      DAY    = 1

1Ø    TODAY  = Ø
      SUBTOT = Ø

2Ø    TODAY  = TODAY + 1
      SUBTOT = SUBTOT + TODAY
      GIFTS  = GIFTS + TODAY
      IF ( TODAY .LT. DAY ) GO TO 2Ø

      WRITE ( 5, 32 ) DAY, SUBTOT, GIFTS
32       FORMAT ( ' ', 3I8 )
      DAY = DAY + 1
      IF ( DAY .LE. 12 ) GO TO 1Ø

      END

[BEGIN EXECUTION]

     DAY   TODAY TO DATE
       1       1       1
       2       3       4
       3       6      1Ø
       4      1Ø      2Ø
       5      15      35
       6      21      56
       7      28      84
       8      36     12Ø
       9      45     165
      1Ø      55     22Ø
      11      66     286
      12      78     364
```

# Chap. 3

## Sec. 3-1

***Problem No. 2***

```
C  **  FIRST WE MUST KNOW THAT 1ØØ1 IS THE INTEGER TO START WITH.

      INTEGER COUNT, NUMBER
      REAL  SUM

      SUM    = Ø.Ø
      NUMBER = Ø
```

**Sec. 3-1 (*Problem No. 2 cont'd*)**

```
      DO 40 COUNT = 1001, 2213, 11
        NUMBER = NUMBER + 1
        SUM    = SUM + FLOAT( COUNT )
 40   CONTINUE

      WRITE ( 5, 52 ) NUMBER, SUM
 52      FORMAT ( ' ', 'FROM 1000 TO 2213 DIVISIBLE BY 11' /
     +            ' ', ' THE NUMBER OF NUMBERS IS ', I7 /
     +            ' ', 'THE SUM OF THE NUMBERS IS ', F8.0 )

      END

[BEGIN EXECUTION]

FROM 1000 TO 2213 DIVISIBLE BY 11
 THE NUMBER OF NUMBERS IS      111
THE SUM OF THE NUMBERS IS  178266.
```

***Problem No. 4***

```
      INTEGER NUMBER
      REAL RECIP

      WRITE ( 5, 12 )
 12      FORMAT ( ' ', 'NUMBER RECIPROCAL' )

      DO 90 NUMBER = 75, 100
        RECIP = 1.0 / FLOAT( NUMBER )
        WRITE ( 5, 42 ) NUMBER, RECIP
 42        FORMAT ( ' ', I6, 3X, F8.6 )
 90   CONTINUE

      END

[BEGIN EXECUTION]

NUMBER RECIPROCAL
    75    .013333
    76    .013158
    77    .012987
    78    .012821
    79    .012658
    80    .012500
    81    .012346
    82    .012195
    83    .012048
```

```
 90   CONTINUE

      WRITE ( 5, 102 ) SUM
 102     FORMAT ( ' ', 'THE SUM OF THE SQUARES OF RECIPROCALS' /
     +            ' ', 'FROM 1 TO 1000 IS ',  F8.6 )

      END

[BEGIN EXECUTION]

THE SUM OF THE SQUARES OF RECIPROCALS
FROM 1 TO 1000 IS 1.643935
```

**Sec. 3-2**

***Problem No. 2***

```
C  **  FIND LARGEST NUMBER AND LOCATION

      INTEGER ARRAY(10), INDEX, LARGE, SAVE, PLACE

      DATA  ARRAY/ 17, 18, 281, -722, 0, -5, -16, 11, -1, 10/

      LARGE = ARRAY(1)
      PLACE = 1

      DO 90 INDEX = 2, 10
        IF ( ARRAY( INDEX ) .LE. LARGE )  GO TO 90
          PLACE = INDEX
          LARGE = ARRAY( PLACE )
 90   CONTINUE

      WRITE ( 5, 102 ) LARGE, PLACE
 102     FORMAT ( ' ', 'LARGEST NUMBER IS', I6 /
     +            ' ', '      IN POSITION', I6 )

      SAVE         = ARRAY(1)
      ARRAY(1)     = ARRAY(PLACE)
      ARRAY(PLACE) = SAVE

      WRITE ( 5, 112 ) ARRAY
 112     FORMAT ( '0', 'AFTER EXCHANGE' /
     +            ' ', 10I5 )

      END
```

```
 84    .Ø119Ø5
 85    .Ø11765
 86    .Ø11628
 87    .Ø11494
 88    .Ø11364
 89    .Ø11236
 9Ø    .Ø11111
 91    .Ø1Ø989
 92    .Ø1Ø87Ø
 93    .Ø1Ø753
 94    .Ø1Ø638
 95    .Ø1Ø526
 96    .Ø1Ø417
 97    .Ø1Ø3Ø9
 98    .Ø1Ø2Ø4
 99    .Ø1Ø1Ø1
1ØØ    .Ø1ØØØØ
```

***Problem No. 6***

```
      INTEGER NUMBER
      REAL SUM

      SUM = Ø.Ø

      DO 9Ø NUMBER = 9ØØ, 1ØØØ
        SUM    = SUM + FLOAT( NUMBER )
9Ø    CONTINUE

      WRITE ( 5, 1Ø2 ) SUM
1Ø2       FORMAT ( ' ', 'THE SUM OF THE INTEGERS FROM'
     +           ' 9ØØ TO 1ØØØ IS ', F8.Ø )

      END
```

```
[BEGIN EXECUTION]

THE SUM OF THE INTEGERS FROM 9ØØ TO 1ØØØ IS    9595Ø.
```

***Problem No. 8***

```
      INTEGER NUMBER
      REAL RECIP, SUM

      DO 9Ø NUMBER = 1, 1ØØØ
        RECIP = 1.Ø / FLOAT( NUMBER )
        SUM   = SUM + RECIP**2
```

```
[BEGIN EXECUTION]

LARGEST NUMBER IS    281
      IN POSITION      3

AFTER EXCHANGE
  281   18   17 -722    Ø   -5  -16   11   -1   1Ø
```

***Problem No. 4***

```
C  **  GENERATE FIBONACCI NUMBERS
C  **   NOTE THAT TO GO PAST THE 23RD FIBONACCI NUMBER
C  **    A REAL ARRAY WILL BE REQUIRED.

      INTEGER FIB(2Ø), INDEX

      FIB(1) = 1
      FIB(2) = 1

      DO 9Ø INDEX = 3, 2Ø
        FIB( INDEX ) = FIB( INDEX-1 ) + FIB( INDEX-2 )
 9Ø   CONTINUE

      WRITE ( 5, 1Ø2 ) FIB
 1Ø2      FORMAT ( ' ', 'FIBONACCI NUMBERS' /
     +             2( ' ', 1ØI6 / ) )

      END
```

```
[BEGIN EXECUTION]

FIBONACCI NUMBERS
     1     1     2     3     5     8    13    21    34    55
    89   144   233   377   61Ø   987  1597  2584  4181  6765
```

***Problem No. 6***

```
C  **  ADDING CORRESPONDNG ELEMENTS OF TWO ARRAYS

      INTEGER FIRST(6), SECOND(6), THIRD(6), INDEX

      DATA FIRST/ 6, 1, 3, 7, 2, 9/
     +    SECOND/ 8, 2, 3, 9, 7, 4/

      DO 35 INDEX = 1, 6
        THIRD( INDEX ) = FIRST( INDEX ) + SECOND( INDEX )
 35   CONTINUE
```

**Sec. 3-2 (*Problem No. 6 cont'd*)**

```
      WRITE ( 5, 52 ) THIRD
 52      FORMAT ( ' ', 6I3 )

      END
```

```
[BEGIN EXECUTION]

 14  3  6 16  9 13
```

### *Problem No. 8*

```
C  **  ADDING CORRESPONDING ELEMENTS OF TWO ARRAYS WITH CARRY

       INTEGER FIRST(1Ø), SECOND(1Ø), SUM(1Ø), INDEX, J1

      DATA FIRST / Ø, 6, 1, 3, 7, 2, 3, 1, 4, 9/
     +     SECOND/ Ø, 8, 2, 3, 9, 7, 4, 1, 2, 4/

      DO 3Ø INDEX = 1, 1Ø
        SUM( INDEX ) = FIRST( INDEX ) + SECOND( INDEX )
 3Ø   CONTINUE

      DO 4Ø INDEX = 1, 9
        J1 = 11 - INDEX
        IF ( SUM( J1 ) .LT. 1Ø ) GO TO 4Ø
         SUM( J1 )     = SUM( J1 ) - 1Ø
         SUM( J1 - 1 ) = SUM( J1 - 1 ) + 1
 4Ø   CONTINUE

      WRITE ( 5, 62 ) FIRST, SECOND, SUM
 62      FORMAT ( ' ', 1ØI1 )

      WRITE ( 5, 72 )
 72      FORMAT ( 'Ø', 'WE HAVE ADDED TWO NINE DIGIT INTEGERS' )

      END
```

```
[BEGIN EXECUTION]

Ø613723149
Ø823974124
1437697273

WE HAVE ADDED TWO NINE DIGIT INTEGERS
```

```
 51   16
 17   51
 17   12
 17   11
 17   16
```

### *Problem No. 4*

```
C  **  CREATE AN ARRAY CONTAINING
C  **   VALUES FOUND IN TWO OTHER ARRAYS

      INTEGER ONE(7), TWO(7), THREE(7), INDEX1, INDEX2, COUNT

      DATA  ONE/ 1, 6, 11, 71, 32, 89, 21/
     +      TWO/ 1, 26, 6, 93, 71, 2, 7/

      WRITE ( 5, 12 ) ONE, TWO
 12      FORMAT ( ' ', 14X, 'TWO ARRAYS' /
     +         2( ' ', 7I5 / )  )

      COUNT = Ø

      DO 1ØØ INDEX1 = 1, 7
        DO 9Ø INDEX2 = 1, 7
          IF ( ONE( INDEX1 ) .NE. TWO( INDEX2 ) )  GO TO 9Ø
           COUNT = COUNT + 1
           THREE( COUNT ) = ONE( INDEX1 )
 9Ø     CONTINUE
 1ØØ  CONTINUE

      WRITE ( 5, 112 ) COUNT
 112     FORMAT ( ' ', 'THE NUMBER OF DUPLICATES IS ', I1 )

C  **  WE MAKE SURE THAT THERE ARE VALUES TO WRITE OUT
      IF ( COUNT .EQ. Ø )  GO TO 999
       DO 15Ø INDEX1 = 1, COUNT
         WRITE ( 5, 122 ) THREE(INDEX1)
 122        FORMAT ( ' ', I5 )
 15Ø   CONTINUE

 999  END
```

```
[BEGIN EXECUTION]

                TWO ARRAYS
    1    6   11   71   32   89   21
```

## Sec. 3-3

### *Problem No. 2*

```
C  **  WRITE ALL UNEQUAL PAIRS OF ELEMENTS FROM TWO ARRAYS

      INTEGER ONE(5), TWO(4), INDX1, INDX2

      DATA  ONE/ 6, 4, 11, 51, 17/
     +      TWO/ 51, 12, 11, 16/

      WRITE ( 5, 12 ) ONE, TWO
 12      FORMAT ( ' ', 'TWO ARRAYS' /
     +            ' ', 5I5 /
     +            ' ', 4I5 //
     +            ' ', 'ALL UNEQUAL PAIRS OF ELEMENTS' )

      DO 8Ø INDX1 = 1, 5
        DO 7Ø INDX2 = 1, 4
          IF ( ONE(INDX1) .EQ. TWO(INDX2) )  GO TO 7Ø
           WRITE ( 5, 32 ) ONE(INDX1), TWO(INDX2)
 32           FORMAT ( ' ', 2I5 )
 7Ø     CONTINUE
 8Ø   CONTINUE

      END

[BEGIN EXECUTION]

 TWO ARRAYS
    6    4   11   51   17
   51   12   11   16

 ALL UNEQUAL PAIRS OF ELEMENTS
    6   51
    6   12
    6   11
    6   16
    4   51
    4   12
    4   11
    4   16
   11   51
   11   12
   11   16
   51   12
   51   11
```

```
    1   26    6   93   71    2    7

THE NUMBER OF DUPLICATES IS 3
    1
    6
   71
```

### *Problem No. 6*

```
C  **  EXTEND THE RANGE FOR PYTHAGOREAN TRIPLES

      INTEGER LEG1, LEG2, HYPOT, K1, K3

      DO 4Ø LEG1 = 1, 25
        DO 3Ø LEG2 = LEG1, 1ØØ
          DO 2Ø HYPOT = LEG2, 125
            K1 = LEG1*LEG1 + LEG2*LEG2
            K3 = HYPOT*HYPOT
            IF ( K3 .GT. K1 )  GO TO 3Ø
             IF ( K3 .LT. K1 )  GO TO 2Ø
              WRITE ( 5, 12 ) LEG1, LEG2, HYPOT
 12              FORMAT ( ' ', 3I5 )
              GO TO 3Ø
 2Ø       CONTINUE
 3Ø     CONTINUE
 4Ø   CONTINUE

      END

[BEGIN EXECUTION]

    3    4    5
    5   12   13
    6    8   1Ø
    7   24   25
    8   15   17
    9   12   15
    9   4Ø   41
   1Ø   24   26
   11   6Ø   61
   12   16   2Ø
   12   35   37
   13   84   85
   14   48   5Ø
   15   2Ø   25
   15   36   39
   16   3Ø   34
```

**Sec. 3-3** ***(Problem No. 6 cont'd)***

```
 16   63   65
 18   24   3Ø
 18   8Ø   82
 2Ø   21   29
 2Ø   48   52
 2Ø   99  1Ø1
 21   28   35
 21   72   75
 24   32   4Ø
 24   45   51
 24   7Ø   74
 25   6Ø   65
```

## Sec. 3-4

### *Problem No. 2*

```
C  **  DO NOT PRINT DUPLICATES AFTER ARRANGING IN INCRESING ORDER

      DIMENSION ARRAY(5)
      INTEGER   ARRAY, LAST, NUMBER, FIRST, BEGIN, SECOND, SAVE
      DATA ARRAY/ 45, 76, -76, 45, 98/
     +    NUMBER/ 5/

      WRITE ( 5, 12 )
 12      FORMAT ( ' ', 'ORIGINAL ORDER' )
      WRITE ( 5, 22 ) ARRAY
 22      FORMAT ( ' ', 1ØI5 )

      LAST = NUMBER - 1
      DO 2ØØ FIRST = 1, LAST
        BEGIN = FIRST + 1
        DO 1ØØ SECOND = BEGIN, NUMBER
          IF ( ARRAY( FIRST ) .LE. ARRAY( SECOND ) ) GO TO 1ØØ
           SAVE           = ARRAY( FIRST )
           ARRAY( FIRST )  = ARRAY( SECOND )
           ARRAY( SECOND ) = SAVE
 1ØØ    CONTINUE
 2ØØ  CONTINUE

      WRITE ( 5, 3Ø2 )
 3Ø2     FORMAT ( ' ', 'THE LIST IN INCREASING ORDER' )
      WRITE ( 5, 952 ) ARRAY(1)
      DO 32Ø FIRST = 2, 5
        IF ( ARRAY( FIRST ) .EQ. ARRAY( FIRST - 1 ) )  GO TO 32Ø
         WRITE ( 5, 952 ) ARRAY( FIRST )
```

```
 3Ø2     FORMAT ( ' ', 'THE LIST IN INCREASING ORDER' )
      WRITE ( 5, 944 ) ARRAY, POSN

 944     FORMAT ( ' ', 11I5 )

      END

[BEGIN EXECUTION]

ORIGINAL ORDER
    1   92 -981   89  -21    Ø -111  111   92 -929 1ØØ1
    1    2    3    4    5    6    7    8    9   1Ø   11
THE LIST IN INCREASING ORDER
 -981 -929 -111  -21    Ø    1   89   92   92  111 1ØØ1
    3   1Ø    7    5    6    1    4    9    2    8   11
```

# Chap. 4

## Sec. 4-1

### *Problem No. 2*

```
C  **  WE MODIFY PROGRAM FACTOR

      INTEGER INDEX, NUMBER, N1, FACTOR
      REAL    DIVIDE, FNUM

 1Ø   WRITE ( 5, 12 )
 12      FORMAT ( 'Ø', 'ENTER AN INTEGER ' )
      READ ( 5, 22 ) NUMBER
 22      FORMAT ( I5 )
      IF ( NUMBER .EQ. Ø ) STOP
      FNUM = FLOAT ( NUMBER )

C  **  WE TEST FROM TWO TO THE SQUARE ROOT OF NUMBER
      N1 = INT( SQRT(FNUM) )
      DO 1ØØ INDEX = 2, N1
        DIVIDE = FNUM / FLOAT( INDEX )
        IF ( DIVIDE .EQ. AINT( DIVIDE ) ) GO TO 3ØØ
 1ØØ  CONTINUE

      WRITE ( 5, 112 )
 112     FORMAT ( '+', ' IS PRIME ' )
      GO TO 1Ø

 3ØØ  FACTOR = INT( DIVIDE )
```

```
320  CONTINUE

952     FORMAT ( ' ', I4 )

     END
```

```
[BEGIN EXECUTION]

ORIGINAL ORDER
   45   76  -76   45   98
THE LIST IN INCREASING ORDER
 -76
  45
  76
  98
```

### Problem No. 4

```
C  **  ARRANGING IN INCREASING ORDER
C  **   KEEPING TRACK OF THE ORIGINAL POSITION OF EACH ELEMENT

      DIMENSION ARRAY(11), POSN(11)
      INTEGER   ARRAY, LAST, NUMBER, FIRST, BEGIN, SECOND, SAVE,
     +    POSN

      DATA ARRAY/ 1, 92, -981, 89, -21, 0, -111, 111, 92, -929, 1001/
     +      POSN/ 1, 2, 3, 4, 5, 6, 7, 8, 9, 10, 11/
     +    NUMBER/ 11/

     WRITE ( 5, 12 )
 12     FORMAT ( ' ', 'ORIGINAL ORDER' )
     WRITE ( 5, 944 ) ARRAY, POSN

     LAST = NUMBER - 1
     DO 200 FIRST = 1, LAST
       BEGIN = FIRST + 1
       DO 100 SECOND = BEGIN, NUMBER
         IF ( ARRAY( FIRST ) .LE. ARRAY( SECOND ) ) GO TO 100
          SAVE              = ARRAY( FIRST )
          ARRAY( FIRST )  = ARRAY( SECOND )
          ARRAY( SECOND ) = SAVE
            SAVE             = POSN( FIRST )
            POSN( FIRST )  = POSN( SECOND )
            POSN( SECOND ) = SAVE
100    CONTINUE
200  CONTINUE

     WRITE ( 5, 302 )
```

```
     WRITE ( 5, 312 ) FACTOR
312     FORMAT ( '+', 'LARGEST FACTOR: ', I5 )
     GO TO 10

     END
```

```
[BEGIN EXECUTION]

ENTER AN INTEGER 336
LARGEST FACTOR:   168

ENTER AN INTEGER 32707
 IS PRIME

ENTER AN INTEGER 1001
LARGEST FACTOR:   143

ENTER AN INTEGER 0

STOP
```

### Problem No. 4

```
C  **  EMULATE THE ABS FORTRAN FUNCTION
C  **   EXCEPT - USE THE ZERO VALUE TO EXIT THE PROGRAM

      REAL NUMBER

 10   WRITE ( 5, 12 )
 12      FORMAT ( ' ', 'ENTER A REAL NUMBER ' )
      READ ( 5, 22 ) NUMBER
 22      FORMAT( F14.6 )
      IF ( NUMBER .EQ. 0.0 ) STOP

      IF ( NUMBER .LT. 0.0 ) NUMBER = -NUMBER

      WRITE ( 5, 32 ) NUMBER
 32      FORMAT ( '+', 'ABSOLUTE VALUE IS ', F14.6 / )
      GO TO 10

      END
```

```
[BEGIN EXECUTION]

ENTER A REAL NUMBER 23.1
ABSOLUTE VALUE IS      23.100000
```

**Sec. 4-1 (*Problem No. 4 cont'd*)**

```
ENTER A REAL NUMBER -101.231
ABSOLUTE VALUE IS     101.231000

ENTER A REAL NUMBER 0.0

STOP
```

***Problem No. 6***

```
      INTEGER MNUTES, HOURS, MNITS1

 10   WRITE ( 5, 12 )
 12      FORMAT ( ' ', 'ENTER MINUTES ' )
      READ ( 5, 22 ) MNUTES
 22      FORMAT ( I6 )
      IF ( MNUTES .EQ. 0 ) STOP

      MNITS1 = MOD( MNUTES, 60 )
      HOURS  = MNUTES / 60

      WRITE ( 5, 42 ) HOURS, MNITS1
 42      FORMAT ( '+', I6, ' HOURS', I6, ' MINUTES' / )
      GO TO 10

      END

[BEGIN EXECUTION]

ENTER MINUTES 666
    11 HOURS      6 MINUTES

ENTER MINUTES 123
     2 HOURS      3 MINUTES

ENTER MINUTES 0

STOP
```

## Sec. 4-2

***Problem No. 2***

```
      INTEGER INPFAH
      REAL CELSUS, FAH, OUTCEL

      CELSUS( FAH ) = 5.0/9.0 * ( FAH - 32.0 )
```

```
      END

[BEGIN EXECUTION]

   -4  -79
   -3  -51
   -2  -29
   -1  -13
    0   -3
    1    1
    2   -1
    3   -9
    4  -23
    5  -43
```

***Problem No. 6***

```
      INTEGER X, Y, FUNCT, X1

      FUNCT( X ) = 2 * X**2 + 8*X - 1

      DO 100 X1 = 1, 9
        X = X1 - 7
        Y = FUNCT( X )
        WRITE ( 5, 22 ) X, Y
22         FORMAT ( ' ', 2I5 )
100   CONTINUE

      END

[BEGIN EXECUTION]

   -6   23
   -5    9
   -4   -1
   -3   -7
   -2   -9
   -1   -7
    0   -1
    1    9
    2   23
```

## Sec. 4-3

***Problem No. 2***

```
C  **  USE FUNCTION IPRIME TO FIND ALL PRIME FACTORS
```

```
      WRITE ( 5, 902 )
902      FORMAT ( ' ', 'ENTER  -999  TO TERMINATE' / )

10    WRITE ( 5, 12 )
12       FORMAT ( '0', 'ENTER FAHRENHEIT TEMPERATURE ' )
      READ ( 5, 22 ) INPFAH
22       FORMAT ( I5 )
      IF ( INPFAH .EQ. -999 ) STOP

      FAH    = FLOAT( INPFAH )
      OUTCEL = CELSUS( FAH )
      WRITE ( 5, 42 ) OUTCEL
42       FORMAT ( '+', 'CELSIUS TEMPERATURE IS ', F6.2 )
      GO TO 10

      END
```

```
[BEGIN EXECUTION]

ENTER  -999  TO TERMINATE


ENTER FAHRENHEIT TEMPERATURE 32
CELSIUS TEMPERATURE IS   0.00

ENTER FAHRENHEIT TEMPERATURE -40
CELSIUS TEMPERATURE IS -40.00

ENTER FAHRENHEIT TEMPERATURE 70
CELSIUS TEMPERATURE IS  21.11

ENTER FAHRENHEIT TEMPERATURE -999

STOP
```

***Problem No. 4***

```
      INTEGER X, Y, FUNCT, X1

      FUNCT( X ) = -3 * X**2 + 7*X - 3

      DO 100 X1 = 1, 10
        X = X1 - 5
        Y = FUNCT( X )
        WRITE ( 5, 22 ) X, Y
22         FORMAT ( ' ', 2I5 )
100   CONTINUE
```

```
      INTEGER NUMBER, N1

      WRITE ( 5, 12 )
12       FORMAT ( ' ', 'FIND PRIMES   ENTER 0 TO TERMINATE' // )

20    WRITE ( 5, 22 )
22       FORMAT ( ' ', 'ENTER AN INTEGER ' )
      READ ( 5, 32 ) NUMBER
32       FORMAT ( I6 )
      IF ( NUMBER .EQ. 0 ) STOP

40    N1 = IPRIME( NUMBER )
      WRITE ( 5, 52 ) N1
52        FORMAT ( '+', I5 / )

60    NUMBER = NUMBER / N1
      IF ( NUMBER .EQ. 1 )  GO TO 20
      IF ( MOD( NUMBER, N1 )  .NE.  0 )  GO TO 40
       GO TO 60

      END
```

```
[BEGIN EXECUTION]

FIND PRIMES   ENTER 0 TO TERMINATE


ENTER AN INTEGER 7777
    7
   11
  101

ENTER AN INTEGER 1946
    2
    7
  139

ENTER AN INTEGER 32707
32707

ENTER AN INTEGER 0

STOP
```

```
      INTEGER FUNCTION GCF( N1, N2 )
C  **  FIND GREATEST FACTOR FOR TWO INTEGERS

      INTEGER N1, N2, K1, INDEX
```

**Sec. 4-3 (*Problem No. 2 cont'd*)**

```
C  **  WE LOOK FOR ALL FACTORS, NOT JUST PRIMES
      DO 100 INDEX = 2, N1
        K1 = N1 + 2 - INDEX
        IF ( MOD( N1, K1 )  .NE. 0 )  GO TO 100

C  **    WE HAVE A FACTOR OF THE FIRST NUMBER
C  **    NOW SEE IF IT IS ALSO A FACTOR OF THE SECOND NUMBER
         IF ( MOD( N2, K1 )  .NE. 0 )  GO TO 100

         GCF = K1
         GO TO 988

100   CONTINUE
      GCF = 1

988   RETURN

      END
```

***Problem No. 4***

```
C  **  TEST GREATEST COMMON FACTOR FUNCTION SUBPROGRAM

      INTEGER GCF, FACT1, FACT2, COMON

      WRITE ( 5, 12 )
 12      FORMAT ( ' ', 'FIND GREATEST COMMON FACTOR --',
     +          ' ENTER ''0,0'' TO END' / )
 20   WRITE ( 5, 22 )
 22      FORMAT ( '0', 'ENTER TWO INTEGERS ' )
      READ ( 5, 32 ) FACT1, FACT2
 32      FORMAT ( 2I6 )
      IF ( FACT1 .EQ. 0 ) STOP

      COMON = GCF( FACT1, FACT2 )
      WRITE ( 5, 62 ) COMON
 62      FORMAT ( '+', 'GREATEST COMMON FACTOR IS ', I6 )
      GO TO 20

      END

[BEGIN EXECUTION]

FIND GREATEST COMMON FACTOR -- ENTER '0,0' TO END
```

```
22       FORMAT ( '0', 'ENTER NUMBER OF CENTS ' )
      READ ( 5, 32 ) CENTS
32       FORMAT ( I2 )
      IF ( CENTS .EQ. 0 ) STOP
      IF ( CENTS .LT. 0  .OR.  CENTS .GT. 99 )  GO TO 20

      CALL CHANGE( CENTS, PEN, NIC, DIM, QUA, HAL )

      WRITE ( 5, 62 ) PEN, NIC, DIM, QUA, HAL
62       FORMAT ( '+', 'CHANGES TO:' /
     +             ' ', I2, 2X, 'PENNIES' /
     +             ' ', I2, 2X, 'NICKELS' /
     +             ' ', I2, 2X, 'DIMES' /
     +             ' ', I2, 2X, 'QUARTERS' /
     +             ' ', I2, 2X, 'HALF-DOLLAR'  )
      GO TO 20

      END
[BEGIN EXECUTION]

MAKING CHANGE  --  ENTER 0 TO EXIT

ENTER NUMBER OF CENTS 26
CHANGES TO:
 1  PENNIES
 0  NICKELS
 0  DIMES
 1  QUARTERS
 0  HALF-DOLLAR

ENTER NUMBER OF CENTS 99
CHANGES TO:
 4  PENNIES
 0  NICKELS
 2  DIMES
 1  QUARTERS
 1  HALF-DOLLAR

ENTER NUMBER OF CENTS 74
CHANGES TO:
 4  PENNIES
 0  NICKELS
 2  DIMES
 0  QUARTERS
```

```
ENTER TWO INTEGERS 633,128
GREATEST COMMON FACTOR IS        1

ENTER TWO INTEGERS 1ØØ1,2222
GREATEST COMMON FACTOR IS       11

ENTER TWO INTEGERS Ø,Ø

STOP
```

## Sec. 4-4

### *Problem No. 2*

```
      SUBROUTINE CHANGE( CENTS, PS, NS, DS, QS, HS )
C  **  MAKING CHANGE FOR 1 TO 99 CENTS
C  **   BEWARE THAT THE VALUE OF CENTS IS MODIFIED HERE

      INTEGER CENTS, PS, NS, DS, QS, HS

C  **  WE TAKE ADVANTAGE OF INTEGER DIVISION HERE
      HS = CENTS / 5Ø
      CENTS = CENTS - HS*5Ø

      QS = CENTS / 25
      CENTS = CENTS - QS*25

      DS = CENTS / 1Ø
      CENTS = CENTS - DS*1Ø

      NS = CENTS / 5
      CENTS = CENTS - NS*5

      PS = CENTS

      RETURN

      END


C  **  TEST CHANGE MAKING SUBROUTINE

      INTEGER CENTS, PEN, NIC, DIM, QUA, HAL

      WRITE ( 5, 12 )
 12      FORMAT ( ' ', 'MAKING CHANGE  --  ENTER Ø TO EXIT' / )

 2Ø   WRITE ( 5, 22 )
```

```
 1  HALF-DOLLAR

ENTER NUMBER OF CENTS Ø

STOP
```

# Chap. 5

## Sec. 5-3

### *Problem No. 2*

```
C  **  SIMPLY FILL A 3 BY 6 ARRAY WITH ONES AND WRITE IT OUT

      INTEGER ARRAY(3,6), ROW, COL

      DO 2Ø ROW = 1, 3
        DO 1Ø COL = 1, 6
          ARRAY( ROW, COL ) = 1
 1Ø     CONTINUE
 2Ø   CONTINUE

C  **  NOTE THAT FORMAT STATEMENT 22 IS 'REUSED' 3 TIMES
      WRITE ( 5, 22 ) ((ARRAY(ROW,COL),COL=1,6),ROW=1,3)
 22      FORMAT ( ' ', 6I4 )

      END

[BEGIN EXECUTION]

   1   1   1   1   1   1
   1   1   1   1   1   1
   1   1   1   1   1   1
```

### *Problem No. 4*

```
      INTEGER ARRAY(3,7), ROW, COL, COUNT

      COUNT = Ø
      DO 1ØØ ROW = 1, 3
        DO 9Ø COL = 1, 7
          ARRAY( ROW, COL ) = COUNT
          COUNT = COUNT + 1
9Ø      CONTINUE
1ØØ   CONTINUE

      WRITE ( 5, 112 )
112      FORMAT ( ' ', 'Ø THROUGH 2Ø IN A 3 BY 7 ARRAY' )
```

**Sec. 5-3 (*Problem No. 4 cont'd*)**

```
      WRITE ( 5, 922 ) ((ARRAY(ROW,COL),COL=1,7),ROW=1,3)

C  **  NOW MULTIPLY BY THE SUM OF THE ROW AND COLUMN NUMBER
      DO 200 ROW = 1, 3
        DO 190 COL = 1, 7
          ARRAY( ROW, COL ) = ARRAY( ROW, COL ) * (ROW + COL)
 190    CONTINUE
 200  CONTINUE

      WRITE ( 5, 222 )
 222    FORMAT ( // ' ', 'AFTER MULTIPLYING' )
      WRITE ( 5, 922 ) ((ARRAY(ROW,COL),COL=1,7),ROW=1,3)

C  **     STATEMENT 922 IS REFERENCED TWICE AND 'REUSED' 3 TMES
C  **     IN EACH CASE.
 922    FORMAT ( ' ', 7I4 )

      END
```

[BEGIN EXECUTION]

```
Ø THROUGH 2Ø IN A 3 BY 7 ARRAY
   Ø   1   2   3   4   5   6
   7   8   9  1Ø  11  12  13
  14  15  16  17  18  19  2Ø


AFTER MULTIPLYING
   Ø   3   8  15  24  35  48
  21  32  45  6Ø  77  96 117
  56  75  96 119 144 171 2ØØ
```

***Problem No. 6***

```
C  **  BUILD THE 12 BY 12 MULTIPLICATION TABLE

      INTEGER TABLE(12,12), ROW, COL

      DO 1ØØ ROW = 1, 12
        DO 9Ø COL = 1, 12
          TABLE( ROW, COL ) = ROW * COL
 9Ø     CONTINUE
 1ØØ  CONTINUE

C  **  FORMAT STATEMENT 122 IS 'REUSED' 12 TIMES
```

```
  ?   4   1   3   Ø
  3   1   4   2   Ø
  4   3   2   1   Ø
  Ø   Ø   Ø   Ø   Ø
```

# Chap. 6

## Sec. 6-1

***Problem No. 2***

```
C  **  IN COURS1 FIND THE NUMER OF PEOPLE WHO WANT
C  **   CHEMISTRY AND PHYSICS

      INTEGER  DATA1(7Ø), J1, N

      DATA  DATA1/ 1,Ø,1,1,Ø, Ø,Ø,1,1,Ø, 1,1,Ø,1,1, 1,Ø,1,1,Ø,
     +             Ø,Ø,1,Ø,1, 1,Ø,1,1,Ø, 1,1,1,Ø,Ø, 1,Ø,1,Ø,1,
     +             1,Ø,1,1,Ø, 1,1,Ø,1,Ø, 1,1,Ø,1,1, 1,1,Ø,1,Ø,
     +             1,1,Ø,Ø,Ø, -1/

      N = Ø
      DO 1ØØ J1 = 1, 65, 5
        IF ( DATA1(J1) .EQ. -1 ) GO TO 12Ø

C  **    CHEMISTRY IS AT DATA1(J1) - PHYSICS AT DATA1(J1+1)
        IF ( (DATA1(J1).EQ.1) .AND. (DATA1(J1+1).EQ.1) ) N=N+1

 1ØØ  CONTINUE

 12Ø  WRITE ( 5, 122 ) N
 122    FORMAT ( ' ', I2, ' PEOPLE REQUESTED CHEM AND PHYSICS' )

      END
```

[BEGIN EXECUTION]

```
 6 PEOPLE REQUESTED CHEM AND PHYSICS
```

***Problem No. 4***

```
C  **  MODIFY TVS TO TABULATE TV'S, CARS AND BATHS
C  **  ASSUME AT LEAST ONE OF EACH HERE

      INTEGER  DATA1(15Ø), TVS(5), CARS(5), BATHS(5), J1
```

```
      WRITE ( 5, 122 ) ((TABLE(ROW,COL),COL=1,12),ROW=1,12)
122      FORMAT ( ' ', 12I4 )

      END
```

[BEGIN EXECUTION]

```
   1   2   3   4   5   6   7   8   9  10  11  12
   2   4   6   8  10  12  14  16  18  20  22  24
   3   6   9  12  15  18  21  24  27  30  33  36
   4   8  12  16  20  24  28  32  36  40  44  48
   5  10  15  20  25  30  35  40  45  50  55  60
   6  12  18  24  30  36  42  48  54  60  66  72
   7  14  21  28  35  42  49  56  63  70  77  84
   8  16  24  32  40  48  56  64  72  80  88  96
   9  18  27  36  45  54  63  72  81  90  99 108
  10  20  30  40  50  60  70  80  90 100 110 120
  11  22  33  44  55  66  77  88  99 110 121 132
  12  24  36  48  60  72  84  96 108 120 132 144
```

### *Problem No. 8*

```
C  **  BUILD THE 5 BY 5 MOD 5 MULTIPLICATION TABLE

       INTEGER TABLE(5,5), ROW, COL

       DO 100 ROW = 1, 5
         DO 90 COL = 1, 5
           TABLE( ROW, COL ) = MOD( ROW * COL, 5 )
 90      CONTINUE
 100   CONTINUE

       WRITE ( 5, 112 )
 112      FORMAT ( ' ', 'MOD 5 MULTIPLICATON TABLE' / )

C  **  HERE THE FORMAT STATEMENT IS 'REUSED' 5 TIMES
       WRITE ( 5, 122 ) ((TABLE(ROW,COL),COL=1,5),ROW=1,5)
 122      FORMAT ( ' ', 5I4 )

       END
```

[BEGIN EXECUTION]

```
MOD 5 MULTIPLICATON TABLE

   1   2   3   4   0
```

```
      DATA  DATA1/ 1,1,2, 2,1,1, 4,2,3, 3,1,1, 5,2,1, 2,1,1, 3,1,3,
     +             4,2,4, 3,1,1, 2,2,2, 1,1,1, 2,2,1, 3,3,2, 4,1,3,
     +             5,1,2, 3,2,4, 2,1,2, 3,2,1, 2,2,5, 2,1,1, 2,2,1,
     +             1,4,3, 2,5,3, 4,3,2, 1,2,3, 2,1,4, 2,3,1, 1,2,1,
     +             4,2,1, 3,1,2, 2,1,1, 1,2,1, -1/
     +      TVS  / 5*0/ CARS/ 5*0/ BATHS/ 5*0/

      DO 100 J1 = 1, 148, 3
        N = DATA1( J1 )
        IF ( N .EQ. -1 )  GO TO 200
         TVS( N )   = TVS( N ) + 1
         N = DATA1( J1 + 1 )
         CARS( N )  = CARS( N ) + 1
         N = DATA1( J1 + 2 )
         BATHS( N ) = BATHS( N ) + 1
100   CONTINUE

200   WRITE ( 5, 202 )
202      FORMAT ( ' ', ' NO. OF   NUMBER OF FAMILIES WITH' /
     +            ' ', '  ITEMS   TV''S   CARS  BATHS' )

      DO 210 J1 = 1, 5
        WRITE ( 5, 204 ) J1, TVS(J1), CARS(J1), BATHS(J1)
204        FORMAT ( ' ', 4I7 )
210   CONTINUE

      END
```

[BEGIN EXECUTION]

```
 NO. OF   NUMBER OF FAMILIES WITH
  ITEMS   TV'S   CARS  BATHS
      1      6     14     15
      2     12     13      7
      3      7      3      6
      4      5      1      3
      5      2      1      1
```

## Sec. 6-2

### *Problem No. 2*

```
C  **  WE ARE MODIFYING COURS2 WITH NAMES IN A REAL ARRAY
C  **  FINDING THE NUMBER OF STUDENTS REQUESTING
C  **   EACH PAIR OF COURSES

       INTEGER  DATA1(5,14), K1, C1, C2, N, FIRST
```

**Sec. 6-2 (*Problem No. 2 cont'd*)**

```
      REAL NAMES(5)

      DATA  DATA1/ 1,0,1,1,0, 0,0,1,1,0, 1,1,0,1,1, 1,0,1,1,0,
     +             0,0,1,0,1, 1,0,1,1,0, 1,1,1,0,0, 1,0,1,0,1,
     +             1,0,1,1,0, 1,1,0,1,0, 1,1,0,1,1, 1,1,0,1,0,
     +             1,1,0,0,0, -1/
     +      NAMES / 'CHEM', 'PHYS', 'FRE ', 'SPAN', 'CALC'/

      DO 150 C1 = 1, 4
        FIRST = C1 + 1

        DO 140 C2 = FIRST, 5
          N = 0

          DO 100 K1 = 1, 14
            IF ( DATA1( 1, K1 ) .LT. 0 )              GO TO 110
             IF ( DATA1(C1,K1).EQ.1 .AND. DATA1(C2,K1).EQ.1 ) N=N+1
100       CONTINUE

110       WRITE ( 5, 112 ) NAMES(C1), NAMES(C2), N
112          FORMAT ( ' ', A4, 2X, A4, 2X, I4 )
140     CONTINUE

150   CONTINUE

      END
```

[BEGIN EXECUTION]

```
CHEM  PHYS    6
CHEM  FRE     6
CHEM  SPAN    8
CHEM  CALC    3
PHYS  FRE     1
PHYS  SPAN    4
PHYS  CALC    2
FRE   SPAN    5
FRE   CALC    2
SPAN  CALC    2
```

***Problem No. 4***

```
C  **  TABULATING TOTAL YES RESPONSES

       INTEGER  DATA1(9,10), RESULT(8,5), K1, K2, K3
     +             2,1,1,0,0,1,0,0,1, 1,1,1,0,0,1,0,1,0,
     +             1,1,0,0,1,1,0,1,1, 3,0,0,1,0,1,1,0,1,
     +             3,0,0,1,0,1,1,0,0, 2,0,1,1,1,0,0,0,1/
       DATA RESULT/ 64*0/

C  **  NOW TABULATE THE FOUR CATEGORIES
       DO 100 K1 = 1, 10
         K2 = DATA1( 1, K1 )
         DO 90 K3 = 1, 8
           K4 = DATA1( K3 + 1, K1 )
           RESULT( K3, K2 ) = RESULT( K3, K2 ) + K4

C  **  HERE WE ACCOMMODATE THE FOUR NEW CATEGORIES
           IF (K2.EQ.1 .OR. K2.EQ.2 ) RESULT(K3,5)=RESULT(K3,5)+K4
           IF (K2.EQ.1 .OR. K2.EQ.3 ) RESULT(K3,8)=RESULT(K3,8)+K4
           IF (K2.EQ.2 .OR. K2.EQ.4 ) RESULT(K3,7)=RESULT(K3,7)+K4
           IF (K2.EQ.3 .OR. K2.EQ.4 ) RESULT(K3,6)=RESULT(K3,6)+K4

 90      CONTINUE
100    CONTINUE

200   WRITE ( 5, 202 )
202      FORMAT ( ' ', '  QUEST   MALE   MALE FEMALE FEMALE',
    +              '   MALE FEMALE  UNDER  21 OR' /
    +         ' ', ' NUMBER    21+  UNDER    21+  UNDER',
    +              '                   21   OVER' )
      WRITE ( 5, 204 ) (K1, (RESULT(K1,K2),K2 = 1, 8),K1 = 1, 8)
204      FORMAT ( ' ', 9I7 )

      END
```

[BEGIN EXECUTION]

| QUEST NUMBER | MALE 21+ | MALE UNDER | FEMALE 21+ | FEMALE UNDER | MALE | FEMALE | UNDER 21 | 21 OR OVER |
|---|---|---|---|---|---|---|---|---|
| 1 | 2 | 2 | 2 | 1 | 4 | 3 | 3 | 4 |
| 2 | 1 | 3 | 0 | 1 | 4 | 1 | 4 | 1 |
| 3 | 0 | 2 | 3 | 1 | 2 | 4 | 3 | 3 |
| 4 | 1 | 2 | 1 | 0 | 3 | 1 | 2 | 2 |
| 5 | 2 | 1 | 3 | 0 | 3 | 3 | 1 | 5 |
| 6 | 0 | 0 | 3 | 0 | 0 | 3 | 0 | 3 |
| 7 | 2 | 1 | 1 | 1 | 3 | 2 | 2 | 3 |
| 8 | 1 | 2 | 2 | 0 | 3 | 2 | 2 | 3 |

```
C  **  TYPING GUIDE  1,2,3,4,5,6,7,8    1,2,3,4,5,6,7,8
     DATA  DATA1/ 3,1,Ø,1,1,1,Ø,Ø,1, 3,1,Ø,Ø,Ø,Ø,1,1,Ø,
    +             2,1,1,1,1,Ø,Ø,1,Ø, 4,1,1,1,Ø,Ø,Ø,1,Ø,
    +             2,1,1,Ø,Ø,1,Ø,Ø,1, 1,1,1,Ø,Ø,1,Ø,1,Ø,
    +             1,1,Ø,Ø,1,1,Ø,1,1, 3,Ø,Ø,1,Ø,1,1,Ø,1,
    +             3,Ø,Ø,1,Ø,1,1,Ø,Ø, 2,Ø,1,1,1,Ø,Ø,Ø,1/
     DATA RESULT/ 4Ø*Ø/

C  **  NOW TABULATE THE FOUR CATEGORIES
     DO 1ØØ K1 = 1, 1Ø
       K2 = DATA1( 1, K1 )
       DO 9Ø K3 = 1, 8
         RESULT( K3, K2 ) = RESULT( K3, K2 ) + DATA1(K3 + 1, K1)
         RESULT( K3, 5  ) = RESULT( K3, 5  ) + DATA1(K3 + 1, K1)
 9Ø    CONTINUE
 1ØØ CONTINUE

 2ØØ WRITE ( 5, 2Ø2 )
 2Ø2    FORMAT ( ' ', '  QUEST    MALE    MALE FEMALE FEMALE  TOTAL' /
    +            ' ', ' NUMBER     21+  UNDER     21+  UNDER' )
     WRITE ( 5, 2Ø4 ) (K1, (RESULT(K1,K2),K2 = 1, 5),K1 = 1, 8)
 2Ø4    FORMAT ( ' ', 6I7 )

     END
```

[BEGIN EXECUTION]

```
  QUEST    MALE    MALE FEMALE FEMALE   TOTAL
 NUMBER     21+  UNDER     21+  UNDER
      1       2      2       2      1       7
      2       1      3       Ø      1       5
      3       Ø      2       3      1       6
      4       1      2       1      Ø       4
      5       2      1       3      Ø       6
      6       Ø      Ø       3      Ø       3
      7       2      1       1      1       5
      8       1      2       2      Ø       5
```

### *Problem No. 6*

```
C  **  MODIFYING SURVY1 BY ADDING FOUR NEW CATEGORIES

     INTEGER  DATA1(9,1Ø), RESULT(8,8), K1, K2, K3, K4

C  **  TYPING GUIDE  1,2,3,4,5,6,7,8    1,2,3,4,5,6,7,8
     DATA  DATA1/ 3,1,Ø,1,1,1,Ø,Ø,1, 3,1,Ø,Ø,Ø,Ø,1,1,Ø,
    +             2,1,1,1,1,Ø,Ø,1,Ø, 4,1,1,1,Ø,Ø,Ø,1,Ø,
```

### *Problem No. 8*

```
C  **  ADD A THIRD RESPONSE TO SURVY1

     INTEGER  DATA1(9,1Ø), RESULT(8,4,3), K1, K2, K3, J1, R1
     REAL  LABELS(3)

C  **  TYPING GUIDE  1,2,3,4,5,6,7,8    1,2,3,4,5,6,7,8
     DATA  DATA1/ 3,2,3,1,3,2,3,3,2, 3,1,3,2,1,3,3,2,1,
    +             2,2,2,1,1,3,3,2,3, 4,1,2,2,1,2,3,2,1,
    +             2,2,2,1,2,3,2,3,3, 1,3,1,3,2,3,1,1,2,
    +             1,2,1,1,1,2,2,1,2, 3,3,1,2,3,2,3,2,1,
    +             3,2,3,3,3,3,2,2,1, 2,3,3,1,1,1,2,3,2/
     DATA  LABELS / ' NO ', 'YES ', 'OTHR'/
     DATA  RESULT / 96*Ø/

C  **  NOW TABULATE THE FOUR CATEGORIES -- IN THREE DIMENSIONS
     DO 1ØØ K1 = 1, 1Ø
       K2 = DATA1( 1, K1 )
       DO 9Ø K3 = 1, 8
         R1 = DATA1(K3 + 1, K1 )
         RESULT( K3, K2, R1 ) = RESULT( K3, K2, R1 ) + 1
 9Ø    CONTINUE
 1ØØ CONTINUE

     DO 3ØØ J1 = 1, 3
       WRITE ( 5, 152 ) LABELS( J1 )
 152      FORMAT ( // ' ', 6X, 'TABULATE ', A4, ' RESPONSES' / )
 2ØØ   WRITE ( 5, 2Ø2 )
 2Ø2      FORMAT ( ' ', '  QUEST   MALE    MALE FEMALE FEMALE' /
    +              ' ', ' NUMBER     21+  UNDER     21+  UNDER' )
       WRITE ( 5, 2Ø4 ) (K1, (RESULT(K1,K2,J1),K2=1,4),K1=1,8)
 2Ø4      FORMAT ( ' ', 5I7 )

 3ØØ CONTINUE

     END
```

[BEGIN EXECUTION]

```
     TABULATE  NO  RESPONSES

  QUEST    MALE    MALE FEMALE FEMALE
 NUMBER     21+  UNDER     21+  UNDER
      1       Ø      Ø       1      1
```

## Sec. 6-2 (*Problem No. 8 cont'd*)

```
       2      2      Ø      1      Ø
       3      1      3      1      Ø
       4      1      2      1      1
       5      Ø      1      Ø      Ø
       6      1      Ø      Ø      Ø
       7      2      Ø      Ø      Ø
       8      Ø      Ø      3      1


    TABULATE YES  RESPONSES

  QUEST   MALE   MALE FEMALE FEMALE
 NUMBER    21+  UNDER    21+  UNDER
      1      1      2      2      Ø
      2      Ø      2      Ø      1
      3      Ø      Ø      2      1
      4      1      1      Ø      Ø
      5      1      Ø      2      1
      6      1      2      1      Ø
      7      Ø      1      3      1
      8      2      1      1      Ø


    TABULATE OTHR RESPONSES

  QUEST   MALE   MALE FEMALE FEMALE
 NUMBER    21+  UNDER    21+  UNDER
      1      1      1      1      Ø
      2      Ø      1      3      Ø
      3      1      Ø      1      Ø
      4      Ø      Ø      3      Ø
      5      1      2      2      Ø
      6      Ø      1      3      1
      7      Ø      2      1      Ø
      8      Ø      2      Ø      Ø
```

## Sec. 6-3

### *Problem No. 2*

```
C  **  MODIFY SURVY2 TO TOTAL YES RESPONSES

      INTEGER  DATA1(8), RESULT(8,5), K1, K2, K3
      DATA  RESULT/ 4Ø*Ø/
```

```
1Ø     READ ( 7, 12 ) K2, DATA1
12        FORMAT ( 9I3 )
       IF ( K2 .EQ. Ø )  GO TO 15Ø

        DO 9Ø K3 = 1, 8
          IF ( DATA1( K3 ) .NE. J1 - 1 )  GO TO 9Ø
           RESULT( K3, K2 ) = RESULT( K3, K2 ) + 1
9Ø      CONTINUE
        GO TO 1Ø

15Ø    WRITE ( 5, 152 ) LABELS( J1 )
152       FORMAT ( // ' ', 6X, 'TABULATE ', A4, ' RESPONSES' / )
2ØØ    WRITE ( 5, 2Ø2 )
2Ø2       FORMAT ( ' ', '  QUEST   MALE   MALE FEMALE FEMALE' /
    +               ' ', ' NUMBER    21+  UNDER    21+  UNDER' )
       WRITE ( 5, 2Ø4 ) (K1, (RESULT(K1,K2),K2 = 1, 4),K1 = 1, 8)
2Ø4       FORMAT ( ' ', 5I7 )

C  **  NOTE THE USE OF THE REWIND STATEMENT TO MAKE THE FILE
C  **  READABLE AGAIN FROM THE BEGINNING
        REWIND 7

 3ØØ  CONTINUE

      END

[BEGIN EXECUTION]



      TABULATE  NO  RESPONSES

  QUEST   MALE   MALE FEMALE FEMALE
 NUMBER    21+  UNDER    21+  UNDER
      1      Ø      Ø      1      1
      2      2      Ø      1      Ø
      3      1      3      1      Ø
      4      1      2      1      1
      5      Ø      1      Ø      Ø
      6      1      Ø      Ø      Ø
      7      2      Ø      Ø      Ø
      8      Ø      Ø      3      1
```

```
10   READ ( 6, 12 ) K2, DATA1
12      FORMAT ( 9I3 )
     IF ( K2 .EQ. Ø )  GO TO 2ØØ
      DO 9Ø K3 = 1, 8
        RESULT( K3, K2 ) = RESULT( K3, K2 ) + DATA1( K3 )
        RESULT( K3,  5 ) = RESULT( K3,  5 ) + DATA1( K3 )
9Ø    CONTINUE
      GO TO 1Ø

2ØØ  WRITE ( 5, 2Ø2 )
2Ø2     FORMAT ( ' ', '  QUEST   MALE   MALE FEMALE FEMALE  YESES' /
    +             ' ', ' NUMBER    21+  UNDER    21+  UNDER' )
     WRITE ( 5, 2Ø4 ) (K1, (RESULT(K1,K2),K2 = 1, 5),K1 = 1, 8)
2Ø4     FORMAT ( ' ', 6I7 )

     END
```

```
[BEGIN EXECUTION]

 QUEST   MALE   MALE FEMALE FEMALE  YESES
NUMBER    21+  UNDER    21+  UNDER
     1      2      2      2      1      7
     2      1      3      Ø      1      5
     3      Ø      2      3      1      6
     4      1      2      1      Ø      4
     5      2      1      3      Ø      6
     6      Ø      Ø      3      Ø      3
     7      2      1      1      1      5
     8      1      2      2      Ø      5
```

***Problem No. 4***

```
C  **  WE MODIFY SURVY2 BY ADDING A CATEGORY OF RESPONSE
C  **  TWO FOR 'OTHER'

      INTEGER  DATA1(8), RESULT(8,4), K1, K2, K3, J1, R1
      REAL  LABELS( 3 )
      DATA  LABELS / ' NO ', 'YES ', 'OTHR'/

C  **  SET UP HERE TO DO THREE SCANS OF THE DATA
      DO 3ØØ J1 = 1, 3
        DO 3Ø K1 = 1, 8
          DO 25 K2 = 1, 4
            RESULT( K1, K2 ) = Ø
25        CONTINUE
3Ø      CONTINUE
```

```
    TABULATE YES  RESPONSES

 QUEST   MALE   MALE FEMALE FEMALE
NUMBER    21+  UNDER    21+  UNDER
     1      1      2      2      Ø
     2      Ø      2      Ø      1
     3      Ø      Ø      2      1
     4      1      1      Ø      Ø
     5      1      Ø      2      1
     6      1      2      1      Ø
     7      Ø      1      3      1
     8      2      1      1      Ø

    TABULATE OTHR RESPONSES

 QUEST   MALE   MALE FEMALE FEMALE
NUMBER    21+  UNDER    21+  UNDER
     1      1      1      1      Ø
     2      Ø      1      3      Ø
     3      1      Ø      1      Ø
     4      Ø      Ø      3      Ø
     5      1      2      2      Ø
     6      Ø      1      3      1
     7      Ø      2      1      Ø
     8      Ø      2      Ø      Ø
```

# Chap. 7

## Sec. 7-1

***Problem No. 2***

```
C  **  REQUIRES SUBROUTINE IENTER  **

C  **  WE MODIFY DIGIT1 TO PRINT ONLY ONE MINUS SIGN.
C  **  TO DO THIS WE ALSO ELIMINATE LEADING ZEROS

      INTEGER DIGITS(5), INDEX, INTEGR, EXP, DIGIT, REMAIN,
     +         PFIRST, SIGNE

 1Ø   CALL IENTER ( INTEGR )

C  **  SET SIGNE TO +1 OR -1
      SIGNE  = ISIGN( 1, INTEGR )
      INTEGR = IABS( INTEGR )

C  **  ENTER THE DIGITS IN ARRAY DIGITS
      DO 1ØØ INDEX = 1, 5
        EXP             = 5 - INDEX
```

**Sec. 7-1 (*Problem No. 2 cont'd*)**

```
       DIGIT              = INTEGR / 10**EXP
       DIGITS( INDEX ) = DIGIT
       REMAIN             = INTEGR - DIGIT * 10**EXP
       INTEGR             = REMAIN
 100  CONTINUE

C  **  DETERMINE PFIRST HERE
      DO 40 INDEX = 1, 5
        PFIRST = INDEX
        IF ( DIGITS( INDEX ) .NE. 0 )  GO TO 50
 40   CONTINUE

 50   DIGITS( PFIRST ) = SIGNE * DIGITS( PFIRST )
      WRITE ( 5, 102 ) (DIGITS(INDEX), INDEX=PFIRST,5)
 102     FORMAT ( '+', 5( 1X, I2 ) )
      GO TO 10

      END

[BEGIN EXECUTION]

ENTER AN INTEGER 1234
  1  2  3  4

ENTER AN INTEGER -1235
 -1  2  3  5

ENTER AN INTEGER 0

STOP
```

***Problem No. 4***

```
C  **  REQUIRES SUBROUTINE IENTER  **

C  **  WE MODIFY DIGIT2 TO USE THE MOD FUNCTION, SUPPRESS
C  **  PRINTING LEADING ZEROS, AND PRINT A SINGLE MINUS SIGN.

      INTEGER DIGITS(5), INDEX, PFIRST, SIGNE, PLACE

 10   CALL IENTER ( INTEGR )

C  **  SET SIGNE TO +1 OR -1
      SIGNE  = ISIGN( 1, INTEGR )
      INTEGR = IABS( INTEGR )
```

***Problem No. 6***

```
C  **  REQUIRES FUNCTION SUBPROGRAM ISPRIM  **

C  **  REVERSE ALL THREE DIGIT INTEGERS AND CHECK FOR BOTH PRIME

      INTEGER INDEX, INTEGR, REVERS, DIGIT, PLACE, DIGITS(5),
     +        PFIRST, INDEX1, INDEX2

C  **  WE NEED NOT CONSIDER THE EVEN HUNDREDS - THE REVERSE
C  **   NUMBERS WILL ALL BE COMPOSITE.
      DO 500 INDEX1 = 100, 900, 200
        DO 490 INDEX2 = 1, 99, 2
          NUMBER = INDEX1 + INDEX2
          INTEGR = NUMBER

C  **      IS INTEGR PRIME? - IF NOT, GET THE NEXT VALUE OF INTGER
          IF ( ISPRIM( INTEGR )  .EQ.  0 )  GO TO 490

           DO 100 INDEX = 1, 5
             PLACE             = 6 - INDEX
             DIGITS( PLACE ) = MOD( INTEGR, 10 )
             INTEGR            = INTEGR / 10
 100       CONTINUE

           REVERS = 0
           DO 200 INDEX = 1, 5
            PFIRST = INDEX
             IF ( DIGITS( INDEX ) .NE. 0 ) GO TO 250
 200       CONTINUE
 250       K1 = -1
           DO 350 INDEX = PFIRST, 5
             K1 = K1 + 1
             REVERS = REVERS + DIGITS(INDEX) * 10**K1
 350       CONTINUE

C  **       NOW MAKE SURE THAT REVERS IS PRIME
          IF ( ISPRIM(REVERS) .EQ. 0 )  GO TO 490

           WRITE ( 5, 402 ) NUMBER, REVERS
 402       FORMAT ( ' ', 2I7 )

 490    CONTINUE
```

```
C  **  ENTER THE DIGITS IN ARRAY DIGITS
      DO 100 INDEX = 1, 5
        PLACE            = 6 - INDEX
        DIGITS( PLACE ) = MOD( INTEGR, 10 )
        INTEGR           = INTEGR / 10
 100  CONTINUE

C  **  DETERMINE PFIRST HERE
      DO 40 INDEX = 1, 5
        PFIRST = INDEX
        IF ( DIGITS( INDEX ) .NE. 0 )  GO TO 50
 40   CONTINUE

 50   DIGITS( PFIRST ) = SIGNE * DIGITS( PFIRST )
      WRITE ( 5, 102 ) (DIGITS(INDEX), INDEX=PFIRST,5)
 102     FORMAT ( '+', 5( 1X, I2 ) )
      GO TO 10

      END

[BEGIN EXECUTION]

ENTER AN INTEGER 1236
  1  2  3  6

ENTER AN INTEGER -5284
 -5  2  8  4

ENTER AN INTEGER 0

STOP

      INTEGER FUNCTION ISPRIM( N1 )
C  **  RETURN ISPRIM = 1 IF N1 IS PRIME
C  **  RETURN ISPRIM = 0 IF N1 IS COMPOSITE

      INTEGER N1, LAST, INDEX

      ISPRIM = 0
      IF ( MOD( N1, 2 ) .EQ. 0  )  GO TO 998

       LAST = INT( SQRT( FLOAT(N1) ) )
       DO 100 INDEX = 3, LAST, 2
         IF ( MOD( N1, INDEX )  .EQ. 0 )  GO TO 998
 100   CONTINUE

       ISPRIM = 1

 998  RETURN

      END
```

```
 500  CONTINUE

        END

[BEGIN EXECUTION]

    101    101
    107    701
    113    311
    131    131
    149    941
    151    151
    157    751
    167    761
    179    971
    181    181
    191    191
    199    991
    311    113
    313    313
    337    733
    347    743
    353    353
    359    953
    373    373
    383    383
    389    983
    701    107
    709    907
    727    727
    733    337
    739    937
    743    347
    751    157
    757    757
    761    167
    769    967
    787    787
    797    797
    907    709
    919    919
    929    929
    937    739
    941    149
    953    359
    967    769
    971    179
    983    389
    991    199
```

## Sec. 7-2

### *Problem No. 2*

```
C  **  THIS PROGRAM CONVERTS DECIMAL TO BINARY

       INTEGER DIGIT(16), BASE10, INDEX, PLACE

 10    CALL IENTER( BASE10 )
       DO 20 INDEX = 1, 16
         DIGIT( INDEX ) = 0
 20    CONTINUE

C  **  LOAD DIGIT ARRAY WITH BINARY DIGITS
       DO 50 INDEX = 1, 16
         PLACE          = 17 - INDEX
         DIGIT( PLACE ) = MOD( BASE10, 2 )
         BASE10         = BASE10 / 2
         IF ( BASE10 .EQ. 0 )  GO TO 100
 50    CONTINUE

 100   WRITE ( 5, 102 ) (DIGIT(INDEX), INDEX=PLACE,16)
 102     FORMAT ( '+', 16I1 )
       GO TO 10

       END

[BEGIN EXECUTION]

ENTER AN INTEGER 16383
11111111111111

ENTER AN INTEGER 255
11111111

ENTER AN INTEGER 256
100000000

ENTER AN INTEGER 0

STOP
```

### *Problem No. 4*

```
C  **  CONVERT BASE TWO TO OCTAL NOTATION

      INTEGER BASE2(16), BASE10, INDEX, DIGIT2(2),
     +        LAST, INDEX1, EXIT, DIGIT8(5), PLACE

C  **  WHILE WE DO THIS AS A SINGLE PROGRAM, IT MIGHT BE A GOOD
C  **    IDEA TO WRITE A SET OF SUBROUTINES WHICH CONVERT FROM
C  **    AND TO BASE TEN AND SIMPLY CALL THEM AS NEEDED.

       END

[BEGIN EXECUTION]

CONVERT BASE TWO TO OCTAL NOTATION
TERMINATE EACH ENTRY WITH 'E'


ENTER A BASE TWO NUMBER 111E
IN OCTAL NOTATION IS 7

ENTER A BASE TWO NUMBER 111000111000E
IN OCTAL NOTATION IS 7070

ENTER A BASE TWO NUMBER JE

BAD DIGIT ENTERED -- TRY AGAIN

ENTER A BASE TWO NUMBER E

STOP
```

### *Problem No. 6*

```
C  **  CONVERT HEX TO BNARY
C  **   POSSIBLE METHODS:
C  **      1) CONVERT HEX TO BASE TEN THEN BASE TEN TO BINARY
C  **      2) CONVERT EACH HEX DIGIT TO FOUR BINARY DIGITS
C  **   THE SECOND METHOD IS USED HERE

      INTEGER HEX(5), HEXNUM(5), DG16(16), LAST, DIGIT2(16),
     +        H, BNUM, HNUM, J1, J2, HDIGIT, BPOSN

      DATA  DG16/ '0','1','2','3','4','5','6','7',
     +            '8','9','A','B','C','D','E','F'/
     +         H/ 'H'/

      WRITE ( 5, 12 )
 12      FORMAT ( ' ', 'CONVERT UP TO 4 HEX DIGITS TO BASE TEN' /
     +            ' ', 'TERMINATE EACH ENTRY WITH AN ''H''' / )

 20   WRITE ( 5, 22 )
```

```
      DATA DIGIT2/ '1','Ø'/
     +      EXIT/ 'E'/

C  **  BY REQUESTING A TERMINATING CHARACTER, WE DO NOT HAVE
C  **   TO DEMAND LEADING ZEROS IN INPUT.
      WRITE ( 5, 12 )
 12      FORMAT ( ' ', 'CONVERT BASE TWO TO OCTAL NOTATION' /
     +              ' ', 'TERMINATE EACH ENTRY WITH ''E''' / )

 2Ø   WRITE ( 5, 22 )
 22      FORMAT ( 'Ø', 'ENTER A BASE TWO NUMBER ' )
      READ ( 5, 32 ) BASE2
 32      FORMAT ( 16A1 )
      IF ( BASE2(1) .EQ. EXIT )  STOP

      DO 5Ø INDEX = 1, 16
        IF ( BASE2( INDEX ) .EQ. EXIT ) GO TO 1ØØ
 5Ø   CONTINUE
      WRITE ( 5, 52 )
 52      FORMAT ( ' ', 'MISSING TERMINATING CHARACTER' )
      GO TO 2Ø

C  **  FIRST CONVERT TO BASE TEN  **
 1ØØ  BASE1Ø = Ø
      LAST   = INDEX - 1
      DO 15Ø INDEX1 = 1, LAST
        IF ( BASE2( INDEX1 ) .EQ.  DIGIT2(2) )  GO TO 15Ø
        IF ( BASE2( INDEX1 ) .EQ.  DIGIT2(1) )  GO TO 14Ø
        WRITE ( 5, 122 )
 122       FORMAT ( ' ', 'BAD DIGIT ENTERED -- TRY AGAIN' )
        GO TO 2Ø

 14Ø    BASE1Ø = BASE1Ø + 2**(LAST - INDEX1)
 15Ø  CONTINUE

C  **  NOW CONVERT BASE1Ø TO OCTAL NOTATION  **
      DO 2ØØ INDEX = 1, 5
        PLACE             = 6 - INDEX
        DIGIT8( PLACE ) = MOD( BASE1Ø, 8 )
        BASE1Ø            = BASE1Ø / 8
        IF ( BASE1Ø .EQ. Ø )  GO TO 21Ø
 2ØØ  CONTINUE

 21Ø  WRITE ( 5, 212 ) (DIGIT8(INDEX), INDEX=PLACE,5)
 212     FORMAT ( '+', 'IN OCTAL NOTATION IS ', 5I1 )
      GO TO 2Ø
```

```
 22      FORMAT ( 'Ø', 'ENTER UP TO FOUR HEX DIGITS ' )
      READ ( 5, 32 ) HEX
 32      FORMAT ( 5A1 )

C  **  FIND THE TERMINATNG CHARACTER, CHECK FOR HEX DIGITS,
C  **    AND STORE DECIMAL VALUES OF HEX DIGITS IN HEXNUM.
      DO 6Ø J1 = 1, 5
        IF ( HEX(J1) .EQ. H ) GO TO 1ØØ
         DO 4Ø J2 = 1, 16
           IF ( HEX(J1) .EQ. DG16(J2) ) GO TO 5Ø
 4Ø      CONTINUE
         WRITE ( 5, 42 ) HEX(J1)
 42         FORMAT ( ' ', '** ', A1, ' ** IS NOT A HEX DIGIT' )
         GO TO 2Ø

 5Ø   HEXNUM( J1 ) = J2 - 1

 6Ø   CONTINUE
      WRITE ( 5, 62 )
 62      FORMAT ( ' ', 'MISSING TERMINATOR CHARACTER' )
      GO TO 2Ø

 1ØØ  IF ( J1 .EQ. 1 ) STOP

C  **  AT THIS POINT THE NUMBER IS VALIDATED
C  **    AND THERE ARE J1-1 HEX DIGITS  - EACH IS 4 BINARY DIGITS
      HNUM = J1 - 1
      BNUM = 4 * HNUM
      DO 11Ø J2 = 1, BNUM
        DIGIT2( J2 ) = Ø
 11Ø  CONTINUE

      DO 2ØØ J1 = 1, HNUM
        HDIGIT = HEXNUM( J1 )
        BPOSN  = 4*J1
 13Ø      DIGIT2( BPOSN ) = MOD( HDIGIT, 2 )
          HDIGIT          = HDIGIT / 2
          BPOSN           = BPOSN - 1
          IF ( HDIGIT .NE. Ø ) GO TO 13Ø
 2ØØ  CONTINUE

      WRITE ( 5, 222 ) (DIGIT2(J1), J1=1,BNUM)
 222     FORMAT ( '+', 'CONVERTS TO BINARY ', 16I1 )
      GO TO 2Ø

      END
```

**Sec. 7-2 (*Problem No. 6 cont'd*)**

```
[BEGIN EXECUTION]

CONVERT UP TO 4 HEX DIGITS TO BASE TEN
TERMINATE EACH ENTRY WITH AN 'H'


ENTER UP TO FOUR HEX DIGITS 1AB4H
CONVERTS TO BINARY ØØØ11Ø1Ø1Ø11Ø1ØØ

ENTER UP TO FOUR HEX DIGITS FFFFH
CONVERTS TO BINARY 1111111111111111

ENTER UP TO FOUR HEX DIGITS H
```

**Sec. 7-3**

***Problem No. 2***

```
C  **  PROGRAM THE EUCLIDEAN ALGORITHM

       INTEGER NUM, DENOM, REMAIN

       WRITE ( 5, 12 )
 12       FORMAT ( ' ', 'FIND THE GREATEST COMMON FACTOR' /
     +             ' ', 'ENTER ''Ø,Ø'' TO TERMINATE' / )

 2Ø    WRITE ( 5, 22 )
 22       FORMAT ( 'Ø', 'ENTER TWO INTEGERS ' )
       READ ( 5, 32 ) NUM, DENOM
 32       FORMAT ( 2I6 )
       IF ( NUM .EQ. Ø )  STOP

 5Ø    REMAIN = MOD( NUM, DENOM )
       IF ( REMAIN .EQ. Ø ) GO TO 1ØØ
        NUM    = DENOM
        DENOM  = REMAIN
        GO TO 5Ø

 1ØØ   WRITE ( 5, 1Ø2 ) DENOM
 1Ø2      FORMAT ( '+', 'THE GREATEST COMMON FACTOR IS ', I6 )
       GO TO 2Ø

       END

[BEGIN EXECUTION]
```

```
          IF ( COUNT .EQ. 4 ) STOP
 2ØØ   CONTINUE

       END

[BEGIN EXECUTION]


   6 IS PERFECT     1    2    3

  28 IS PERFECT     1    2   14    4    7

 496 IS PERFECT     1    2  248    4  124    8   62   16
                   31

8128 IS PERFECT     1    2 4Ø64    4 2Ø32    8 1Ø16   16
                  5Ø8   32  254   64  127
STOP
```

***Problem No. 6***

```
C  **  SOLVE THE EIGHT QUEENS PUZZLE

       INTEGER ROW(8), COL, PIECE, TEMP

       COL = Ø

 2Ø    COL = COL + 1
       ROW( COL ) = Ø
 4Ø    IF ( ROW( COL ) .LT. 8 ) GO TO 6Ø
 5Ø     COL = COL - 1
        IF ( COL .EQ. Ø ) STOP
        GO TO 4Ø
 6Ø    ROW( COL ) = ROW( COL ) + 1
       TEMP = COL - 1
       IF ( TEMP .LT. 1 ) GO TO 9Ø

        DO 8Ø PIECE = 1, TEMP
          IF ( ROW( COL ) .EQ. ROW( PIECE )
     +      .OR.  ROW( COL ) + COL .EQ. ROW( PIECE ) + PIECE
     +      .OR.  ROW( COL ) - COL .EQ. ROW( PIECE ) - PIECE )
     +         GO TO 4Ø
 8Ø     CONTINUE
```

```
FIND THE GREATEST COMMON FACTOR
ENTER 'Ø,Ø' TO TERMINATE

ENTER TWO INTEGERS 33,333
THE GREATEST COMMON FACTOR IS       3

ENTER TWO INTEGERS 1ØØ1,22
THE GREATEST COMMON FACTOR IS      11

ENTER TWO INTEGERS Ø,Ø

STOP
```

***Problem No. 4***

```
C  **  FINDING PERFECT NUMBERS

      INTEGER NUMBER, INDEX, FACTOR(5Ø), F1, LAST, SUM, J1,
     +        FACT, COUNT

      COUNT = Ø
C  **  THERE ARE NO KNOWN ODD PERFECT NUMBERS.
      DO 2ØØ NUMBER = 2, 32766, 2
        LAST          = INT( SQRT( FLOAT( NUMBER ) ) )

C  **  TABULATE FACTORS HERE
        SUM           = 1
        F1            = 1
        FACTOR( F1 ) = 1
        DO 1ØØ INDEX = 2, LAST
          IF ( MOD( NUMBER, INDEX ) .NE. Ø ) GO TO 1ØØ
           FACT             = NUMBER / INDEX
           FACTOR( F1 + 1 ) = INDEX
           FACTOR( F1 + 2 ) = FACT
           F1               = F1 + 2
           SUM              = SUM + INDEX + FACT
           IF ( SUM .GT. NUMBER )  GO TO 2ØØ
 1ØØ    CONTINUE
        IF ( SUM .NE. NUMBER ) GO TO 2ØØ

C  **   WRITE OUT THE FACTORS IF A PERFECT NUMBER
        WRITE( 5, 1Ø2 ) NUMBER, (FACTOR( J1 ), J1 = 1, F1 )
 1Ø2       FORMAT( 'Ø', I5, ' IS PERFECT', 2( 8I5 / 17X ) )

        COUNT = COUNT + 1
```

```
 9Ø     IF ( COL .LT. 8 ) GO TO 2Ø
        WRITE( 5,1Ø2) ROW
 1Ø2       FORMAT( ' ', 8I3 )
        GO TO 5Ø

        END
```

```
[BEGIN EXECUTION]

  1  5  8  6  3  7  2  4
  1  6  8  3  7  4  2  5
  1  7  4  6  8  2  5  3
  1  7  5  8  2  4  6  3
  2  4  6  8  3  1  7  5
  2  5  7  1  3  8  6  4
  2  5  7  4  1  8  6  3
  2  6  1  7  4  8  3  5
  2  6  8  3  1  4  7  5
  2  7  3  6  8  5  1  4
  2  7  5  8  1  4  6  3
  2  8  6  1  3  5  7  4
  3  1  7  5  8  2  4  6
  3  5  2  8  1  7  4  6
  3  5  2  8  6  4  7  1
  3  5  7  1  4  2  8  6
  3  5  8  4  1  7  2  6
  3  6  2  5  8  1  7  4
  3  6  2  7  1  4  8  5
  3  6  2  7  5  1  8  4
  3  6  4  1  8  5  7  2
  3  6  4  2  8  5  7  1
  3  6  8  1  4  7  5  2
  3  6  8  1  5  7  2  4
  3  6  8  2  4  1  7  5
  3  7  2  8  5  1  4  6
  3  7  2  8  6  4  1  5
  3  8  4  7  1  6  2  5
  4  1  5  8  2  7  3  6
  4  1  5  8  6  3  7  2
  4  2  5  8  6  1  3  7
  4  2  7  3  6  8  1  5
  4  2  7  3  6  8  5  1
  4  2  7  5  1  8  6  3
  4  2  8  5  7  1  3  6
  4  2  8  6  1  3  5  7
  4  6  1  5  2  8  3  7
  4  6  8  2  7  1  3  5
```

**Sec. 7-3 (*Problem No. 6 cont'd*)**

```
4 6 8 3 1 7 5 2
4 7 1 8 5 2 6 3
4 7 3 8 2 5 1 6
4 7 5 2 6 1 3 8
4 7 5 3 1 6 8 2
4 8 1 3 6 2 7 5
4 8 1 5 7 2 6 3
4 8 5 3 1 7 2 6
5 1 4 6 8 2 7 3
5 1 8 4 2 7 3 6
5 1 8 6 3 7 2 4
5 2 4 6 8 3 1 7
5 2 4 7 3 8 6 1
5 2 6 1 7 4 8 3
5 2 8 1 4 7 3 6
5 3 1 6 8 2 4 7
5 3 1 7 2 8 6 4
5 3 8 4 7 1 6 2
5 7 1 3 8 6 4 2
5 7 1 4 2 8 6 3
5 7 2 4 8 1 3 6
5 7 2 6 3 1 4 8
5 7 2 6 3 1 8 4
5 7 4 1 3 8 6 2
5 8 4 1 3 6 2 7
5 8 4 1 7 2 6 3
6 1 5 2 8 3 7 4
6 2 7 1 3 5 8 4
6 2 7 1 4 8 5 3
6 3 1 7 5 8 2 4
6 3 1 8 4 2 7 5
6 3 1 8 5 2 4 7
6 3 5 7 1 4 2 8
6 3 5 8 1 4 2 7
6 3 7 2 4 8 1 5
6 3 7 2 8 5 1 4
6 3 7 4 1 8 2 5
6 4 1 5 8 2 7 3
6 4 2 8 5 7 1 3
6 4 7 1 3 5 2 8
6 4 7 1 8 2 5 3
6 8 2 4 1 7 5 3
7 1 3 8 6 4 2 5
7 2 4 1 8 5 3 6
7 2 6 3 1 4 8 5
```

```
      WRITE ( 5, 1Ø2 ) X1, X2
1Ø2      FORMAT ( '+', 'REAL ZEROS ARE', F6.2, ' AND', F6.2, )
      GO TO 1Ø

      END

[BEGIN EXECUTION]


ENTER QUADRATIC COEFFICIENTS 1,2,3
NONREAL ZEROS:  -1.ØØ +  1.41I  AND -1.ØØ -  1.41I

ENTER QUADRATIC COEFFICIENTS 6,13,6
REAL ZEROS ARE  -.67 AND -1.5Ø

ENTER QUADRATIC COEFFICIENTS Ø,Ø,Ø

STOP
```

***Problem No. 4***

```
C  **  FIND TWO NUMBERS WHOSE SUM AND PRODUCT ARE GIVEN

      INTEGER NØ1, DØ1, NØ2, DØ2
      REAL    X1, X2, S1, D1, A1, B1, C1

 1Ø   WRITE ( 5, 12 )
 12      FORMAT ( 'Ø', 'ENTER SUM AND PRODUCT AS FRACTIONS',
     +               ' ''N,D,N,D'' ' )
      READ ( 5, 22 ) NØ1, DØ1, NØ2, DØ2
 22      FORMAT ( 4I5 )
      IF ( NØ1 .EQ. Ø  .AND.  DØ1 .EQ. Ø )  STOP

      A1 = FLOAT( DØ1 * DØ2 )
      B1 = FLOAT( -NØ1 * DØ2 )
      C1 = FLOAT( NØ2 * DØ1 )

C  **  SAVE THE DISCRIMINANT AND TEST FOR NEGATIVE VALUE
      D1 = B1**2 - 4.Ø * A1 * C1
      IF ( D1 .GE. Ø.Ø ) GO TO 6Ø
       WRITE ( 5, 42 )
 42       FORMAT ( '+', 'NONREAL:' )
       GO TO 1Ø

 6Ø   S1 = SQRT( D1 )
```

```
  7  3  1  6  8  5  2  4
  7  3  8  2  5  1  6  4
  7  4  2  5  8  1  3  6
  7  4  2  8  6  1  3  5
  7  5  3  1  6  8  2  4
  8  2  4  1  7  5  3  6
  8  2  5  3  1  7  4  6
  8  3  1  6  2  5  7  4
  8  4  1  3  6  2  7  5
STOP
```

# Chap. 8

## Secs. 8-1 to 8-3

### *Problem No. 2*

```
C  **  CALCULATE REAL ZEROS AND NON-REAL ZEROS OF A QUADRATIC

       INTEGER A, B, C
       REAL    X1, X2, S1, D1, A1, B1, C1

 10    WRITE ( 5, 12 )
 12       FORMAT ( '0', 'ENTER QUADRATIC COEFFICIENTS ' )
       READ ( 5, 22 ) A, B, C
 22       FORMAT ( 3I5 )
       IF ( A .EQ. 0 ) STOP

       A1 = FLOAT( A )
       B1 = FLOAT( B )
       C1 = FLOAT( C )

C  **  SAVE THE DISCRIMINANT AND TEST FOR NEGATIVE VALUE
       D1 = B1**2 - 4.0 * A1 * C1
       IF ( D1 .GE. 0.0 ) GO TO 60
        S1 = SQRT( ABS(D1) )
        X1 = -B1 / (2.0*A1)
        X2 = ABS( S1 / (2.0*A1) )
        WRITE ( 5, 42 ) X1, X2, X1, X2
 42        FORMAT ( '+', 'NONREAL ZEROS: ', F6.2, ' +', F6.2,
     +                           'I  AND', F6.2, ' -', F6.2, 'I' )
        GO TO 10

 60    S1 = SQRT( D1 )

C  **  NOW CALCULATE THE TWO REAL ZEROS
       X1 = (-B1 + S1) / (2.0 * A1)
       X2 = (-B1 - S1) / (2.0 * A1)

C  **  NOW CALCULATE THE TWO REALS
       X1 = (-B1 + S1) / (2.0 * A1)
       X2 = (-B1 - S1) / (2.0 * A1)

       WRITE ( 5, 102 ) X1, X2
 102      FORMAT ( '+', 'THE NUMBERS ARE', F6.2, ' AND', F6.2, )
       GO TO 10

       END

[BEGIN EXECUTION]

ENTER SUM AND PRODUCT AS FRACTIONS 'N,D,N,D' 5,1,6,1
THE NUMBERS ARE  3.00 AND  2.00

ENTER SUM AND PRODUCT AS FRACTIONS 'N,D,N,D' 2,3,3,2
NONREAL:

ENTER SUM AND PRODUCT AS FRACTIONS 'N,D,N,D' -3,2,-2,3
THE NUMBERS ARE   .36 AND -1.86

ENTER SUM AND PRODUCT AS FRACTIONS 'N,D,N,D' 0,0,0,0

STOP
```

### *Problem No. 6*

```
C  **  SHADING A GRAPH

       INTEGER VLINE(65), INDEX, K1, Y,
     +         DASH, EYE, SPACE, STAR, DOT
       DATA   DASH/ '-'/ EYE/ 'I'/ SPACE/ ' '/ STAR/ '*'/
     +        DOT/ '.'/
       IFUNCT( Y ) = Y**2

C  **  SETUP PRINTING THE Y-AXIS LABELS
       DO 10 INDEX = 1, 6
         VLINE( INDEX ) = 10 * ( INDEX - 1 )
 10    CONTINUE

C  **  WRITE OUT THE NUMERIC LABELS
       WRITE ( 5, 22 ) (VLINE( K1 ), K1 = 1, 6 )
 22       FORMAT ( ' ', 6( 8X, I2 ) )

C  **  SETUP Y-AXIS ITSELF
       DO 30 INDEX = 1, 65
```

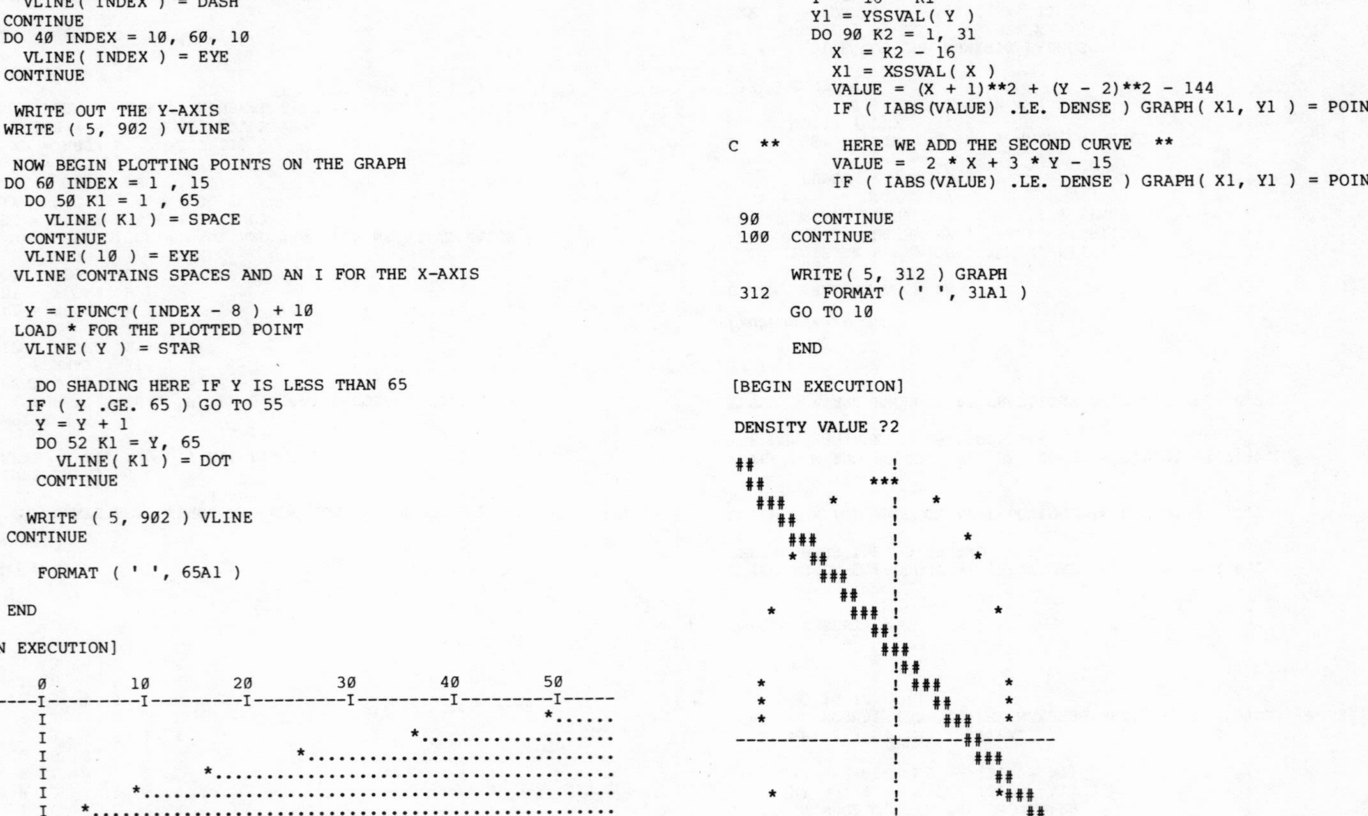

```
          VLINE( INDEX ) = DASH
   30   CONTINUE
        DO 40 INDEX = 10, 60, 10
          VLINE( INDEX ) = EYE
   40   CONTINUE

C  **   WRITE OUT THE Y-AXIS
        WRITE ( 5, 902 ) VLINE

C  **   NOW BEGIN PLOTTING POINTS ON THE GRAPH
        DO 60 INDEX = 1 , 15
          DO 50 K1 = 1 , 65
            VLINE( K1 ) = SPACE
   50     CONTINUE
          VLINE( 10 ) = EYE
C  **   VLINE CONTAINS SPACES AND AN I FOR THE X-AXIS

          Y = IFUNCT( INDEX - 8 ) + 10
C  **   LOAD * FOR THE PLOTTED POINT
          VLINE( Y ) = STAR

C  **     DO SHADING HERE IF Y IS LESS THAN 65
          IF ( Y .GE. 65 ) GO TO 55
           Y = Y + 1
           DO 52 K1 = Y, 65
             VLINE( K1 ) = DOT
   52      CONTINUE

   55     WRITE ( 5, 902 ) VLINE
   60   CONTINUE

  902     FORMAT ( ' ', 65A1 )

        END
```

[BEGIN EXECUTION]

```
         0         10        20        30        40        50
---------I---------I---------I---------I---------I---------I-----
         I                                                 *.....
         I                                    *..................
         I                           *...........................
         I                  *....................................
         I           *...........................................
         I    *..................................................
```

```
        Y  = 16 - K1
        Y1 = YSSVAL( Y )
        DO 90 K2 = 1, 31
          X  = K2 - 16
          X1 = XSSVAL( X )
          VALUE = (X + 1)**2 + (Y - 2)**2 - 144
          IF ( IABS(VALUE) .LE. DENSE ) GRAPH( X1, Y1 ) = POINT1
C  **       HERE WE ADD THE SECOND CURVE  **
          VALUE =  2 * X + 3 * Y - 15
          IF ( IABS(VALUE) .LE. DENSE ) GRAPH( X1, Y1 ) = POINT2

   90     CONTINUE
  100   CONTINUE

        WRITE( 5, 312 ) GRAPH
  312     FORMAT ( ' ', 31A1 )
        GO TO 10

        END
```

[BEGIN EXECUTION]

DENSITY VALUE ?2

```
##             !
 ##          ***
  ###    *     !   *
    ##         !
     ###       !      *
     * ##      !       *
        ###    !
          ##   !
   *       ### !         *
             ##!
              ###
               !##
  *            !  ###      *
  *            !   ##      *
  *            !    ###    *
---------------+------##-------
               !       ###
               !         ##
   *           !         *###
               !            ##
```

```
I*.........................................................................................
*..........................................................................................
I*.........................................................................................
I    *.....................................................................................
I          *...............................................................................
I                  *.......................................................................
I                             *............................................................
I                                          *...............................................
I                                                           *..............................
```

## Sec. 8-4

### *Problem No. 2*

```
C  **  TWO DIFFERENT CURVES ON THE SAME GRAPH
C  **  WE SET UP TWO PLOT CHARACTERS IN POINT1 AND POINT2

      INTEGER GRAPH(31,31), YAXIS, XAXIS, ORIGIN, SPACE,
     +        K1, K2, YSSVAL, XSSVAL, X, Y, VALUE, X1, Y1, DENSE,
     +        POINT1, POINT2
      DATA  YAXIS/ '!'/ XAXIS/ '-'/ ORIGIN/ '+'/ POINT1/ '*'/
     +      SPACE/ ' '/ POINT2/ '#'/

C  **  DEFINE FUNCTIONS TO CONVERT (Ø,Ø) TO (16,16)
      YSSVAL( Y ) = 16 - Y
      XSSVAL( X ) = 16 + X

 1Ø   WRITE ( 5, 12 )
 12      FORMAT ( 'Ø', 'DENSITY VALUE ?' )
      READ ( 5, 14 ) DENSE
 14      FORMAT ( I5 )
      IF ( DENSE .LT. Ø ) STOP

      DO 3Ø K1 = 1, 31
        DO 2Ø K2 = 1, 31
          GRAPH( K1, K2 ) = SPACE
 2Ø     CONTINUE
 3Ø   CONTINUE

      DO 4Ø K1 = 1, 31
        GRAPH( 16, K1 ) = YAXIS
        GRAPH( K1, 16 ) = XAXIS
 4Ø   CONTINUE
      GRAPH( 16, 16 ) = ORIGIN

C  **  LOADING POINTS TO BE PLOTTED
      DO 1ØØ K1 = 1, 31
```

```
                  !                ##
  *               !           *
   *              !          *
                  !
      *           !      *
               ***
                  !
                  !
                  !
                  !
                  !
```

```
DENSITY VALUE ?-1

STOP
```

### *Problem No. 4*

```
C  **  GRAPHING WITH 'SHADING'

      INTEGER GRAPH(31,31), YAXIS, XAXIS, ORIGIN, POINT, SPACE,
     +        K1, K2, YSSVAL, XSSVAL, X, Y, VALUE, X1, Y1, DENSE
      DATA  YAXIS/ '!'/ XAXIS/ '-'/ ORIGIN/ '+'/ POINT/ '*'/
     +      SPACE/ ' '/

C  **  DEFINE FUNCTIONS TO CONVERT (Ø,Ø) TO (16,16)
      YSSVAL( Y ) = 16 - Y
      XSSVAL( X ) = 16 + X

 1Ø   WRITE ( 5, 12 )
 12      FORMAT ( 'Ø', 'DENSITY VALUE ?' )
      READ ( 5, 14 ) DENSE
 14      FORMAT ( I5 )
      IF ( DENSE .LT. Ø ) STOP

      DO 3Ø K1 = 1, 31
        DO 2Ø K2 = 1, 31
          GRAPH( K1, K2 ) = SPACE
 2Ø     CONTINUE
 3Ø   CONTINUE

      DO 4Ø K1 = 1, 31
        GRAPH( 16, K1 ) = YAXIS
        GRAPH( K1, 16 ) = XAXIS
 4Ø   CONTINUE
      GRAPH( 16, 16 ) = ORIGIN
```

```
C  **  LOADING POINTS TO BE PLOTTED
      DO 100 K1 = 1, 31
        Y  = 16 - K1
        Y1 = YSSVAL( Y )
        DO 90 K2 = 1, 31
          X  = K2 - 16
          X1 = XSSVAL( X )
          VALUE = (X + 1)**2 + (Y - 2)**2 - 144

C  **      HERE IS THE ONLY CHANGE FROM PROGRAM GRAPH1  **
          IF ( VALUE .LE. DENSE ) GRAPH( X1, Y1 ) = POINT

 90       CONTINUE
 100  CONTINUE

      WRITE( 5, 312 ) GRAPH
 312     FORMAT ( ' ', 31A1 )
      GO TO 10

      END
```

[BEGIN EXECUTION]

```
DENSITY VALUE ?20

                !
          *********
        *************
      *****************
     *******************
    *********************
    *********************
   ***********************
   ***********************
  *************************
  *************************
  *************************
  *************************
  *************************
  *************************
--*************************----
  *************************
  *************************
   ***********************
   ***********************
```

```
      WRITE ( 5, 12 )
 12      FORMAT ( ' ', 'THE ACUTE ANGLES OF A 3, 4, 5 TRIANGLE ARE:' /
     +            ' ', 'DEGREES OR  DEGREES MINUTES SECONDS' )
      WRITE ( 5, 22 ) ANGLE3, DEG3, MIN3, SEC3
      WRITE ( 5, 22 ) ANGLE4, DEG4, MIN4, SEC4
 22      FORMAT ( ' ', F7.2, 4X, 2I8, F8.2 )

      END
```

[BEGIN EXECUTION]

```
THE ACUTE ANGLES OF A 3, 4, 5 TRIANGLE ARE:
DEGREES OR  DEGREES MINUTES SECONDS
  36.87         36      52    11.75
  53.13         53       7    48.25
```

***Problem No. 4***

```
C  **  EXPRESS ANGLES TO THE NEAREST MINUTE
C  **  FOR A 10, 10, 4 TRIANGLE

      REAL  ANGLE3, ANGLE4, RADIAN, TEMP
      INTEGER DEG3, MIN3, DEG4, MIN4

C  **  THIS IS AN ISOSCELES TRIANGLE.  SO DROP A PERPENDICULAR TO
C  **   THE '4' SIDE TO FORM A 10, 2, SQRT( 100 - 4) RT. TRIANGLE.
      RADIAN = ATAN( SQRT( 96.0 ) / 2.0 )

C  **  CALCULATE FOR A BASE ANGLE
      ANGLE3 = RADIAN * 180.0 / 3.14159
      DEG3   = INT( ANGLE3 )
      TEMP   = ANGLE3 - FLOAT( DEG3 )
      MIN3   = INT( TEMP * 60.0 + .5 )

C  **  CALCULATE FOR THE VERTEX ANGLE
C  **   WE BISECTED THIS VERTEX ANGLE WHEN WE DROPPED THE ALTITUDE
      ANGLE4 = 2.0 * ( 90.0 - ANGLE3 )
      DEG4   = INT( ANGLE4 )
      TEMP   = ANGLE4 - FLOAT( DEG4 )
      MIN4   = INT( TEMP * 60.0 + .5 )

      WRITE ( 5, 12 )
 12      FORMAT ( ' ', 'THE ANGLES OF A 10, 10, 4 TRIANGLE ARE:' /
     +            ' ', 'DEGREES OR  DEGREES MINUTES' )
      WRITE ( 5, 22 ) ANGLE3, DEG3, MIN3
```

```
*********************
*********************
*******************
*****************
**************
*********
         !
         !
         !
         !
         !

DENSITY VALUE ?
               -1

STOP
```

## Chap. 9

### Sec. 9-2

*Problem No. 2*

```
C  **  EXPRESS ANGLES IN DEGREES, MINUTES AND SECONDS
C  **  FOR A 3, 4, 5 RIGHT TRIANGLE

      REAL  ANGLE3, ANGLE4, RADIAN, SEC3, SEC4, TEMP
      INTEGER DEG3, MIN3, DEG4, MIN4

      RADIAN = ATAN( 0.75 )

C  **  CALCULATE FOR ANGLE3
      ANGLE3 = RADIAN * 180.0 / 3.14159
      DEG3   = INT( ANGLE3 )
      TEMP   = ANGLE3 - FLOAT( DEG3 )
      MIN3   = INT( TEMP * 60.0 )
      TEMP   = TEMP * 60.0  -  FLOAT( MIN3 )
      SEC3   = TEMP * 60.0

C  **  CALCULATE FOR ANGLE4
C  **  THIS MIGHT BE A PLACE FOR A SUBROUTINE  **
      ANGLE4 = 90.0 - ANGLE3
      DEG4   = INT( ANGLE4 )
      TEMP   = ANGLE4 - FLOAT( DEG4 )
      MIN4   = INT( TEMP * 60.0 )
      TEMP   = TEMP * 60.0  -  FLOAT( MIN4 )
      SEC4   = TEMP * 60.0

      WRITE ( 5, 22 ) ANGLE3, DEG3, MIN3
      WRITE ( 5, 22 ) ANGLE4, DEG4, MIN4
 22      FORMAT ( ' ', F7.2, 4X, 2I8 )

      END

[BEGIN EXECUTION]

THE ANGLES OF A 10, 10, 4 TRIANGLE ARE:
DEGREES OR  DEGREES MINUTES
  78.46          78       28
  78.46          78       28
  23.07          23        4
```

*Problem No. 6*

```
C  **  GIVEN A RIGHT TRIANGLE WITH ONE ANGLE 42 DEG AND 25 MIN,
C  **   THE SIDE OPPOSITE HAS LENGTH 10.0, FIND THE OTHER
C  **   SIDES OF THE TRIANGLE

      REAL ANGLEA, SIDEA, SIDEB, SIDEC, TAN
      TAN( ANGLEA ) = SIN( ANGLEA ) / COS( ANGLEA )

      SIDEA  = 10.0
      ANGLEA = ( 42.0 + 25.0/60.0 ) * 3.14159 / 180.0
      SIDEB  = SIDEA / TAN( ANGLEA )
      SIDEC  = SQRT( SIDEA**2 + SIDEB**2 )

      WRITE ( 5, 12 ) SIDEA, SIDEB, SIDEC
 12      FORMAT ( ' ', 'THE THREE SIDES ARE: ', 3F6.2 )

      END

[BEGIN EXECUTION]

THE THREE SIDES ARE:  10.00 10.95 14.83
```

### Sec. 9-3

*Problem No. 2*

```
C  **  SOLVE THE ANGLE-SIDE-ANGLE AND
C  **   THE ANGLEA-ANGLEB-SIDEA CASES

      REAL  AREA, ANGLEA, ANGLEB, ANGLEC, SIDEA, SIDEB, SIDEC,
     +      DECIDE(3), SELECT
      DATA  DECIDE/ 'ASA', 'AAS', 'END'/
```

**Sec. 9-3** (***Problem No. 2 cont'd***)

```
C  **  COMBINE DEGREES TO RADIANS AND SIN CALCULATION
      SINE(X) = SIN( 3.14159 / 180.0 * X )

 10   WRITE ( 5, 12 )
 12      FORMAT ( ' ', 'ENTER ''ASA'', ''AAS'', ''END'' ' )
      READ ( 5, 22 ) SELECT
 22      FORMAT ( A3 )
      IF ( SELECT .EQ. DECIDE(1) ) GO TO 100
      IF ( SELECT .EQ. DECIDE(2) ) GO TO 150
      IF ( SELECT .EQ. DECIDE(3) ) GO TO 9900
      GO TO 10

C  **  HANDLE THE ASA CASE HERE
 100  WRITE ( 5, 102 )
 102     FORMAT ( ' ', 'ENTER ANGLE-SIDE-ANGLE ' )
      READ ( 5, 112 ) ANGLEB, SIDEA, ANGLEC
 112     FORMAT ( 3F6.2 )

      ANGLEA = 180.0 - ( ANGLEC + ANGLEB )
      GO TO 200

C  **  HANDLE THE AAS CASE HERE
 150  WRITE ( 5, 152 )
 152     FORMAT ( ' ', 'ENTER ANGLEA-ANGLEB-SIDEA ' )
      READ ( 5, 162 ) ANGLEA, ANGLEB, SIDEA
 162     FORMAT ( 3F6.2 )

      ANGLEC = 180.0 - ( ANGLEA + ANGLEB )
      GO TO 200

 200  SIDEB  = SIDEA * SINE( ANGLEB ) / SINE( ANGLEA )
      SIDEC  = SIDEB * SINE( ANGLEC ) / SINE( ANGLEB )

      AREA   = .5 * SIDEA * SIDEB * SINE( ANGLEC )

      WRITE ( 5, 202 )
 202     FORMAT ( '+', 25X, 'A', 9X, 'B', 9X, 'C' )
      WRITE ( 5, 204 ) ANGLEA, ANGLEB, ANGLEC
 204     FORMAT ( ' ', 'THE ANGLES ARE   ', 3F10.2 )
      WRITE ( 5, 206 ) SIDEA, SIDEB, SIDEC
 206     FORMAT ( ' ', 'THE SIDES ARE    ', 3F10.2 )
      WRITE ( 5, 208 ) AREA
 208     FORMAT ( ' ', ' AND THE AREA IS ', F10.2 / )

      GO TO 10
```

```
      POLAR(5) = SIN( 3.0 * RADIAN )
      POLAR(6) = SIN( RADIAN ) + COS( RADIAN )

      TEMP     = COS(RADIAN)
      POLAR(7) = SIGN( 999.99, TEMP )
      IF ( TEMP .EQ. 0.0 ) POLAR( 7 ) = 999.99
      IF ( ABS( TEMP ) .GT. 0.001 ) POLAR(7) = 1.0 / TEMP

      TEMP     = 1.0 - COS( RADIAN )
      POLAR(8) = SIGN( 999.99, TEMP )
      IF ( TEMP .EQ. 0.0 ) POLAR( 8 ) = 999.99
      IF ( ABS( TEMP ) .GT. 0.001 ) POLAR(8) = 1.0 / TEMP

      DO 150 K1 = 1, 8
        POLAR( K1 ) = ROUND( POLAR(K1) )
150   CONTINUE

C  **   WE SELECT THE FIRST EQUATION AS A SAMPLE HERE
C  **   TO SEE EQUATIONS 2 THRU 8, SIMPLY ASSIGN EQU
C  **   AND CHANGE THE COLUMN LABEL IN STATEMENT 102
        EQU = 1
        X = POLAR(EQU) * COS( RADIAN )
        Y = POLAR(EQU) * SIN( RADIAN )

        WRITE ( 5, 162 ) DEGREE, X, Y
 162       FORMAT ( ' ', I5, 2F7.2 )

 200  CONTINUE

      END

[BEGIN EXECUTION]

ANGLE  (A) X  (A) Y
    0   1.00   0.00
   15    .84    .23
   30    .43    .25
   45   0.00   0.00
   60   -.25   -.43
   75   -.23   -.84
   90   -.00  -1.00
  105    .23   -.84
  120    .25   -.43
  135   0.00   0.00
  150   -.43    .25
```

```
 9900 END

[BEGIN EXECUTION]

ENTER 'ASA', 'AAS', 'END' ASA

ENTER ANGLE-SIDE-ANGLE 45.0,10.0,45.0
                          A          B          C
THE ANGLES ARE          90.00      45.00      45.00
THE SIDES ARE           10.00       7.07       7.07
 AND THE AREA IS        25.00

ENTER 'ASA', 'AAS', 'END' AAS

ENTER ANGLEA-ANGLEB-SIDEA 15.0,20.0,14.0
                          A          B          C
THE ANGLES ARE          15.00      20.00     145.00
THE SIDES ARE           14.00      18.50      31.03
 AND THE AREA IS        74.28

ENTER 'ASA', 'AAS', 'END' END
```

## Sec. 9-4

### *Problem No. 2*

```
C  **  CALCULATE VALUES OF R FOR THE EQUATIONS (A) - (H)
C  **  AND CONVERT TO ( X, Y ) FOR A RECTANGULAR COORDINATE
C  **  SYSTEM PLOT.

      REAL      POLAR(8), CONVRT, RADIAN, ROUND, TEMP, X, Y
      INTEGER   INDEX, DEGREE, K1, EQU

      ROUND( X ) = AINT( 100.0 * X + SIGN( .5, X ) ) / 100.0
      CONVRT = 3.14159 / 180.0

      WRITE ( 5, 102 )
 102     FORMAT ( ' ', 'ANGLE   (A) X   (A) Y' )

      DO 200 INDEX = 1, 361, 15
        DEGREE = INDEX - 1
        RADIAN = CONVRT * DEGREE

        POLAR(1) = COS( 2.0 * RADIAN )
        POLAR(2) = COS( 3.0 * RADIAN )
        POLAR(3) = COS( 4.0 * RADIAN )
        POLAR(4) = SIN( 2.0 * RADIAN )
```

```
 165    -.84     .23
 180   -1.00     .00
 195    -.84    -.23
 210    -.43    -.25
 225    0.00    0.00
 240     .25     .43
 255     .23     .84
 270     .00    1.00
 285    -.23     .84
 300    -.25     .43
 315    0.00    0.00
 330     .43    -.25
 345     .84    -.23
 360    1.00    -.00
```

# Chap. 10

## Sec. 10-1

### *Problem No. 2*

```
      INTEGER POLY1(10), POLY2(10), DIF(10), J1, N1, N2, J2, N3

      WRITE ( 5, 12 )
 12      FORMAT ( ' ', 'SUBTRACTING TWO POLYNOMIALS' /
     +            ' ', 'ENTER NUMBER OF TERMS AND TERMS -',
     +            ' ''0'' TO QUIT' / )

 20   WRITE ( 5, 22 )
 22      FORMAT ( '0', 'FROM         ' )
      READ ( 5, 902 ) N1,(POLY1(J1), J1 = 1, N1)
      IF ( N1 .GT. 10  .OR.  N1 .LT. 0 )  GO TO 20
      IF ( N1 .EQ. 0 ) STOP

 30   WRITE ( 5, 32 )
 32      FORMAT ( '+', 'SUBTRACT ' )
      READ ( 5, 902 ) N2,(POLY2(J1), J1 = 1, N2)
      IF ( N2 .GT. 10  .OR.  N2 .LT. 0 )  GO TO 30
      IF ( N2 .EQ. 0 )  STOP

      N3 = MAX0( N1, N2 )
      DO 50 J1 = 1, N3
        DIF( J1 ) = 0
 50   CONTINUE

      DO 60 J1 = 1, N1
        J2 = N3 - N1 + J1
```

**Sec. 10-1** (***Problem No. 2 cont'd***)

```
      DIF( J2 ) =  POLY1( J1 )
 6Ø   CONTINUE

      DO 7Ø J1 = 1, N2
        J2 = N3 - N2 + J1
        DIF( J2 ) = DIF( J2 ) - POLY2( J1 )
 7Ø   CONTINUE

C  **  REMOVE UNWANTED LEADING ZEROS HERE  **
 8Ø   IF ( DIF( 1 ) .NE. Ø  .OR.  N3 .EQ. 1 ) GO TO 1ØØ
       N3 = N3 - 1
       DO 9Ø J1 = 1, N3
         DIF( J1 ) = DIF( J1 + 1 )
 9Ø    CONTINUE
       GO TO 8Ø

 1ØØ  WRITE ( 5, 1Ø2 ) (DIF(J1), J1 = 1, N3)
 1Ø2     FORMAT ( '+', 'DIFFERENCE: ', 1ØI5 )

      GO TO 2Ø

 9Ø2     FORMAT ( 2ØI4 )

      END
```

```
[BEGIN EXECUTION]

SUBTRACTING TWO POLYNOMIALS
ENTER NUMBER OF TERMS AND TERMS - 'Ø' TO QUIT


FROM      4,1,2,3,5
SUBTRACT 4,-1,-6,9,4
DIFFERENCE:      2    8   -6    1

FROM     Ø

STOP
```

***Problem No. 4***

```
      INTEGER POLY1(1Ø), POLY2(1Ø), PRDUCT(19), J1, J2, J3,
     +        N1, N2, N3

      WRITE ( 5, 12 )
```

```
SECOND 2,3,2
PRODUCT:     9   39   7Ø   68   24

FIRST  Ø

STOP
```

***Problem No. 6***

```
      INTEGER POLY1(1Ø), POLY2, ANS(9), REMAIN, J1, N1, N3

      WRITE ( 5, 12 )
 12      FORMAT ( ' ', 'DO SYNTHETIC DIVISION - ''Ø'' TO QUIT' / )

 2Ø   WRITE ( 5, 22 )
 22      FORMAT ( 'Ø', 'NUMBER OF TERMS, TERMS:' /
     +           ' ', 'DIVIDE: ' )
      READ ( 5, 9Ø2 ) N1,(POLY1(J1), J1 = 1, N1)
      IF ( N1 .GT. 1Ø  .OR.  N1 .LT. Ø )  GO TO 2Ø
      IF ( N1 .EQ. Ø ) STOP

      WRITE ( 5, 32 )
 32      FORMAT ( '+', 'BY X - ' )
      READ ( 5, 9Ø2 ) POLY2

C  **  DO THE DIVISION HERE  **
      ANS( 1 ) = POLY1( 1 )
      DO 1ØØ J1 = 2, N1
        ANS( J1 ) = POLY1( J1 ) + ANS( J1 - 1 ) * POLY2
 1ØØ  CONTINUE
      REMAIN = ANS( N1 )
      N3     = N1 - 1

      WRITE ( 5, 2Ø2 ) (ANS(J1), J1 = 1, N3)
 2Ø2     FORMAT ( '+', 'YIELDS: ', 1ØI4 )
      WRITE ( 5, 2Ø4 ) REMAIN
 2Ø4     FORMAT ( ' ', 'REMAINDER = ', I4 )

      GO TO 2Ø

 9Ø2     FORMAT ( 2ØI4 )

      END
```

[BEGIN EXECUTION]

```
12      FORMAT ( ' ', 'MULTIPLY TWO POLYNOMIALS' /
     +           ' ', 'ENTER NUMBER OF TERMS AND TERMS -',
     +         ' ''Ø'' TO QUIT' / )

 2Ø   WRITE ( 5, 22 )
 22      FORMAT ( 'Ø', 'FIRST  ' )
      READ ( 5, 9Ø2 ) N1,(POLY1(J1), J1 = 1, N1)
      IF ( N1 .GT. 1Ø  .OR.  N1 .LT. Ø )  GO TO 2Ø
      IF ( N1 .EQ. Ø ) STOP

 3Ø   WRITE ( 5, 32 )
 32      FORMAT ( '+', 'SECOND ' )
      READ ( 5, 9Ø2 ) N2,(POLY2(J1), J1 = 1, N2)
      IF ( N2 .GT. 1Ø  .OR.  N2 .LT. 1 )  GO TO 3Ø

      N3 = N1 + N2 - 1
      DO 4Ø J1 = 1, N3
        PRDUCT( J1 ) = Ø
 4Ø   CONTINUE

      DO 6Ø J1 = 1, N1
        DO 5Ø J2 = 1, N2
          J3 = J1 + J2 - 1
          PRDUCT( J3 ) = PRDUCT( J3 ) + POLY1( J1 ) * POLY2( J2 )
 5Ø     CONTINUE
 6Ø   CONTINUE

      WRITE ( 5, 1Ø2 ) (PRDUCT(J1), J1 = 1, N3)
 1Ø2     FORMAT ( '+', 'PRODUCT: ', 1ØI5 )

      GO TO 2Ø

 9Ø2     FORMAT ( 2ØI4 )

      END
```

[BEGIN EXECUTION]

```
MULTIPLY TWO POLYNOMIALS
ENTER NUMBER OF TERMS AND TERMS - 'Ø' TO QUIT


FIRST  2,1,4
SECOND 2,1,7
PRODUCT:     1   11   28

FIRST  4,3,11,16,12
DO SYNTHETIC DIVISION - 'Ø' TO QUIT

NUMBER OF TERMS, TERMS:
DIVIDE: 4,1,1,-5,-2
BY X - 2
YIELDS:     1   3   1
REMAINDER =     Ø

NUMBER OF TERMS, TERMS:
DIVIDE: 4,1,1,-5,-2
BY X - -2
YIELDS:     1  -1  -3
REMAINDER =     4

NUMBER OF TERMS, TERMS:
DIVIDE: Ø

STOP
```

## Sec. 10-2

### *Problem No. 2*

```
      INTEGER FUNCTION PNEST( N1, P1, X1 )
C  **  CHAPTER 1Ø  SECTION 2  PROBLEM 2
C  **  USING NESTED FORM TO EVALUATE A POLYNOMIAL
C  **  P1 OF N1 TERMS FOR THE VALUE OF X EQUALS X1.

      INTEGER P1(N1), N1, X1, J1

      PNEST = P1(1)
      DO 1ØØ J1 = 2, N1
        PNEST = PNEST * X1  +  P1( J1 )
 1ØØ  CONTINUE

      RETURN

      END
```

### *Problem No. 4*

```
      SUBROUTINE SYNDIV( N1, P1, P2, N3, ANS, R1 )
C  **  THIS IS A SUBROUTINE TO PERFORM SYNTHETIC DIVISION.
C  **   DIVIDE POLYNOMIAL P1 OF N1 TERMS BY (X - P2),
C  **   RETURN THE QUOTIENT IN N3 TERMS OF ANS AND
```

**Sec. 10-2 (*Problem No. 4 cont'd*)**

```
C  **   THE REMANDER IN ANS( N1 ).

      INTEGER P1(10), P2, ANS(9), R1, J1, N1, N3

C  **  DO THE DIVISION HERE  **
      ANS( 1 ) = P1( 1 )
      DO 100 J1 = 2, N1
        ANS( J1 ) = P1( J1 ) + ANS( J1 - 1 ) * P2
  100 CONTINUE
      N3 = N1 - 1

      RETURN

      END
```

## Sec. 10-3

### *Problem No. 2*

```
      REAL FUNCTION RPNEST( N1, P1, X1 )
C  **  USING NESTED FORM TO EVALUATE A REAL POLYNOMIAL
C  **  P1 OF N1 TERMS FOR THE VALUE OF X EQUALS X1.

      INTEGER N1, J1
      REAL P1(N1), X1

      RPNEST = P1(1)
      DO 100 J1 = 2, N1
        RPNEST = RPNEST * X1  +  P1( J1 )
  100 CONTINUE

      RETURN

      END
```

# Chap. 11

## Sec. 11-2

### *Problem No. 2*

```
C  **  PRINTING COMBINATIONS OF N LETTERS TAKEN R AT A TIME.

      INTEGER WORD(20), PRINT(20), RECORD(20), J1, J2, J3, HPOS,
     +        N, R, J0
```

```
         IF ( RECORD( HPOS ) .LE. N )                       GO TO 30
         HPOS = HPOS - 1
         IF ( HPOS .GT. 0 )                                 GO TO 90
         GO TO 10

         END

[BEGIN EXECUTION]

TAKING N LETTERS R AT A TIME
20 LETTER MAXIMUM
ENTER '0,0' TO TERMINATE

ENTER N,R 4,3
ENTER THE LETTERS NAME

NAM
NAE
NMA
NME
NEA
NEM
ANM
ANE
AMN
AME
AEN
AEM
MNA
MNE
MAN
MAE
MEN
MEA
ENA
ENM
EAN
EAM
EMN
EMA

ENTER N,R 0,0

STOP
```

```
      WRITE ( 5, 8 )
 8       FORMAT ( ' ', 'TAKING N LETTERS R AT A TIME' /
     +            ' ', '2Ø LETTER MAXIMUM'//
     +            ' ', 'ENTER ''Ø,Ø'' TO TERMINATE' // )
 1Ø   WRITE ( 5, 12 )
 12      FORMAT ( 'Ø', 'ENTER N,R ' )
      READ ( 5, 14 ) N, R
 14      FORMAT ( 2I3 )
      IF ( N .GT. 2Ø  .OR.  N .LT. Ø )  GO TO 1Ø
      IF ( R .GT. 2Ø  .OR.  R .GT. N )  GO TO 1Ø
      IF ( N .EQ. Ø ) STOP

      WRITE ( 5, 16 )
 16      FORMAT ( '+', 'ENTER THE LETTERS ' )
      READ ( 5, 18 ) (WORD(J1), J1 = 1, N )
 18      FORMAT ( 2ØA1 )

C  **  SET UP THE RECORD ARRAY WITH THE POSITIONS FROM
C  **  WHICH THE LETTERS WILL BE TAKEN FOR OUTPUT
      HPOS = Ø
 2Ø   HPOS = HPOS + 1
      RECORD( HPOS ) = 1
 3Ø   IF ( HPOS .LT. R )                         GO TO 2Ø

C  **  TEST TO SEE IF WE ARE USING ANY OF THE ORIGINAL LETTERS
C  **  MORE THAN ONCE.
      JØ = R - 1
      DO 6Ø J1 = 1, JØ
        J2 = J1 + 1
        DO 5Ø J3 = J2, R

C  **       SAVE WHERE ANY DUPLICATE OCCURS
          HPOS = J3
          IF ( RECORD( J1 ) .EQ. RECORD( J3 )) GO TO 9Ø
 5Ø     CONTINUE
 6Ø   CONTINUE

C  **  NOW LOAD PRINT AND WRITE OUT THIS PERMUTATION
      DO 8Ø J1 = 1, R
        J2 = RECORD( J1 )
        PRINT( J1 ) = WORD( J2 )
 8Ø   CONTINUE
      WRITE ( 5, 82 ) (PRINT(J1), J1 = 1, R )
 82      FORMAT ( ' ', 2ØA1 )

C  **  NOW WE CHANGE THE LAST LETTER
 9Ø   RECORD( HPOS ) = RECORD( HPOS ) + 1
```

### *Problem No. 4*

```
C  **  CARS:
C  **   18 COLORS, 7 MODELS, 4 ENGINES, AND
C  **   15 OPTIONS.

      REAL NCARS

      NCARS = 18.Ø * 7.Ø * 4.Ø * 2.Ø**15

      WRITE ( 5, 12 ) NCARS
 12      FORMAT ( ' ', F9.Ø, ' DIFFERENT CARS AVAILABLE' )

      END
```

[BEGIN EXECUTION]

16515Ø7Ø. DIFFERENT CARS AVAILABLE

### *Problem No. 6*

```
C  **  FUNCTION SUBPROGRAM COMB REQUIRED  **

      REAL COMB1, COMB2

C  **  IN A CLASS OF 3Ø:
C  **  CALCULATE THE NUMBER OF SIX MEMBER COMMITTEES
      COMB1 = COMB( 3Ø, 6 )
      WRITE ( 5, 12 ) COMB1
 12      FORMAT ( ' ', E1Ø.4, ' SIX MEMBER COMMITTEES FROM 3Ø' )

      COMB2 = COMB( 15, 6 )
      WRITE ( 5, 22 ) COMB2
 22      FORMAT ( ' ', E1Ø.4, ' OF THEM ARE ALL GIRLS' )

      END
```

[BEGIN EXECUTION]

.5938E+Ø6 SIX MEMBER COMMITTEES FROM 3Ø
.5ØØ5E+Ø4 OF THEM ARE ALL GIRLS

### *Problem No. 8*

```
C  **  5 AND 1Ø DIFFERENT BIRTHDAYS

      INTEGER J1, J2
```

**Sec. 11-2** (***Problem No. 8 cont'd***)

```
      REAL BRTHØ5, BRTH1Ø

C  **  A) 5 PEOPLE WITH DIFFERENT BIRTHDAYS
      BRTHØ5 = 1.Ø
      DO 8Ø J1 = 1, 5
        J2 = 365 + 1 - J1
        BRTHØ5 = BRTHØ5 * FLOAT( J2 )
 8Ø   CONTINUE
      WRITE ( 5, 92 ) BRTHØ5
 92      FORMAT ( ' ', 'NUMBER OF WAYS FIVE PEOPLE CAN HAVE'/
     +            ' ', 'FIVE DIFFERENT BIRTHDAYS: ', E1Ø.4 / )

C  **  B) 1Ø PEOPLE WITH DIFFERENT BIRTHDAYS
      BRTH1Ø = 1.Ø
      DO 18Ø J1 = 1, 1Ø
        J2 = 365 + 1 - J1
        BRTH1Ø = BRTH1Ø * FLOAT( J2 )
 18Ø  CONTINUE
      WRITE ( 5, 192 ) BRTH1Ø
 192     FORMAT ( ' ', 'NUMBER OF WAYS TEN PEOPLE CAN HAVE' /
     +            ' ', 'TEN DIFFERENT BIRTHDAYS: ', E1Ø.4 )

      END
```

[BEGIN EXECUTION]

```
NUMBER OF WAYS FIVE PEOPLE CAN HAVE
FIVE DIFFERENT BIRTHDAYS:   .63Ø3E+13

NUMBER OF WAYS TEN PEOPLE CAN HAVE
TEN DIFFERENT BIRTHDAYS:   .37Ø6E+26
```

### *Problem No. 10*

```
C  **  5 FLAGS FOR FORMING SIGNALS

      INTEGER SGNALS, J1, J2, J3, TOTAL, NFLAGS

C  **  A) NUMBER OF SIGNALS USING ALL 5 FLAGS
      SGNALS = 1
      DO 8Ø J1 = 1, 5
        J2     = 6 - J1
        SGNALS = SGNALS * J2
 8Ø   CONTINUE
      WRITE ( 5, 92 ) SGNALS
```

```
      END
```

[BEGIN EXECUTION]

```
 .126411E+15 GUEST LISTS OF 25 FROM AMONG 5Ø
```

### *Problem No. 14*

```
C  **  VARIOUS COMMITTEES FROM 3Ø STUDENTS WITH 17 GIRLS.

C  **  REQUIRES FUNCTION SUBPROGRAM COMB  **

      INTEGER COMB1

      COMB1 = INT( COMB( 3Ø, 4 ) )
      WRITE ( 5, 12 ) COMB1
 12      FORMAT ( ' ', I6, ' STRAIGHT COMMITTEES OF 4' )

      COMB1 = INT( COMB( 13, 2 ) * COMB( 17, 2 ) )
      WRITE ( 5, 22 ) COMB1
 22      FORMAT ( ' ', I6, ' TWO BOYS AND TWO GIRLS' )

      COMB1 = INT( COMB( 13, 1 ) * COMB( 17, 3 ) )
      WRITE ( 5, 32 ) COMB1
 32      FORMAT ( ' ', I6, ' ONE BOY AND THREE GIRLS' )

      COMB1 = INT( COMB( 17, 4 ) )
      WRITE ( 5, 42 ) COMB1
 42      FORMAT ( ' ', I6, ' FOUR GIRLS' )

      COMB1 = INT( COMB( 13, 4 ) )
      WRITE ( 5, 52 ) COMB1
 52      FORMAT ( ' ', I6, ' FOUR BOYS' )

      END
```

[BEGIN EXECUTION]

```
 274Ø5 STRAIGHT COMMITTEES OF 4
 1Ø6Ø8 TWO BOYS AND TWO GIRLS
  884Ø ONE BOY AND THREE GIRLS
  238Ø FOUR GIRLS
   715 FOUR BOYS
```

```
 92       FORMAT ( ' ', 'NUMBER OF SIGNALS WITH 5 FLAGS: ', I5 // )

C  **  B) NUMBER OF SIGNALS USING UP TO FIVE FLAGS
      TOTAL = Ø

C  **  SET UP TO USE Ø THROUGH 5 FLAGS
      DO 1ØØ J1 = 1, 6
        NFLAGS = J1 - 1
        SGNALS = 1
        IF ( NFLAGS .EQ. Ø ) GO TO 6Ø
         DO 5Ø J2 = 1, NFLAGS
           J3 = 5 + 1 - J2
           SGNALS = SGNALS * J3
 5Ø      CONTINUE
 6Ø     TOTAL = TOTAL + SGNALS
        WRITE ( 5, 62 ) NFLAGS, SGNALS
 62        FORMAT ( ' ', I2, ' FLAGS ', I6, ' SIGNALS' )
 1ØØ  CONTINUE

      WRITE ( 5, 112 ) TOTAL
 112     FORMAT ( ' ', 'TOTAL IS ', I6, ' SIGNALS POSSIBLE' )

      END
```

[BEGIN EXECUTION]

```
NUMBER OF SIGNALS WITH 5 FLAGS:   12Ø


 Ø FLAGS      1 SIGNALS
 1 FLAGS      5 SIGNALS
 2 FLAGS     2Ø SIGNALS
 3 FLAGS     6Ø SIGNALS
 4 FLAGS    12Ø SIGNALS
 5 FLAGS    12Ø SIGNALS
TOTAL IS    326 SIGNALS POSSIBLE
```

### *Problem No. 12*

```
C  **  REQUIRES FUNCTION SUBPROGRAM COMB  **

      REAL COMB1

      COMB1 = COMB( 5Ø, 25 )
      WRITE ( 5, 12 ) COMB1
 12      FORMAT ( ' ', E12.6, ' GUEST LISTS OF 25 FROM AMONG 5Ø' )
```

### *Problem No. 16*

```
C  **  NUMBER OF SETS OF TWO 5 CARD HANDS FROM 52 CARDS

C  **  REQUIRES FUNCTION SUBPROGRAM COMB  **

      REAL NWAYS

      NWAYS = COMB( 52, 5 ) * COMB( 47, 5 )
      WRITE ( 5, 12 ) NWAYS
 12      FORMAT ( ' ', E12.6, ' SETS OF TWO 5 CARD HANDS' )

      END
```

[BEGIN EXECUTION]

```
 .398665E+13 SETS OF TWO 5 CARD HANDS
```

## Sec. 11-3

### *Problem No. 2*

```
C  **  2 PEOPLE IN A ROW OF TEN

      REAL PROB2, NWAYS, DWAYS
      INTEGER J1, J2

C  **  TWO WAYS TO ARRANGE THE TWO PEOPLE
      NWAYS = 2.Ø

C  **  9*8*7*...*2*1 WAYS TO ARRANGE THE RESULTING GROUPS -
C  **    ONE GROUP OF TWO AND 8 GROUPS OF ONE.
      DO 4Ø J1 = 1, 9
        J2    = 1Ø - J1
        NWAYS = NWAYS * FLOAT( J2 )
 4Ø   CONTINUE

C  **  1Ø*9*...*2*1 WAYS TO ARRANGE TEN PEOPLE
      DWAYS = 1.Ø
      DO 8Ø J1 = 1, 1Ø
        J2    = 11 - J1
        DWAYS = DWAYS * FLOAT( J2 )
 8Ø   CONTINUE

      PROB2 = NWAYS / DWAYS
      WRITE ( 5, 92 ) PROB2
 92      FORMAT ( ' ', '2 PEOPLE NEXT TO EACH OTHER IN 1Ø: ', F7.6 )
```

**Sec. 11-3 (*Problem No. 2 cont'd*)**

```
      END
```

```
[BEGIN EXECUTION]

2 PEOPLE NEXT TO EACH OTHER IN 1Ø: .2ØØØØØ
```

*Problem No. 4*

```
C  **  FIND THE PROBABILITY OF A PARTICULAR FIVE CARD HAND
C  **  A ROYAL STRAIGHT FLUSH THIS TIME

C  **   REQUIRES FUNCTION SUBPROGRAM COMB  **

      REAL NWAYS, DWAYS, PROB

C  **  THERE IS ONE WAY TO GET THAT HAND
      NWAYS = 1.Ø

C  **  THE NUMBER OF 5 CARD HANDS:
      DWAYS = COMB( 52, 5 )

      PROB = NWAYS / DWAYS
      WRITE ( 5, 12 ) PROB
 12      FORMAT ( ' ', 'ACE, KING, QUEEN, JACK, 1Ø -',
     +        ' ALL SPADES' /
     +              ' ', 'PROBABILITY: ', E12.6 )

      END
```

```
[BEGIN EXECUTION]

ACE, KING, QUEEN, JACK, 1Ø - ALL SPADES
PROBABILITY:  .384769E-Ø6
```

*Problem No. 6*

```
C  **  ALL HEADS IN TEN FLIPS

      REAL PROB1Ø

      PROB1Ø = (Ø.5)**1Ø
      WRITE ( 5, 12 ) PROB1Ø
 12      FORMAT ( ' ', '1Ø HEADS IN 1Ø FLIPS' /
     +              ' ', 'PROBABILITY: ', E12.6 )
```

```
32       FORMAT ( ' ', 'ROLL NO. ', I3, ' PROBABILITY: ', F7.6 )

4Ø    CONTINUE

      END
```

```
[BEGIN EXECUTION]

ROLL NO.   1 PROBABILITY: .166667
ROLL NO.   2 PROBABILITY: .138889
ROLL NO.   3 PROBABILITY: .115741
ROLL NO.   4 PROBABILITY: .Ø96451
ROLL NO.   5 PROBABILITY: .Ø8Ø376
ROLL NO.   6 PROBABILITY: .Ø6698Ø
ROLL NO.   7 PROBABILITY: .Ø55816
ROLL NO.   8 PROBABILITY: .Ø46514
ROLL NO.   9 PROBABILITY: .Ø38761
ROLL NO.  1Ø PROBABILITY: .Ø323Ø1
```

*Problem No. 12*

```
C  **  SOMEBODY FROM AMONG 29 HAS YOUR BIRTHDAY

      REAL PROB29

      PROB29 = 1.Ø - (364.Ø/365.Ø)**29
      WRITE ( 5, 12 ) PROB29
 12      FORMAT ( ' ', 'AT LEAST ONE PERSON WITH YOUR BIRTHDAY' /
     +              ' ', 'IN A ROOM WITH 29 OTHER PEOPLE' /
     +              ' ', 'PROBABILITY: ', F7.6 )

      END
```

```
[BEGIN EXECUTION]

AT LEAST ONE PERSON WITH YOUR BIRTHDAY
IN A ROOM WITH 29 OTHER PEOPLE
PROBABILITY: .Ø76478
```

## Sec. 11-4

*Problem No. 4*

```
      INTEGER J1, BULB, OPENER, DE(4)
```

```
      END
```

```
[BEGIN EXECUTION]

10 HEADS IN 10 FLIPS
PROBABILITY:  .976563E-03
```

*Problem No. 8*

```
C  **  DRAW UNTIL AN ACE APPEARS

      REAL PROB4

C  **  GUARANTEE NO ACE ON THE FIRST 3 DRAWS AND
C  **    AN ACE ON THE FOURTH DRAW
      PROB4 = (48.0/52.0)*(47.0/51.0)*(46.0/50.0)*(4.0/49.0)
      WRITE ( 5, 12 ) PROB4
 12      FORMAT ( ' ', 'ACE ON THE FOURTH DRAW' /
     +            ' ', 'PROBABILITY: ', F7.6 )

      END
```

```
[BEGIN EXECUTION]

ACE ON THE FOURTH DRAW
PROBABILITY: .063888
```

*Problem No. 10*

```
C  **  2 ON ROLLS 1 THROUGH 10

      INTEGER J1, J2, J3
      REAL PROBJ1, NUMBS, TWOS, NONTWO

      DO 40 J1 = 1, 10
        NUMBS  = 6.0
        TWOS   = 1.0
        NONTWO = 5.0
        PROBJ1 = 1.0
        J2     = J1 - 1
        IF ( J2 .EQ. 0 ) GO TO 30
         DO 20 J3 = 1, J2
           PROBJ1 = PROBJ1 * (NONTWO / NUMBS)
 20      CONTINUE

 30     PROBJ1 = PROBJ1 * (TWOS/NUMBS)
        WRITE ( 5, 32 ) J1, PROBJ1
```

```
      DO 10 J1 = 1, 4
        DE( J1 ) = 0
 10   CONTINUE

C  **  SELECT 1000 TIMES AT RANDOM - 1 CAN OPENER AND 1 BULB
      DO 100 J1 = 1, 1000

C  **    VALUE = 1  IMPLIES DEFECTIVE
C  **    VALUE > 1  IMPLIES SATISFACTORY
        BULB   = INT( 20.0 * RND( 23 ) ) + 1
        OPENER = INT( 25.0 * RND( 31 ) ) + 1

        IF (BULB .GT. 1  .AND.  OPENER .GT. 1) DE(1) = DE(1) + 1
        IF (BULB .EQ. 1  .AND.  OPENER .EQ. 1) DE(2) = DE(2) + 1
        IF ( BULB   .EQ. 1 ) DE(3) = DE(3) + 1
        IF ( OPENER .EQ. 1 ) DE(4) = DE(4) + 1

 100  CONTINUE

      WRITE ( 5, 122 ) DE
 122     FORMAT ( ' ', 'NEITHER   BOTH   BULB OPENER' /
     +            ' ', 4I7 )

      END
```

```
[BEGIN EXECUTION]

NEITHER   BOTH   BULB OPENER
    924      1     50     27
```

*Problem No. 6*

```
C  **  ROLL A DIE AND TABULATE '1 OR 5'

      INTEGER J1, J2, COUNT

      COUNT = 0
      DO 100 J1 = 1, 500

        J2 = INT( 6.0 * RND( 7 ) ) + 1
        IF ( J2 .EQ. 1  .OR.  J2 .EQ. 5 ) COUNT = COUNT + 1

 100  CONTINUE

      WRITE ( 5, 112 ) COUNT
 112     FORMAT ( ' ', 'ONE OR FIVE ', I4, ' TIMES IN 500' )
```

**Sec. 11-4** (*Problem No. 6 cont'd*)

```
      END

[BEGIN EXECUTION]

ONE OR FIVE  163 TIMES IN 500
```

*Problem No. 8*

```
C  **  ROLLING A DIE UNTIL A '1' COMES UP

      INTEGER J1, J2, COUNT, EXCESS, TAB(50)

      EXCESS = 0
      DO 30 J1 = 1, 50
        TAB( J1 ) = 0
 30   CONTINUE

C  **  PERFORM THE EXPERIMENT 500 TIMES
      DO 100 J1 = 1, 500
        COUNT = 0

 40     J2 = INT( 6.0 * RND( 11 ) ) + 1
        COUNT = COUNT + 1
        IF ( J2 .NE. 1 ) GO TO 40

        IF ( COUNT .LT. 51 ) TAB(COUNT) = TAB(COUNT) + 1
        IF ( COUNT .GT. 50 ) EXCESS = EXCESS + 1

 100  CONTINUE

      DO 150 J1 = 1, 50
        J2 = 51 - J1
        IF ( TAB(J2) .NE. 0 ) GO TO 200
 150  CONTINUE

 200  WRITE ( 5, 202 )
 202     FORMAT ( ' ', ' ROLLS TIMES' )
      DO 250 J1 = 1, J2
        WRITE ( 5, 222 ) J1, TAB(J1)
 222       FORMAT ( ' ', 2I6 )
 250  CONTINUE

      IF ( EXCESS .GT. 0 ) WRITE ( 5, 262 ) EXCESS
 262     FORMAT ( ' ', I5, ' EXPERIMENTS REQUIRED MORE THAN 50' )

      DO 100 TRIAL = 1, 500
        ONES = 0

        DO 50 ROLL = 1, 10
          J1 = INT( 6.0 * RND( 3 ) ) + 1
          IF ( J1 .EQ. 1 ) ONES = ONES + 1
 50     CONTINUE
        LIST( ONES + 1 ) = LIST( ONES + 1 ) + 1

 100  CONTINUE

      WRITE ( 5, 112 ) LIST
 112     FORMAT ( ' ', ' ROLLING TEN DICE 500 TIMES' /
     +            ' ', '   0   1   2   3   4   5   6   ',
     +                 '7   8   9  10' /
     +            ' ', 11I4 )

      END

[BEGIN EXECUTION]

 ROLLING TEN DICE 500 TIMES
   0   1   2   3   4   5   6   7   8   9  10
  88 152 144  79  24  10   2   1   0   0   0
```

## Sec. 11-5

*Problem No. 2*

```
C  **  PRINT ACCUMULATED TOTALS FOR ROLLING TEN DICE

      INTEGER R, N, R1
      REAL  PROB, SPROB

      WRITE ( 5, 12 )
 12      FORMAT ( ' ', ' ONES PROBABILITY   SUBTOTALS' )

      N     = 10
      SPROB = 0.0
      DO 100 R1 = 1, 11
        R     = R1 - 1
        PROB  = COMB( N, R ) * (1.0/6.0)**R * (5.0/6.0)**(N-R)
        SPROB = SPROB + PROB
        WRITE ( 5, 62 ) R, PROB, SPROB
 62        FORMAT ( ' ', I5, 2X, F10.8, 2X, F10.8 )
```

```
      END
```

[BEGIN EXECUTION]

```
 ROLLS TIMES
     1    78
     2    55
     3    66
     4    39
     5    43
     6    49
     7    33
     8    19
     9    16
    1Ø    17
    11    11
    12    15
    13    13
    14     9
    15     5
    16     7
    17     6
    18     2
    19     2
    2Ø     1
    21     2
    22     3
    23     2
    24     Ø
    25     Ø
    26     Ø
    27     2
    28     2
    29     1
    3Ø     1
    31     Ø
    32     1
```

### Problem No. 10

```
C  **  ROLL TEN DICE 5ØØ TIMES

       INTEGER TRIAL, ROLL, ONES, LIST(11), J1

       DO 2Ø J1 = 1, 11
         LIST( J1 ) = Ø
 2Ø    CONTINUE
```

```
1ØØ  CONTINUE

     END
```

[BEGIN EXECUTION]

```
 ONES PROBABILITY   SUBTOTALS
    Ø   .1615Ø56Ø   .1615Ø56Ø
    1   .323Ø111Ø   .4845167Ø
    2   .29Ø71ØØØ   .7752267Ø
    3   .155Ø453Ø   .93Ø272ØØ
    4   .Ø5426587   .9845379Ø
    5   .Ø13Ø2381   .9975617Ø
    6   .ØØ217Ø64   .9997323Ø
    7   .ØØØ248Ø7   .99998Ø4Ø
    8   .ØØØØ1861   .999999ØØ
    9   .ØØØØØØ83   .9999998Ø
   1Ø   .ØØØØØØØ2   .9999998Ø
```

### Problem No. 4

```
C  **  FIND THE PROBABILITY THAT TWO PEOPLE FROM 25 HAVE A
C  **  BLOOD TYPE FOUND IN 1% OF THE POPULATION.

       INTEGER N, R
       REAL PROB
       N = 25
       R = 2
       PROB = COMB( N, R ) * (.Ø1)**R * (.99)**(N-R)

       WRITE ( 5, 12 ) PROB
 12       FORMAT ( ' ', '2 PEOPLE IN 25 HAVE A 1% BLOOD TYPE' /
      +           ' ', PROBABILITY: ', F8.7 )

       END
```

[BEGIN EXECUTION]

```
2 PEOPLE IN 25 HAVE A 1% BLOOD TYPE
PROBABILITY: .Ø238Ø84
```

### Problem No. 6

```
C  **  A BOLT COMPANY MAKES 1 DEFECTIVE IN 1ØØØ.  WE BUY 1ØØ.

       INTEGER N, R
       REAL PROB
```

**Sec. 11-5 (*Problem No. 6 cont'd*)**

```
C  **  THE PROBABILITY OF AT LEAST ONE DEFECTIVE BOLT IS
C  **  ONE MINUS THE PROBABLITY OF NONE DEFECTIVE.
      N = 1ØØ
      R = Ø
      PROB = 1.Ø - COMB( N, R ) * (.ØØ1)**R * (.999)**(N-R)

      WRITE ( 5, 12 ) PROB
 12      FORMAT ( ' ', 'AT LEAST 1 BOLT IN 1ØØ IS DEFECTIVE' /
     +            ' ', 'PROBABILITY: ', F8.7 )

      END
```

[BEGIN EXECUTION]

```
AT LEAST 1 BOLT IN 1ØØ IS DEFECTIVE
PROBABILITY: .Ø952Ø52
```

### *Problem No. 8*

```
C  **  A BOLT COMPANY MAKES 1 DEFECTIVE IN 1ØØØ.  WE BUY 1ØØ.

      INTEGER N, R
      REAL PROB

      N = 1ØØ
      R = 1Ø
      PROB = COMB( N, R ) * (.ØØ1)**R * (.999)**(N-R)

      WRITE ( 5, 12 ) PROB
 12      FORMAT ( ' ', 'EXACTLY 1Ø BOLTS IN 1ØØ ARE DEFECTIVE' /
     +            ' ', 'PROBABILITY: ', E12.6 )

      END
```

[BEGIN EXECUTION]

```
EXACTLY 1Ø BOLTS IN 1ØØ ARE DEFECTIVE
PROBABILITY:  .158198E-16
```

### *Problem No. 10*

```
C  **  FIND THE PROBABILITIES OF Ø THROUGH 6 1'S ROLLING 6 DICE
```

### *Problem No. 12*

```
C  **  FIND THE PROBABILITIES OF Ø THROUGH 1Ø HEADS
C  **  FLIPPING 1Ø COINS

      INTEGER N, R, R1
      REAL PROB

      WRITE ( 5, 12 )
 12      FORMAT ( ' ', ' HEADS PROBABILITY' )

      N    = 1Ø
      DO 1ØØ R1 = 1, 11
        R    = R1 - 1
        PROB = COMB( N, R ) * (Ø.5)**R * (Ø.5)**(N-R)
        WRITE ( 5, 112 ) R, PROB
 112       FORMAT ( ' ', I6, F12.8 )
 1ØØ  CONTINUE

      END
```

[BEGIN EXECUTION]

```
HEADS PROBABILITY
    Ø   .ØØØ97656
    1   .ØØ976563
    2   .Ø4394531
    3   .1171875Ø
    4   .2Ø5Ø781Ø
    5   .246Ø938Ø
    6   .2Ø5Ø781Ø
    7   .1171875Ø
    8   .Ø4394531
    9   .ØØ976563
   1Ø   .ØØØ97656
```

### *Problem No. 14*

```
C  **  FLIP A COIN UNTIL IT COMES UP HEADS

      INTEGER N, HEADS, TAILS, PATERN(1Ø), J1, J2
      REAL PROB
      DATA PATERN/ 'T','T','T','T','T','T','T','T','T','H'/

      WRITE ( 5, 12 )
 12      FORMAT ( ' ', ' FLIPS PROBABILITY      PATTERN' )
```

```
      INTEGER N, R, R1
      REAL PROB

      WRITE ( 5, 12 )
12       FORMAT ( ' ', '  ONES PROBABILITY' )

      N    = 6
      DO 100 R1 = 1, 7
        R    = R1 - 1
        PROB = COMB( N, R ) * (1.0/6.0)**R * (5.0/6.0)**(N-R)
        WRITE ( 5, 112 ) R, PROB
112        FORMAT ( ' ', I6, F12.8 )
100   CONTINUE

      END

[BEGIN EXECUTION]

  ONES PROBABILITY
     0    .33489790
     1    .40187750
     2    .20093880
     3    .05358368
     4    .00803755
     5    .00064300
     6    .00002143
```

```
C  **  IN EACH CASE THERE IS ONLY ONE COMBINATION  **
      DO 100 N = 1, 10
        HEADS = 1
        TAILS = N - HEADS
        PROB  = (0.5)**TAILS * (0.5)**HEADS
        J1 = 11 - N
        WRITE ( 5, 112 ) N, PROB, (PATERN(J2), J2 = J1, 10)
112        FORMAT ( ' ', I6, F12.8, 3X, 10A1 )
100   CONTINUE

      END

[BEGIN EXECUTION]

 FLIPS PROBABILITY      PATTERN
     1    .50000000   H
     2    .25000000   TH
     3    .12500000   TTH
     4    .06250000   TTTH
     5    .03125000   TTTTH
     6    .01562500   TTTTTH
     7    .00781250   TTTTTTH
     8    .00390625   TTTTTTTH
     9    .00195313   TTTTTTTTH
    10    .00097656   TTTTTTTTTH
```

# Index

Coláiste Oideachais Mhuire Gan Smál
Luimneach